Sounding/Silence

John D. Caputo, *series editor*

Perspectives in
Continental
Philosophy

DAVID NOWELL SMITH

Sounding/Silence

Martin Heidegger
at the Limits of Poetics

FORDHAM UNIVERSITY PRESS
New York ■ 2013

Fordham University Press has no responsibility for the persistence or accuracy of URLs for external or third-party Internet websites referred to in this publication and does not guarantee that any content on such websites is, or will remain, accurate or appropriate.

Fordham University Press also publishes its books in a variety of electronic formats. Some content that appears in print may not be available in electronic books.

Library of Congress Cataloging-in-Publication Data is available from the publisher.

Printed in the United States of America

15 14 13   5 4 3 2 1

First edition

Contents

Abbreviations

All citations from Heidegger's works are given with the English translation, followed by reference to the German edition (with the exception of untranslated works, which are given by their number from Heidegger's *Gesamtausgabe*).

BPP *Basic Problems of Phenomenology*, trans. Albert Hofstadter (Bloomington: Indiana University Press, 1988); German edition Frankfurt am Main: Klostermann, 1975.

BT *Being and Time,* trans. John Macquarrie and Edward Robinson (Oxford: Blackwell, 1962); German edition Tübingen, M. Niemeyer, 1953.

BW *Basic Writings*, ed. David Farrell Krell (New York: Harper Collins, 1992).

EHP *Elucidations of Hölderlin's Poetry,* trans. Keith Hoeller (Amherst, NY: Humanity Books, 2000); German edition Frankfurt am Main: V. Klostermann, 1951.

EL *On the Essence of Language: The Metaphysics of Language and the Essencing of the Word; Concerning Herder's Treatise On the Origin of Language,* trans. Wanda Torres Gregory and Yvonne Unna (Albany: State University of New York Press, 2004); German edition Frankfurt am Main: V. Klostermann, 1999.

ET *The Essence of Truth: on Plato's cave allegory and Theaetetus,* trans. Ted Sadler (London: Continuum, 2002); German edition Frankfurt am Main: Klostermann, 1988.

FCM   *Fundamental Concepts of Metaphysics,* trans. William McNeill and Nicholas Walker (Bloomington: Indiana University Press, 1995); German edition Frankfurt am Main: Klostermann, 1992.

GA5   *Holzwege* (Frankfurt am Main : Klostermann, 1977).

GA39   *Hölderlins Hymne, 'Germanien' und 'Der Rhein'* (Frankfurt am Main: Klostermann, 1980).

GA52   *Hölderlins Hymne, 'Andenken'* (Frankfurt am Main: Klostermann, 1982).

IM   *Introduction to Metaphysics,* trans. Richard Polt and Gregory Fried (New Haven: Yale Nota Bene, 2000); German edition Tübingen, Niemeyer, 1966.

Ni   *Nietzsche I: The Will to Power as Art,* trans. David Farrell Krell (New York: Harper and Row, 1979); German edition Frankfurt am Main: Klostermann, 1985.

Nii   *Nietzsche II: The Eternal Recurrence of the Same,* trans. David Farrell Krell (New York: Harper and Row, 1981); German edition Frankfurt am Main: Klostermann, 1989.

OBT   *Off the Beaten Track,* trans. Julian Young and Kenneth Haynes (Cambridge: Cambridge University Press, 2002); German edition Frankfurt am Main: Klostermann, 1950.

OL   *On the Way to Language,* trans. Peter Hertz and Joan Stambaugh (New York: Harper and Row, 1971); German edition Pfullingen: Neske, 1959.

P   *Pathmarks,* ed. William McNeill (Cambridge: Cambridge University Press: 2001); German edition Frankfurt am Main: Klostermann, 1967.

Par   *Parmenides,* trans. André Schuwer and Richard Rojcewicz (Bloomington: Indiana University Press, 1992); German edition Frankfurt am Main: Klostermann, 1982.

PLT   *Poetry Language Thought,* trans. Albert Hofstadter (New York: Harper and Row, 1971); "Language" in *Unterwegs zur Sprache;* ". . . poetically man dwells . . ." in *Vorträge und Aufsätze* (Pfullingen: G. Neske, 1954).

PR   *The Principle of Reason,* trans. Reginald Lilly (Bloomington: Indiana University Press, 1991); German edition Pfullingen: G. Neske, 1957.

WCT   *What is Called Thinking?,* trans. J. Glenn Gray and F. Wieck (New York: Harper and Row, 1972); German edition Tübingen: M. Niemeyer, 1954.

Note on the text

All translations of Heidegger's works are reproduced in the form employed by the source being quoted from, unless otherwise stated. Translations are modified either for the sake of consistency between translations or when I wish to highlight an aspect of the original overlooked by the translation cited. All Greek words are transliterated and standardized for the sake of consistency. German terms are reproduced according to the form employed by the source quoted (for example, the term *Riß* (Heidegger's spelling) is also reproduced as *Riss*).

Acknowledgments

I am greatly indebted to the many friends and colleagues without whose support I never would have been able to elaborate, let alone complete, this project. Especial thanks are due to Ruth Abbott, Vincent Broqua, Olivier Brossard, Virgil Brower, Jamie Castell, Nick Chapin, Lizzy Coles, Jonathan Culler, Peter De Bolla, Rosalind Delmar, Amanda Dennis, Alexander García Düttmann, Daniel Jean, Abigail Lang, Drew Milne, Cecily Nowell-Smith, Geoffrey Nowell-Smith, Ian Patterson, Neil Pattison, Liz Pender, Seth Perlow, Paul Volsik, Lola Wilhelm, Ross Wilson, and Jarad Zimbler. My thanks also to the president and fellows of Queens' College, Cambridge, and to the Institut Charles V, Université Paris VII—Denis Diderot, for the many years during which they provided me with intellectual and financial sustenance.

This book and the thinking out of which it has arisen have benefitted immeasurably from the conversation with and friendship of Ben Etherington and Ewan Jones over a period of many years now, as well as from the attentive and patient reading of Christopher Fynsk and Paul Hamilton at an early stage, and later on from my anonymous readers at Fordham. I should also like to thank Thomas Lay at Fordham University Press and Michael Koch for the great meticulousness they have shown in making the manuscript presentable for general consumption. My greatest debt, however, goes to Simon Jarvis, whose guidance and generosity pervades each of the following pages.

This vast array has made *Sounding/Silence* a better book than it would otherwise possibly have been; the failings that remain are, needless to say, my own.

Elements of Chapters 1 and 4 appear in "The Art of Fugue: Heidegger on Rhythm," *Gatherings: The Heidegger Circle Annual* 2 (2012): 41–64; a programmatic summary of some of the book's major claims appeared as "Sounding/Silence" in *Gatherings* 3 (2013): 18–29. An early and abridged incarnation of Chapter 3, entitled, like the chapter itself, "Heidegger's Figures," appears in *Textual Practice* 26, no. 6 (2012): 1045–63; material reused in the introduction was first published in "The Poetry-Verse Distinction Reconsidered," *Thinking Verse* I (2011): 137–60. I would like to thank the editors of these journals for allowing me to republish this work here. Similarly, I would like to thank Pierre Joris for the permission to reproduce his translation of Paul Celan's "Schieferäugige" (Slate-eyed One), from *Breathturn* (New York: Sun and Moon Books, 1995), 234–35.

Introduction

The Limits of Poetics

To set up a limit is a dual gesture, at once instituting difference and indicating a point of contact. Martin Heidegger's critique of the discipline of poetics, a recurrent feature throughout his long engagement with poetry, is just such a gesture. On the one hand, he claims that his own readings of poems or *Erläuterungen* ("soundings-out") can articulate aspects of these poems to which poetics itself is blind. It thus stands beyond the limits of poetics—limits, that is, not simply born of bad critical practices, but which belong to the very "essence" of poetics as a mode of questioning. On the other hand, in his readings of poetry, and his discussions of generic features of poetry such as rhythm or figurative language, he continually finds himself in an encounter not only with poetry, but with those same modes of questioning which he ascribes to poetics. Just as he attempts to stand *outside* the limits of poetics, his thinking brought into contact with these limits.

To suggest—as I have just done and will continue to do throughout the following pages—that Heidegger's writing on poetry involves an engagement with poetics, runs counter to the tone of patrician disdain that characterizes many of Heidegger's own pronouncements on the subject. In the preface to the fourth edition (1971) of his *Elucidations of Hölderlin's Poetry,* he states his opinion boldly: "The present elucidations do not claim to be contributions to research in the history of literature or aesthetics. They spring from a necessity of thought" (EHP 21/7). Echoing the dictum from the 1956 lecture series *What Is Called Thinking?*, that "science does not think," the history of literature and aesthetics (disciplines that converge in poetics) are tacitly opposed to the "necessity of thought," and even, the implication goes, antithetical to "thinking" taking place at all. Discussing Georg Trakl's poem "Ein Winterabend" (A Winter Evening) at the beginning of his lecture on "Language," he observes laconically: "The poem is made up of three stanzas. Their meter and rhyme pattern can be defined accurately according to the schemes of metrics and poetics. The poem's content is comprehensible" (PLT 193/18). Heidegger, by contrast, is not concerned with the "schemes of metrics and poetics" or with dissecting the poem's content; rather, he is "seeking the speaking of language in the poem," something that poetics and its schemes will never grasp.

The "speaking of language," like the "necessity of thought," will draw Heidegger beyond the limits of poetics as a discipline. But this involves a strikingly narrow definition of poetics. In each instance, poetics is seen merely to furnish a metrical "scheme," or to interpret "images" and "symbols" (the camel in Arabian epic being one preferred example), and it is this onus on schemes that prevents poetics from "thinking," and renders it deaf to the "speaking of language." There is nevertheless a broader significance in Heidegger's argument, even for that majority of poeticians and literary critics who will not identify themselves with the furnishing of schemas. This concerns the value of poetic technique. Heidegger's central concern is that in technical or hermeneutic analysis, the poem's "thrust into the extra-ordinary is captured by familiarity and connoisseurship" (OBT 42/56). Ultimately at stake is a means of attending to the "unfamiliar" in poetry without familiarizing it, explaining it without explaining it away. It is by reducing the unfamiliar to a series of analyzable "formal features" (OBT 42/56) that poetics would be blocked off from grasping the "speaking of language" that Heidegger argues we must try to hear in its very unfamiliarity.

This leads poetics into double impasse. Firstly, its schemas familiarize *Dichtung* (poetry) so that it becomes mere *Literatur* (literature), or *Poesie* (poesy), that subsection of literature that employs verse.[1] Once thus familiarized, we encounter nothing more than an "aimless imagining of whimsicalities [and] flight of mere representations and fancies into the unreal" (OBT 45/60). Furthermore, Heidegger argues, the inability to think beyond these schemas means that "even when we are engaged in demonstrating by means of literary history that these works of poetry really are not literature," poetry cannot appear to literary history except as "literature" (WCT 134/139). In other words, poetics might be aware of its own limits, but it cannot overcome them without overcoming poetics itself. The only way in which we can move from a determination of poetry as literature to poetry itself, Heidegger says—the poetry in which we will then be able to hear the "speaking of language"—is if we "release poetry into its essential place [*der Dichtung ihren Wesensort freigeben*]"; and this will happen only when poetry, freed from the "literary" concepts through which we would read it, is allowed to "determine and reach this place" itself (WCT 134/139; translation modified). Heidegger intends his writing on poetry as an attempt to allow poetizing to reach this place, and thereby to hear the "speaking of language" this place renders audible.

To this there is one obvious riposte. How can Heidegger's own readings, valorizing their disregard toward the poems' literary features, to the metrical schemes employed, be so sure that it is they and not poetics that allow poetry to determine and reach this "essential place"? How, indeed, can he know when poetry has in fact determined and reached this "place?" After all, if metrical schemes and recurrent tropes were entirely absent from poetry's "essential place," it would seem strange that so many poems should employ them. Why, even, should it be that poetry's "essential place" is, as Heidegger asserts, that which "allows th[e] open to happen in such a way, indeed, that now, for the first time, in the midst of beings, it brings them to shine and sound" (OBT 45/60)? For Heidegger is making a claim not simply about how we read poetry, as poeticians or as "thinkers," but about poetry itself, contrasting the "essential place" of *Dichtung*, the "projective saying" that "first" brings into the "open," to its determination as *Poesie*, the "linguistic work in the narrow sense" (OBT 45/60).

Obvious as this riposte may appear, it is not one Heidegger confronts head-on. He does, however, offer a more nuanced relation between the poem's "essential place" and its purportedly formal features than his categorical division might suggest. His 1936 lecture on "Hölderlin and the Essence of Poetry," for instance, states that poetry's "harmless exterior belongs to the essence of poetry, just as the valley belongs to the mountain" (EHP 62/41–42). What Heidegger calls the "harmless exterior" are those features, such as rhyme, metrical schemes, metaphor, and so on, which characterize the poem's surface: its "whimsicalities," its "flight of mere fancies." Yet in the valley-mountain simile it ceases to be exterior at all. Not only are valley and mountain mutually dependent and determining; the mountain rises out of the valley, meaning that the "harmless exterior" not only "belongs to the essence of poetry" but it serves as the very ground which gives this essence foundations and shapes its rising-up. That a piece of literature fulfils the *generic* requirements of *Poesie* is not perhaps a sufficient condition for its attaining the ontological vocation of *Dichtung*, but this does not mean that it does not condition this vocation at all.

We thus encounter a tension in Heidegger's thinking on poetry that *Sounding/Silence* will probe throughout. Heidegger effects what I would term an *ontologization* of poetry: that is, he moves away from its "ontic" or generic features, in order to conceive of the poem as a privileged site for the "event" of being.[2] If this leads him at times to dismiss these generic features—the poem's form, its use of trope, fiction, construction of persona and voice—as somehow inessential to this site, we also find him attending to precisely these features in order to articulate how the poem might first furnish such a site. At issue ultimately is not a *denial* of a poem's formal features but a *revaluation* of them. We will encounter this motif throughout the book: Heidegger dismisses form in order to rethink form; he dismisses beauty in order to rethink beauty; he dismisses rhythm in order to rethink rhythm; he dismisses metaphor in order to rethink metaphor. In each case his dismissal starts by branding a feature metaphysical, but this gesture should not sidetrack us from what Heidegger is actually doing. Engaging with what lies at the limits of the metaphysical concept, Heidegger aims to see the problem anew.

This requires that we understand with greater clarity what is meant by Heidegger when he speaks of "metaphysics." While "metaphysics" often appears in Heidegger's vocabulary as a catch-all depreciation of the history of the forgetting of being since the Greeks, we can discern a far more precise meaning. In the 1929 address "What is Metaphysics?" and the 1935 lecture series *Introduction to Metaphysics,* he sees metaphysics as a mode of situating oneself "beyond beings," which grounds his own, "metaphysical" fundamental ontology; in his later work it has become a precipitate scission between sensuous and nonsensuous realms, where the transcendence of "beyond beings" is now situated "beyond" the physical. Central to both is the interpretation of being as *presence.* On the later account, "metaphysical" thought appeals to a nonsensuous realm in order to secure constant presence, and thereby to overcome absence. By contrast, the "metaphysics" of his earlier work involves our exposing ourselves to "the nothing"—that which refuses to be drawn into presence. The "metaphysics" Heidegger at this juncture proposes can only afford or secure presence through an attention to that absencing movement that bounds it. Even when Heidegger discards and disparages the term *metaphysics,* the question of how presence is engendered by an absencing movement will remain a key, perhaps *the* key motif in his thought. It is also the motif that will necessitate an exacting thinking of *limit,* something that guides both his conception of poetry as *Dichtung,* and the way he reads poems.

"Metaphysics," then, brings together the interpretation of being in terms of presence with the question of how to secure this presence. In this respect, it might seem to be very close to the problematic of the "ontico-ontological difference," that is, the difference between *das Seiende* (a being or entity) and *das Sein* (being), where beings can only enter presence insofar as they show themselves "in their being." Heidegger, however, is at pains to distinguish ontological difference from apparently analogous oppositions—such as between the transcendental and the empirical, a priori and a posteriori, substance and accident, or "beingness" and "entity"—and in the 1936–39 *Contributions to Philosophy* goes so far as to claim that ontological difference, setting *das Sein* (being) against *das Seiende* (beings), cannot grasp *das Seyn* (the be-ing) that first gives such a difference to be thought.[3] In his later work, this is the originary movement through which being gives itself, the "it" (*es*) that "gives being" (*es gibt*)[4] that Heidegger will thematize as the *Ereignis,* the "event of appropriation."

This then implies that in his later work, Heidegger moves away from ontological difference as a guiding category in his thought; however, as Thomas Sheehan has argued powerfully, the relation between being and beings was always, for Heidegger, a question of how beings come to disclose themselves in an intelligible manner, and how we can understand such autodisclosure from within a pregiven world.[5] Whether asking after the "being of beings" or the originary event, which "appropriates" beings into the "open region" in which we will encounter them, the guiding concern is how beings might, by virtue of this intelligibility, disclose themselves as "present." Sheehan frames the problematic of a being's autodisclosure in terms of what he calls "pres-absentiality," that is, oscillations between presencing and absencing that structure the way in which a being can appear *in* presence. Sheehan's great insight is to observe how all intelligible appearance is necessarily *kinetic:* that is, it is structured by continual countermovements which set up the open region in which a being can disclose itself as the being it is.

Sheehan's central concern is the articulation of what Heidegger, from the mid-1930s onward, will call *Ereignis;* however, his insight allows us to see how ontological difference is replayed in the distinction between *Dichtung,* and *Poesie.* For if *Dichtung* engenders a singular presence, it does so only as the poem engages with the "ontic" possibilities of its linguistic medium, through verse technique, trope and so on: those features that characterize the singular way in which any poem (or other kind of artwork) discloses itself as the poem it is. Above I said: Heidegger dismisses form in order to rethink form, dismisses beauty in order to rethink beauty, dismisses trope in order to rethink trope, and so on. This dismissal and rethinking would grasp these features in terms of the relations between presencing and absencing that condition the poem's own appearance. These formal features attain "ontological" weight insofar as they are concerned with tracing these relations between presencing and absencing as these countermovements inhere in their medium; it is this tracing which endows the poem with a singular presence. In order to allow poetry to "itself determine and reach [its essential] place," Heidegger's thinking must engage with literature after all. I am far from being the first reader of Heidegger to observe his dependence, in setting up "ontological" claims, on "ontic" features of language and experience; where I differ from many critics, especially those of a "deconstructive" bent, is in saying that, far from this undermining Heidegger's project, and resulting in the unraveling of ontological difference as such, it constitutes a central feature of his project. Indeed, I will argue throughout, it is only by attending to the ontic complexity of poems as the way in which they disclose themselves in presence that Heidegger will be able to articulate their ontological vocation.

■

In this, Heidegger's work is of great relevance to a current trend in poetics and literary theory to attempt to endow a poem's "ontic" features with "ontological" weight. For these thinkers as for Heidegger, Hölderlin is an exemplary figure, although the passage from the "Notes on Oedipus" they focus on is one that Heidegger himself, regrettably, never discusses.[6] Here he elaborates a "law" of tragic drama, in which the "rhythmic sequence of the representations" exists "in tragedy more as a state of balance than as mere succession."[7] At the crux of this "state of balance" is the irreversible event that breaks with the status quo of the beginning of the tragedy and structures the entire tragedy, and he aligns this event with "*what in poetic meter is called caesura,* the pure word, the counter-rhythmic interruption."[8] Extracted from the context of meter, caesura becomes the tragic structure's Archimedian point: tragedy thus follows a "logic of caesura."[9] Behind this, Philippe Lacoue-Labarthe has observed, lies a conception of temporality in which the equilibrium structuring temporal experience is marked by an originary discordance, in which rhythmic continuity is dependent on, and conditioned by, counter-rhythm.[10] Lacoue-Labarthe develops this train of thought further, remarking that these caesura-like events involve "empty" moments, moments that he glosses in terms of "withdrawal" and the "nothing."[11] What we encounter, Lacoue-Labarthe argues, is a "law of finitude" through which "it is perhaps not impossible to raise caesura to the level of a, if not the, concept of historicity."[12]

One might wonder, however, how much of the specifically *metrical* dimension of caesura is preserved when, by virtue of its deployment of temporal continuity and disjunction, identity and difference, it is "raised to the level of a . . . concept of historicity." This is most striking in William S. Allen's recent discussion of this work, which wishes to employ its broadened thinking of caesura as the basis for readings of individual caesurae in poetry. He glosses caesura thus: "the caesura cannot be marked, but can only be recalled as that which has occurred without appearing, thereby leaving a trace of absence, a re-(mark), which neither is nor is not, for it renders such a distinction impossible; rather it is indistinct, inapparent."[13] But if caesura in a poem occurs "without appearing," it is not clear how it would effect its "counter-rhythmic interruption" on the poems themselves. Indeed, when Allen directs his account of caesura back on to Heidegger's readings of individual poems, he identifies one such caesura in a colon at the ending of the penultimate line of Stefan George's "Das Wort." This is, of course, not metrically a caesura at all; and insofar as the colon precedes a final epigram, its "interruption" would, on a formal level, seem far from counter-rhythmic. The metrical dimension of caesura, so important to Hölderlin's analysis, has been disregarded entirely—and at the very moment when he would speak of meter! Allen's reading bears witness to a difficulty for any philosophical poetics that wants to justify its claims both to be "philosophical" and to constitute "poetics." Reading a wider philosophical significance into caesura, and its employment and deployment of relations of difference and identity, presence and absence, it is placed in direct contradiction with caesurae as they actually appear in verse.

In other words, the danger in the analogy between the prosodic disjunction of caesura and its ontological disjunction is that it risks reifying verse technique, something that becomes explicit in Allen's countersensical line-ending caesura. This is the double bind Giorgio Agamben seeks to avoid in his discussion, in "The End of the Poem," of that other mode of interrupting the sameness of rhythm in metrical poetry: enjambment. Starting with an "ontic" analysis of this technical feature of verse, namely that "the possibility of enjambment constitutes the only criterion for distinguishing poetry from prose,"[14] Agamben will eventually make an ontological claim about *poetry*, and indeed *for* poetry, as that mode of writing that will "let language finally communicate itself."[15] The echo of Heidegger's own description of "the speaking of language" is by no means coincidental; yet Agamben, unlike Heidegger, aims to situate this speaking not in the poem's engagement with its medium in general, but in one specific formal feature of this medium.

As with Hölderlin's caesura, Agamben approaches metrical rhythm as a kind of "interruption"; and he too focuses on the negative dimension of a verse feature. Agamben focuses on "the end of the poem" because "there can be no enjambment in the last line," which means that each poem faces the ultimate dissolution of the tension and difference in which it "lives."[16] At this point, the impossibility of enjambment implies an impossibility of poetry as such: each poem must continually confront and negotiate the specter of its own impending impossibility. In its final lines, the poem is left with two options: sound and sense can be reconciled in a "mystical marriage" in which the poem itself would be dismantled, or alternatively the last line can give on to an "empty place in which, according to Mallarmé's phrase, truly *rien n'aura lieu que le lieu*."[17] Agamben develops this either-or into a brief reading of the final five lines of Dante's "Così nel mio parlar voglio esser aspro": "The double intensity animating language does not die away in a final comprehension; instead it collapses into silence, so to speak, in an endless falling. The poem thus reveals the goal of its proud strategy: to let language finally communicate itself, without remaining unsaid in what is said."[18]

It is here that Agamben's analysis shifts from an ontic to an ontological plane, where the poem ceases to be *Poesie* and becomes *Dichtung*. Although less glaring than in Allen's "caesura" line-ending, we once again encounter an ambivalence at this point of transition. Collapsing into "an endless falling," does the poem follow the second of the two possibilities Agamben has suggested, in which nothing takes place except the place itself, or does it serve to suspend this either-or indefinitely? This suspension, as an endless *falling*, would refuse even to "place" itself in the place of where "nothing" will take place. If poetry brings language to communicate itself, it does so only insofar as language itself is ultimately negative. If enjambment in particular can endow poetry with its peculiar negativity, this is by virtue of its peculiar negativity, understood as its tension between the poem's sound patterning and its sense.

This points to a wider worry about Agamben's transition from the generic analysis of *Poesie* to an ontological exposition of *Dichtung*. Language "communicates itself" when it exceeds the sound-sense dichotomy, or tension, in which enjambment "lives." But it is one thing to say that language in essence exceeds a sound-sense dichotomy that has been shown up as insufficient, another thing entirely to claim that language communicates itself as—and ultimately *is*—this excess. This, indeed, is the claim Agamben will make when elsewhere he speaks of a "negative ontological foundation."[19] He does not ask whether another conception of language might allow us to grasp, from within the poem, language's communicating itself on its own terms. For Heidegger, this would simply be one more instance of "demonstrating by means of literary history that these works of poetry really are not literature," but finding that the poem nevertheless continues to be grasped in terms of "literature" (WCT 134/139). The moral of this story, he would conclude, is that this excess must point us toward a thinking of language and poetry beyond the limits of poetics.

There is one further difference between Heidegger's thinking and that of Agamben, Laboue-Labarthe and Allen, and one that should give us pause. Both enjambment and caesura are seen to attain their ontological import through the irruption of negativity into a self-present sphere of meaning. Heidegger, by contrast, insists that poetry, in its vocation as *Dichtung,* is an *opening* of meaning. This is not to ignore the negativity taking place in poetry, but to reframe its significance. As mentioned above, Heidegger is concerned with how presence is shaped by an absencing movement that delimits it; absencing effects an opening of meaning not by undermining it or rendering meaning impossible in advance, but by conditioning the openness through which beings and the world can become meaningful. At the same time, he argues that this open region must not only involve a principle of *difference,* so that we can set beings off from one another, and from the world they inhabit, but also a principle of *jointure* (*Fuge*), which binds them together in such a way that they can enter into relation. Throughout the book I will depict this as an *articulation* that both differentiates and joins. It is as it differentiates and joins beings in a singular manner that a poem can bring beings to show themselves "for the first time."

Moreover, this understanding of difference and jointure coincides with the kinetic conception of the relations between presence and absencing so that all meaning is indelibly *rhythmic.* Lacoue-Labarthe, Allen and Agamben situate the negativity of poetry in its deployment of nonsemantic rhythmic features; rhythm is an "other" to thinking, it is immediately counter-rhythm. Yet Heidegger argues that rhythm rather conditions, and shapes, the openness we inhabit. In this respect the poem does not constitute a "counter-rhythmic interruption" to meaning, but through its rhythmicity performs the entry into meaning itself, opening up the possibility of an encounter with beings. Given Heidegger's onus on the kinetic dimension of beings' autodisclosure, it is unsurprising that poetry should attain such significance in his thought, for in it coincide two modes of rhythmicity: that of the fabric of our experience, and the rhythmicity proper to language itself. Rendering manifest these two rhythms, poetry can shape the countermovements between presencing and absencing as such.

However, here one might ask how such rhythmicity relates to rhythm as a "paralinguistic" feature of language. As we shall see throughout, bodily and verbal openness are approached concomitantly, so that language becomes what I term a *bodily articulation.* Agamben portrays the distinction between sound and sense in the poem as between "semiotic" and "semantic" spheres; the sonority of poetry, for Agamben, is semiotic (or so one can surmise—he himself does not explain this equivalence) in that it is a patterning of individual sounds into recognizable systems (iambs, *terza rima*, and so on). But to do this requires that the sounds of language be abstracted from meaning—it would be "metaphysical" insofar as it imposes on language a strict dualism between language's physical and ideal dimensions. For Heidegger, by contrast, language means insofar as it *sounds* (*lautet*); in other words, the material or physical features of language—which are often called paralinguistic as they coincide with language but are not part of its meaning—should not be conceived of as an interruption of, or aporia for, meaning, but constitute a central moment in meaning's coming to sound. It is at these points of contact, moreover, that we find not only Heidegger's engagement with poetry, but also an engagement with those same "schemas" of poetics that he elsewhere denigrates. A central task of this book will be to probe the potential significance this notion of *sounding* holds for poetics.

■

On June 21, 1934, Heidegger resigned from his post as rector of the University of Freiburg. In the Winter Semester of that year, he gave his first lecture series on the poetry of Friedrich Hölderlin, on the late hymns "Germanien" and "Der Rhein." The close succession of these two events has led much of the writing on Heidegger's readings of poetry, and especially since the "Heidegger controversy" that followed the publications of Victor Farias's and Hugo Ott's biographies,[20] to concern itself with whether we can find, in his engagement with Hölderlin, a way of explaining or salvaging him from his support for the Nazi Party. This line of argument is encouraged by Heidegger himself in his interview with *Der Spiegel*, "Only a God Can Save Us": "After I stepped down as rector I limited myself to teaching. In the summer semester of 1934 I lectured on 'Logic.' In the following semester I gave the first Hölderlin lecture. In 1936, I began the Nietzsche lectures. Anyone with ears to hear heard in these lectures a confrontation (*Auseinandersetzung*) with National Socialism."[21] Following Heidegger's hint, many works—including Miguel de Beistegui's *Heidegger and the Political*, Michael Zimmerman's *Heidegger's Confrontation with Modernity*, and Julian Young's *Heidegger, Philosophy, Nazism*—aim to "hear" in Heidegger's readings of Hölderlin and Nietzsche just such an *Auseinandersetzung*,[22] whereas others—such as James Phillips's *Heidegger's Volk* and Bernhard Radloff's *Heidegger and the Question of National Socialism*—go so far as to identify in Heidegger's writings on poetry a salvaged conception of the "political" as such, in particular in its critique of liberal humanism.[23]

There are then works that approach Heidegger's readings of Hölderlin to prove precisely the opposite—that is, that his philosophy is inherently Nazist, and that his readings of Hölderlin are designed to Nazify a poet whose poetry resists such an operation at every juncture.[24] This focus has coincided for the most part with an emphasis on the thematic aspects of Heidegger's writing, and in particular on questions of the "other," technology, our relation to the earth and to our "homeland," and the relation between the divine and the human. Questions concerning poetry as an artistic medium employing particular expressive features are for the most part overlooked, as are the issues Heidegger's thinking raises for literary theory and poetics more generally.[25]

My focus will be these implications for poetics, and as a result I will restrict questions of Heidegger's political activity to footnotes. Nevertheless, one cannot ignore the extent to which Heidegger's political judgments of the 1930s constitute a real problem for any serious engagement with his thought. To see this, take the following passage, from the *Introduction to Metaphysics* lecture course he gave in 1935, a year after he had resigned the rectorate:

> We lie in the pincers. Our people, as standing in the centre, suffers the most intense pressure—our people, the people richest in neighbors and hence the most endangered people, and in this [*in all dem*] the metaphysical people.[26] We are sure of this vocation; but this people will gain a fate from its vocation only when it creates *in itself* a resonance, a possibility of resonance for this vocation, and grasps its tradition creatively. All this implies that this people, as a historical people, must transpose itself—and with it the history of the West— from the centre of their future happening into the originary realm of the powers of Being. Precisely if the great decision regarding Europe is not to go down the path of annihilation—precisely then can this decision come about only through the development of new, historically *spiritual* forces from the centre. (IM 41/29; translation modified)

When we read the claim that the Germans are "the metaphysical people," we should note that, at this point in his thinking, Heidegger is conceiving of metaphysics as the posing of the question, "why are there beings, rather than nothing at all?," in order to reach "beyond beings," and that Heidegger's warning of Europe's "annihilation" also nods toward his account of "the nothing" which serves as the impetus for asking this question. In this respect, the "great decision" alluded to is our posing of the question as to how we stand with being, and with "the nothing." Indeed, the Germans attain their status as "the metaphysical people" by virtue of their exposed relation to foreign "neighbors." This both continues Heidegger's thinking on the relation between Dasein's uncanniness and its authenticity, and prefigures the role played by "neighborhood" in his later thought, which is understood as a co-belonging foreignness. Heidegger will expand upon this in the 1942 lecture series on Hölderlin's "Ister" hymn, saying that "the law of the encounter between the foreign and one's own is the fundamental truth of history, a truth from out of which the essence of history must unveil itself" (IH 49/61). To call the Germans "the most endangered people" would appear to give fundamental-ontological sustenance to the clamor for remilitarizing the Rhineland, while also recalling Hölderlin's lines from "Patmos": "But where danger threatens / That which saves from it also grows."[27]

Far from being extraneous to, let alone incompatible with, Heidegger's wider philosophy, this passage would appear to be both philosophically consistent, and, more critically, philosophically *sound*, supporting Karl Löwith's observation that Heidegger's supposedly philosophical and political pronouncements overlap to the extent that the rectoral address is "philosophically demanding, a minor stylistic masterpiece."[28] We might note a kinship between the "leaders" of the rectoral address and the "creators" of "The Origin of the Work of Art" and the *Introduction to Metaphysics*,[29] and indeed, this aspect of Heidegger's thinking can be traced further back, firstly to Heidegger's reading of Plato's cave allegory in *On the Essence of Truth*, when he speaks of the "liberators" who make possible free human comportment (ET 83/115), but also to the final passages of the 1929 lecture "What is Metaphysics?": "only because we can question and ground things is the destiny of our existence placed in the hands of the researcher" (P 95–96/18).[30] In short, Heidegger's thinking at this period cannot be extricated from the political choices that led him to join the Nazi Party in 1933, uncomfortable though this truth is for those of us who admire his thinking and find Nazism in all its incarnations abhorrent.[31]

This does not mean that Nazist thinking exhausts these passages, however. Although there is evident overlap between Heidegger's first writings on poetry and these "Nazi" writings, and between Heidegger's philosophical concerns and some of the motifs of Nazi and other right-wing discourse of the period, many of his most important insights, such as his insistence on the work's thingliness and his critique of "symbolic images" as an explanation of art meaning, reach far beyond its political context. Heidegger's account of the artwork is most pointedly political in the infamous comparison between the artwork as a "happening of truth" and other moments when truth takes place: "the state-founding act" and "the essential sacrifice" (OBT 37/51). We also notice unmistakably national-ist overtones when Heidegger speaks of the work's making possible the being-with-one-another of a *Volk* (people), who engage with the "earth" of the artwork as "their earth," and thus become "a historical humanity" (OBT 47/62).[32] This historical dimension, however, is predicated on the artwork's engagement with the modes of appearance of its "work-material" or medium and thereby "transports" thinking "out of the realm of the usual" (OBT 40/54). The *Volk* can only grasp the "earth" as "their earth" because of the artwork's engagement with its own earth. Indeed, although the ways in which Heidegger preserves the artwork undergoes a tangible shift in his later essays, where the language of *Gelassenheit* (releasement) supplants that of *Erschlossenheit* (resoluteness),[33] the understanding of how the artwork renders possible such preservation remains broadly intact. In other words, if Heidegger endows the artwork with nationalistic signifi-cance in his writings of the 1930s, then this is to do with his preservation of the work, rather than the model of the work itself.

This would suggest that one can give, as it were, a formal reading of Heidegger untouched by the particular political gloss he subsequently gave to his own insights. However, I would also claim that the passages cited ac-tually, at crucial junctures, undercut the political gloss Heidegger provides. For instance, when the Germans are deemed "the metaphysical people," it is because of an exposedness or ecstasis that would construct them as a people. Yet the corollary of this is that to overcome this exposedness would be to lose this capacity to pose the question of being. Authentic being-in-the-world does not dissolve ecstasis but rather grasps in ecstasis the pos-sibility most proper to it. In other words, the Germans depend on this exposedness for their status as "the metaphysical people"; to declare war on these "neighbors" would entail closing themselves off from the question of being.

A similar point can be made with reference to Heidegger's discussion of a geologist who attempts to grasp the heaviness of a rock: "While the heaviness weighs down on us, at the same time, it denies us any penetra-tion into it. If we attempt such penetration by smashing the rock, then it shows us its pieces but never anything inward, anything that has been opened up. The stone has instantly withdrawn again into the same dull weight and mass of its fragments" (OBT 24–25/35). The attempt to grasp the rock through penetrating into it fails because what we are searching for continually withdraws from our thinking. Rather, we need to attend to the withdrawal itself, and this requires a mode of thinking that will trace the "earth" of the rock in the "coming-forth concealing" movement by which it withdraws. The human activity that can trace this movement is art, and

thinking can only grasp this movement through its "preservation" of artworks. But this means that if the earth is to become the *Grund* (ground)
for a *Volk,* it can only do insofar as it remains *Ab-grund* (abyss). Again, the
onus is on attending to withdrawal, whatever the voluntaristic vocabulary
and the Faustian allusions of the *staatgründende Tat.* What Heidegger's
thinking exacts at these junctures, quite simply, undermines the direction
that he himself will attempt to take it. Perhaps unsurprisingly, it is those
aspects of his thinking that resist any assimilation into right-wing politics
that are of greatest consequence for poetry and poetics.

■

There is one further difficulty confronting any attempt to give a coherent
account of Heidegger's thinking, namely that it does not easily give itself
to summary or a series of propositions. Heidegger's thinking is continually
in flux, ceaselessly revising itself, calling into question earlier formulations
and ways of framing problems, and his later work in particular is knowingly provisional. In the opening of his lecture entitled "Language," he
admits that the guiding phrase he proposes: "language is—language" is
not going to get us anywhere. His rejoinder is salutary: "But we do not
want to get anywhere. We would like only, for once, to get to just where
we are already" (PLT 188/12). If this is the ethic that motivates much of his
writing on poetry, we will find the significance of his thinking less in the
actual statements he makes than in the shape of the thinking that informs
it, and the recurrent motifs through which he thinks. It is thus that I will
approach his thinking—less to reconstruct a Heideggerian account of poetry, were such a thing even possible, than to look at the ways in which he
approaches poetry, the broader patterns and problematics of his thinking,
and particular junctures in this thinking when these patterns and problematics are most powerfully in evidence.

The book has four chapters. Chapter 1 charts the motif of firstness in
Heidegger's writing on art and poetry in the 1930s. This motif, I argue,
constitutes a confrontation with the traditions of "aesthetics" and "metaphysics" on the one hand, and with the lacunae of his earlier work on the
other. My central claim is that, if the term *being* is used in order to think
the movement of beings into presence, then we do not find, as has often
been argued, an opposition of the formal to the ontological aspects of artworks, but rather a revaluation of the work's engagement with its medium
in terms of this ontological movement. Heidegger's aim is to return to
such features this *aletheic* capacity, and does this through an engagement
with what he terms the earth in the artwork's "work-material," that is, its
medium. Insofar as it inheres in the work's medium, earth is aligned with

the work's formal features, but it further belongs to Heidegger's retrieval of form as a metaphysical concept. In both instances, what is at issue is the limit that conditions all openness. In the artwork, this limit inheres in the opacity of the work's medium; the work's engagement with this medium allows it to "fix in place" this concealing movement so that it attains a particular *Gestalt* (shape). Heidegger thematizes this as a "contest between measure and limit": the work seeks, through the repertoire of modes of artistic articulation open to it, to render manifest that within its medium which would recede from view. It is as it contests its own limits that the work becomes a "setting-into-work of truth": rendering manifest and shifting its own limits, it shifts limit as such, and with it the open region in which beings enter into presence. It is through this shift in the limits of the open that the work brings us to see the world "as though for the first time."

Chapter 2 relates this problematic to Heidegger's analyses of language, taking as its starting point Heidegger's rather enigmatic suggestion that the earth in language lies in "the naming power of the word" (the phrase from which the chapter takes its title). Here I argue that *naming* is not simply an unmediated saying of being, but rather a quasi-performative "bringing-into-name" whereby that which lies beyond the limits of intelligibility is for the first time rendered thinkable. This can be seen through the shifting meaning of *logos* in Heidegger's oeuvre. At first, *logos* denotes discourse, the whole of meaningful verbal practices anterior to language as a lexical and syntactical system. In his later writing, however, *logos* points to the gathering by which this intelligibility is first constituted. On the one hand, we find *die Sage* (a gathering "Saying"); on the other, *das Sprechen* (human speech); *die Sprache* (language) becomes the movement from Saying into speech. The abiding concern, the relation between this originary intelligibility and the verbal language that depends on it, remains throughout, as Heidegger asks how an individual verbal utterance might engender and even transform the intelligibility out of which it arises, and thus "name" being. This happens not simply semantically, but as language becomes articulation, that is, a setting-into-relation that both joins and differentiates. As we shall see, this articulation is indelibly *bodily.*

It is here that poetry attains a particular significance for Heidegger's thinking on language, as that kind of speech that engages with its limits in order to name. This is already present in the account of "poetical discourse" in *Being and Time,* which makes known through vocal expressivity certain affective states that cannot be articulated semantically: voice thus inhabits the limits of discursivity. This coincides with a second voice, the "voice of conscience," which also exceeds the discursive through its disclosure of the nothing. And yet there is a fundamental discrepancy between the two: poetry attains its effect from its vocal sonority, whereas the voice of conscience is silent. When, in his later writings, Heidegger employs the guideword "language speaks as the peal of stillness [*Geläut der Stille*]," it is precisely this antinomy that he aims to resolve, bringing together in this "peal" the *sounding* of poetical discourse and the *silence* of the voice of conscience. Here Heidegger conceives of silence as a dual limit: the "Saying" that renders possible verbal language but also exceeds it on the one hand, and the absencing movement of everything that withdraws from presence (be it as the absence of phenomenal sound or as the resistance to semantic meaning) on the other. Naming takes place at the liminal point between the sounding of verbal language and this double silence, a silence out of which poetry must trace its own entry into presence.

Heidegger's insistence on language as a bodily articulation also motivates his famous dismissal of metaphor, which I turn to in Chapter 3. Here I note that each of Heidegger's denunciations of metaphor arise as digressions from a wider polemic against the "physiological" determination of the body. Why should he link metaphor to the physiological body thus? Because metaphor, Heidegger argues, adheres to the sensuous-nonsensuous dualism: *meta-pherein, Über-tragung* (literally "carrying over"), implies that the nonsensuous content remains stable as its sensuous manifestations alter, just as the physiological understanding of the body assumes in advance an ideal or cognitive realm that remains stable as the physical body changes.

Yet what of Heidegger's own apparent recourse to metaphor? Firstly, I note that "metaphor" can often be used to domesticate a statement that appears aberrant, rather than asking where this aberrance might lead. Indeed, any attempt to think, from within a preexisting idiom, beyond the limits of this idiom, will at first appear aberrant. What is at issue in the question of metaphor is precisely a transformation of what language can do. Again, the bodily dimension is key. Heidegger turns to two metaphors that would undermine the sensuous-nonsensuous opposition and its attendant opposition of bodily experience and linguistic cognition, the first concerned with bodily receptivity, the second, which comes from Hölderlin's "Brot und Wein," "Worte, wie Blumen [words, like flowers]," with the bodily production of words. Rather than approaching this as the physiological production of phonetic matter, Heidegger points to an anterior growth into language, through which language comes to "sound" out of both body and "Saying." Here we also get an implicit account of "poetic language" and its truth: in its exploration, and performance, of such "growth," Hölderlin's metaphor is able to "name" the sounding of language.

Here we start to see the significance of Hölderlin's lines for Heidegger's thinking, and chapter 4 analyzes the role played by poetry within his own argumentation, and the reading practices he employs as he encounters particular poems. I argue that Heidegger's *Erläuterungen* of poems should not be read as exegeses but, following the German more literally, as "soundings-out" of the poems, continuing the project of "preservation" that he had outlined in "The Origin of the Work of Art": a mode of reading, listening, or beholding that, submitting itself to the openness of beings the work brings about, is thereby brought outside of itself. Poetry allows thinking, as it were, to think beyond its own limits.

This raises two questions. Firstly, do Heidegger's readings "stand within" the poems they read? To this end I examine the points of contact, intersection, and divergence, between poem and reading. Secondly, does this standing within accord with Heidegger's own account of it? Indeed, if poetry is a limit to his thinking, his aim is to "submit to the displacement" that the poems come to effect, then it follows that Heidegger must be unable to grasp the full significance of his insights. I thus look to the ways in which the poems inflect—and infect—Heidegger's readings in ways that he himself would deny. Thus I finish by arguing that Heidegger's thinking opens up possibilities for poetics that requires not only that we *read* Heidegger, but that we read *beyond* him. Focusing on his accounts of the artwork's engagement of its medium, of the relation between poem and reading, or language's entry into relationality, I suggest that Heidegger's thinking points—tentatively—toward something like "a poetics of limit" (the subtitle of my conclusion). But it is a poetics of limit that cannot limit itself to Heidegger himself. When Heidegger reads Hölderlin or George, but also Kant or Aristotle, he always reads beyond them, and this is what my book eventually will do with Heidegger himself, by gesturing toward other possible directions for such a poetics of limit.

■

Setting up an encounter between Heidegger's readings of poetry and poetics involves not only disregarding his own dismissals of poetics, but at times reading against the grain of his readings. But it also requires a defense of Heidegger's thinking, both from those for whom his work provokes irritation, and from his most trenchant critics. Heidegger himself anticipated such criticism, saying, in "Why Poets?":

There is the single necessity: by thinking soberly in what is said in [Hölderlin's] poetry, to experience what is unsaid. This is the course of the history of being. If we enter upon this course, it brings thinking and poetry together in a dialogue engaged with the history of being. Researchers in literary history will inevitably see the dialogue as an unscholarly violation of what they take to be the facts. Philosophers will see it as a baffled descent into mysticism. However, destiny pursues its course untroubled by all that. (OBT 204/252)

Heidegger's invocation of "destiny" at this moment is designed, one suspects, to enrage even further the "philosophers" and "researchers in literary history" he feels attacked by. As it happens, literary critics will find far more to take issue with in Heidegger's readings of poems than mere "unscholarly violation of what they take to be the facts." Nevertheless, I would argue that just poetics and literary criticism constitute more than a fact-checking exercise, Heidegger's thinking is far more complex and attentive to the workings of poetry than his critics suggest. Yet if the book will at times appear like a defense of Heidegger, this is not simply a response to his reception by literary theorists and critics. It is only within the internal dynamics of Heidegger's thinking, I would suggest, that we can establish its significance for our understanding of poetry, and to an extent this requires, at least initially, a suspension of disbelief that more skeptical readers might consider to be not only willing, but willful. But as the book progresses, we will also see how Heidegger's most powerful insights are left incomplete, pointing to future directions for a philosophical poetics that would respond to Heidegger's insights, but subsequently take off from them. If this book aims to convince its readers that Heidegger and poetics have far more in common than either party will admit, and to stage a dialogue between them that will benefit both, then ultimately, it also wishes to open up possibilities and exigencies for a philosophical poetics to come.

1

For the First Time

In the introductory remarks to his lecture series on Friedrich Hölderlin's late hymns "Germanien" and "Der Rhein," the first he gave on Hölderlin's poetry, Heidegger discusses the opening lines of "Germanien" and their form: "The form of the poem provides no particular difficulties. The meter does not follow the model of any conventional genre. A poem without meter and rhyme is nevertheless not really a poem at all, not poetry, prose rather. . . . [A]nd yet, [a] common, precise, prosaic 'For' [*Denn*], sounds, as though spoken for the first time, and this apparent prose of the whole poem is more poetic than the smoothest gamboling lines and jingling rhymes of any Goethesque Lieder or other singsong" (GA 39, 16). Prizing the "poetic" away from the generic features of meter or rhyme, Heidegger focuses on the moment at which the word *Denn* "sounds, as though spoken for the first time." Yet this would not render the word's sounding wholly unrelated to questions of "meter and rhyme." Indeed, the "apparent prose" through which this word "sounds" is only "apparent"; it is not prose but the "prosaic" as it irrupts within verse; its sounding cannot be extracted from its prosodic effect within the verse structure of the hymn as a whole. Challenging any peremptory equation of the term "poetic" with euphonic "singsong," Heidegger argues what makes this word *Denn* poetic is precisely its prosaic quality, its dissonance. But it also exacts that we *hear* this dissonance, and the sounding this dissonance effects. If the poem brings the word *Denn* to sound at the moment where the generic characterization of verse breaks down, then we must be able to explain this breakdown as a feature of this very instance of verse.

We might see the relation between the poem's sounding and its meter and rhyme as analogous to the distinction that Heidegger draws, in the 1935–36 triple lecture on "The Origin of the Work of Art," between *Dichtung*, the "projective saying" that is the "essence" of all art, and *Poesie*, the "linguistic work in the narrow sense" (OBT 45/61). This is not the only time Heidegger will invoke, and invert, the prose-verse distinction as a means of showing how *Dichtung* exceeds its determination as *Poesie*. In the 1950 essay "Language," he intones: "Pure prose is never prosaic. It is as poetic [*dichterisch*] . . . as poesy [*Poesie*]" (PLT 205/31, translation modified). What marks this excess of the "poetic" over "poesy" is, in the Hölderlin lecture, aligned with the word's "first" quality, and the motif of "firstness" is deployed throughout "The Origin of the Work of Art" in order to depict the "truly poetizing projection" that, he argues, is at the basis of all great art (OBT 47/63). The artwork (in this instance the temple at Paestum) "*first* makes the storm visible in its violence," "*first* brings forth the light of day, the breadth of the sky, the darkness of night," so that "tree, grass, eagle and bull, snake and cricket *first* enter their distinctive shapes and thus come to appearance as what they are" (OBT 21/31, my emphasis). What is at issue in the work's firstness is the work's status as a "happening of the truth of beings"; that is, the work projects an open region in which beings enter into unconcealment (*aletheia*) in a singular way, thus appearing as though *for the first time*. And this unconcealment is dependent on a prior firstness: the work can "bring forth the light of day" because, in its use of its "work-material," or medium, "the rock comes to bear and to rest and so *first* becomes rock; the metal comes to glimmer and shimmer, the colors to shine, the sounds to ring, the word to say" (OBT 24/35; translation modified, emphasis added). Truth is the truth of medium: the work will only transform, as though for the first time, the presencing of the "light of day" because it has brought forth, for the first time, the modes of presencing proper to stone, rock, metal, color, sound, and word.

This motif of "for the first time" in Heidegger's writings of the 1930s galvanizes not only his account of the work's truth, but also his critique of the "aesthetic" tradition. Rather than being merely an object of beauty, the work becomes a site in which is rendered audible and thinkable an "open" (*das Offene*) into which human beings are thrown, but to whose limits they are deaf and blind, whose parameters they cannot gauge—and consequently, cannot as yet inhabit. And rather than the work's "formal features" being ornamental (OBT 42/56), to be appreciated for their own sake, they are integral to the work's singular "poetizing projection." But this also implies that it is only by looking precisely to such formal features that we can come to trace how the work can, in each case, engender the firstness through which it brings its medium to "shine" and "say." The "sounding" of *Dichtung,* situated variously in "pure" prose and, within verse itself, "apparent" prose, only exceeds formal or generic determinations of *Poesie* through an engagement with the limits of these determinations. In this respect, Heidegger too is engaging with those aspects of poetry that are often understood in terms of its "form."

This would mean that an understanding of how artworks and poems can shape the modalities of beings' presencing or autodisclosure, where these works bring beings to show themselves "for the first time," would necessitate a deep engagement with the work's *formal* dimension. But what of that warning, eloquently expressed by Bruns, that to ask "how [of Heidegger's thinking] is part of the errancy of the modern age, the age of structuralism, of analytic and calculative reason, which has no other interest in things except in how they work or what strategies they employ"?[1] Bruns's fear is, I think, overstated: not only does Heidegger himself continually try to identify this "first" quality in artworks (such as the temple at Paestum or Hölderlin's "Germanien"), but in so doing he aims to think "how" the artwork functions in such a way as to avoid fitting it to the structures of analytic or calculative reason, in order to "see the enigma" of art and not to "solve" it (OBT 51/66). If, as he remarks in "Hölderlin and the Essence of Poetry," Hölderlin calls poetry "the most innocent of all occupations" in part, Heidegger wryly notes, "to spare his mother" (EHP 62/41), it is also because "this harmless exterior belongs to the essence of poetry, just as the valley belongs to the mountain" (EHP 62/41–42). That is, only by inhabiting this "harmless exterior" can the poem first shift our reading and hearing into the presencing that these poems, in their sounding, render manifest. I would in fact go further: Heidegger's thinking necessitates that we ask "how" even when he does not, for it is here that we can see the extent to which his thinking, far from constituting a simple rejection of the categories of aesthetics—such as "form," "beauty," or aesthetic "experience"—is in fact a radical revaluation of these very phenomena that these categories aim to grasp, and here also that we can start to sketch the far-reaching implications his thinking offers for contemporary poetics and criticism.

The chapter has three sections. The first two are concerned with "The Origin of the Work of Art," arguing that its critique of form is central to the attempt to attend to those moments where the work can bring beings to disclose themselves "for the first time." The first of these sections focuses on Heidegger's confrontation both with the tradition of aesthetics and the lacunae he comes to identify in his own earlier work; the second looks in detail at his analyses of the work's "earthly" medium, and the way in which the "coming-forth concealing" movement by which this medium at once irrupts into the phenomenal world and withdraws from it is "fixed" in what Heidegger terms the work's *Gestalt*. In this, we encounter the work as marked by an uncanny movedness (*Bewegtheit*), and in the third section I pursue this question of movement in terms of a constellation of thinking around *rhythm*, both in "The Origin of the Work of Art" and in his later work. The firstness of the work, arising out of the modalities of beings' entry into presence, is paradigmatically rhythmic; yet we must also ask what relation such rhythmicity bears to the rhythmic movement of an individual poem, its prosody, and the formalization of such prosody in versification, meter, and what one might otherwise term a poem's formal features.

Rethinking Form: Aesthetics and the Recovery of Experience

If Heidegger's presents the sounding of Hölderlin's hymn as irreducible to those aspects of it that are normally grouped together as its form, then this avowed opposition to the formal aspect of works has also provided the basis for some of the most trenchant critiques directed at Heidegger's writing on art and poetry. Both Adorno and Meschonnic argue that his disregard of what Adorno terms "the agency of form," far from overcoming the form-content opposition, results in a simplistic enumeration of the poem's "content," now transformed into a message.[2] For de Man, this arises from an even more basic "flaw": "the substitution of ontological for what could well be called formal dimensions of language."[3] The opposition between formal and ontological is not restricted to Heidegger's critics. In one of the most powerful sympathetic accounts of his work, Fynsk distinguishes, in the exposition of the "figure" (*Gestalt*) of the artwork in "The Origin of the Work of Art," between an understanding of this *Gestalt* in "formal terms," concerned with the work's phenomenal features, and one in terms of "the event of truth" that the work traces and opens up.[4]

However, we might be skeptical about making so clear-cut a distinction between the "formal" and the "ontological" dimensions of the artwork. As we have seen, the sounding effected by the opening lines of "Germanien," which is precisely the poem's "ontological" dimension, arises through the poem's supposedly "formal" prosodic dissonance. Indeed, if, as I argued in the introduction, *ontology* for Heidegger describes the ways in which beings can first come to show themselves in an open region—their autodisclosure, and the modalities of such autodisclosure—it would appear that any ontological approach to the artwork necessarily entails and engagement with supposedly formal features of the work. What is at issue is less these features themselves than their value within the work, and in particular the role they play in engendering the firstness that Heidegger takes to be characteristic of "great art." In this, Heidegger finds himself in critical dialogue with some of the guiding tropes of the aesthetic tradition, and what appears initially to be simplificatory dismissal of this tradition turns out in fact to be the catalyst for a far more developed thinking of precisely those phenomena with which "aesthetics" is concerned: form, but also the categories of beauty, artistic technique, the relation between artwork and equipment, the experience of an artwork, amongst others. At the same time, Heidegger's turn to the artwork arises out of the internal dynamics of his thought, and particularly the problematic of "finite transcendence," in which an entity whose existence is bounded by the world it inhabits would succeed in thinking beyond the parameters of this world, so as to shape its own existence, and even the world itself.[5] The status of *limit* becomes crucial to both strands: at once, it explains the movement into appearance effected in and by the artwork, and continues the logic of finitude that pervades Heidegger's thinking of the "open" space in which beings come to presence. It is through this engagement with limit that Heidegger will conceive of those aspects of the artwork that are often approached in terms of its form as constitutive of the work's opening up an encounter with beings, such that "for the first time, in the midst of beings, it brings them to shine and sound" (OBT 45/60).

Form and the Aesthetic Tradition

As we saw in the hymn "Germanien," the poem's firstness cannot be reduced to analyses of imagery and versification, pursuits which Heidegger denigrates as a "beloved occupation of the learned," but from whose "enlightenment . . . nothing comes" (GA39 16). This is echoed in "The Origin of the Work of Art" when Heidegger contrasts the "preservation" of the artwork, which "stand[s] within the openness of beings that happens in the work" (OBT 41/55), to "that merely cultivated connoisseurship of the formal features of the work, its qualities and intrinsic charms [*Reize an sich*]" (OBT 42/56). Behind this penchant for subjecting professional literary critics and art aficionados to ridicule lies a serious point.[6] For if we take the work's formal features in isolation and treat them as "charms," we effect a schematic separation of these formal features from the work itself. The charms *an sich* might be "intrinsically" charming, but by this very token they become extrinsic to the work as a whole. Nothing more than mere ornament, the formal features must be incidental to any "happening" of the "openness of beings" the work might bring about. Yet without these features, such openness is rendered impossible in advance. Listening to the "singsong" alone, we are rendered deaf to the poem's sounding.

In this respect, Heidegger would seem closer to Adorno's account of "the agency of form" than either would imagine (or, for that matter, would wish to admit). And, like Adorno, Heidegger's revaluation of form involves confronting the question of the *truth* of art, however much their conceptions of truth diverge. If our appreciation of the artwork treats its form in isolation, Heidegger argues, we are tacitly accepting an interpretation of truth as *adaequatio intellectus et rei*, the correspondence of a concept to an extant thing. In order that the charms should become charming, they must first of all be freed from any truth claim, and in particular from the exigencies of correspondence. Yet this freedom is in fact nothing of the kind, the work's formal charms serving as the veneer for a historically sedimented impotence that continually replays the inaugurating gesture of "aesthetics": the scission of beauty and truth.[7]

As is the case with "form," Heidegger does not want to dismiss "beauty" as a category, but rather to return it to its place within the conception of truth as *aletheia*, which Heidegger translates as *Unverborgenheit* (unconcealment). Building on the simple observation that we can have a true, or "correct" representation of a being only if this being has in some sense given itself to be so represented, he suggests that anterior to all correspondence or "correctness" must be an open space in which beings enter into unconcealment, or, following the alpha privative of *a-letheia*, nonoblivion. The truth of art would concern not its correct depiction of, say, a pair of peasant shoes,[8] but rather the modes through which beings first enter unconcealment: that which renders something like depiction possible in the first place. And it is here that beauty and truth coincide once more: "The shining [*Scheinen*] which is set into the work is the beautiful [*Schöne*]. *Beauty is one way in which truth as unconcealment comes to presence*" (OBT 32/43). No longer merely decorative, an object of aesthetic pleasure, beauty becomes index of its entry into unconcealment—that is, it becomes the way in which its truth is articulated.

The extraction of an artwork's form to something decorative also, of course, assumes it to have no bearing on the work's "content" or "matter," and running alongside Heidegger's antipathy toward "intrinsic charms" is a developed dismantling of the interpretation of the "thing" as "formed matter" (OBT 8/16). "Formed matter" is but one of three interpretations of thingliness that Heidegger identifies in the history of philosophy, along with "a bearer of traits" and the "unity of a sensory manifold" (OBT 11/20). Heidegger first notes the strengths of this interpretation: not only does it offer, at least initially, to steer a mid-point between the excesses of the other two (the former "holds [the thing], as it were, too far away from the body, the second brings it too close" [OBT 8/16]), but it is especially attractive for aesthetics as it immediately affords an account of the artist's activity as giving form to an otherwise formless mass. However, Heidegger suggests, it might be precisely this attractiveness that leads it to be an "assault on the thing" in general (OBT 11/20), and on the thingly dimension of artworks in particular.

There is something anomalous about the thingliness of the artwork, and indeed, it is from this difficulty that the problem of form first issues. If Hölderlin's poems were found in a soldier's knapsack in World War I along with "cleaning equipment," and Beethoven's string quartets are routinely stored "like potatoes in a cellar" (OBT 3/9), we nevertheless believe these works to be constitutively different from disinfectant or tubers. We might, for example, point to "something" in the artwork "over and above its thingliness" (OBT 3/9). This "over and above" would then be understood as a content that "says something other than the mere thing"; the artwork becomes *allo agoreuei:* allegory or symbol. When we recognize an object depicted in a painting, or identify and flesh out a recurrent trope in a corpus of poetry (the camel in Arabic epic, rivers in Hölderlin's late hymns), we interpret them in terms of this "over and above."

This, Heidegger argues, would be to assume both a hard-and-fast dichotomy between sensuous and nonsensuous realms, and the model of meaning as correspondence, something made explicit in his lecture series on Hölderlin's "Ister" hymn, where he offers a critique of the interpretation of artworks in terms of "symbolic images" (*Sinnbilder*): sensuous tokens (be it as individual verbal signs or as wider tropes) that point to an ideal content (IH 16/17–18). And, although he approaches them separately, the positing of an artwork's meaning over and above its thingliness is seen to be intimately related to the dichotomy between form and matter through which thingliness itself is grasped. This latter is in fact a double dichotomy: we might contrast the work's formal features—for example a poem's prosody, trope and image—to the content that this prosodic and figural repertoire of images is employed in order to evoke, decorate, or "echo";[9] but we might equally set up a distinction between the inanimate verbal matter that is arranged prosodically and the animating artistic intention that forms it into meaningful prosodic and semantic units. In either case, Heidegger wishes to ask whether this need to turn to the nonthingly aspect of the work might not be precipitate, in fact indicative not of the singularity of artworks as being more than mere things, but of an impoverished understanding of this thingliness. Maybe it is not an ideal content, but rather its treatment of its thingly work-material (*Werkstoff*) that separates the *Grosse Fuge* from the Jersey Royal. Moreover, he will suggest, that which is most proper to thingliness is precisely what the very invocation of something "over and above" is deployed to explain.

This leads to a radically nonmimetic account of art meaning. No longer a content that supervenes over the thingly dimension of the work, "meaning" would describe the way in which the thing's entry into appearance is set into motion in and by the work. The question here is one of how, for example, pigment can first come not to be mere color, but to "shine" (OBT 24/35). This might be seen in figurative painting as the question as to how a configuration of shape and color attains the value of "depiction," although, as first Clement Greenberg and then Michael Fried have argued, this is also a question for abstract modernist painting, Greenberg pointing to how a flat support can engender the illusion of depth, and Fried to the tension between "literal" and "depicted" shape.[10] Fried's subsequent claim that this tension allows the painting to "defeat or suspend its own object-hood" is, like Heidegger, concerned with how the work, as a thing, should be able to exceed its own thingliness. Both, moreover, look to a meaningful layer in art that precedes, and indeed opens up the possibility of, figural representation. In a work such as Cézanne's *Portrait du jardinier Vallier* for example, a painting whose importance to Heidegger I will discuss below, it is the question of how, in the texture of the brushstrokes, the painting oscillates between figuration and abstraction, both constructing a central figure and yet overwhelming it; the brushstrokes at once render palpable the gardener Vallier's flesh and yet, depicting and evoking this flesh, give onto an experience with its pigment that is subsequently irreducible to depiction or evocation. Indeed, not only does it transform the way we see skin and flesh but it brings us to see pigment *as pigment;* it grasps, and even performs, the moment at which color "comes to shine" (OBT 25/36). That the painting is depicting a particular thing—the gardener's face—is secondary to the movement and texture of the paint itself; indeed, the depiction only arises out of this movement, and the painting's "over and above" out of its engagement with the thingliness of its medium, or "work-material" (OBT 24/35).[11] This opening of meaning, moreover, is precisely what Heidegger attempts to capture as the work's firstness, the supposedly formal movement of pigment transformed into the disclosive movement that Heidegger will term *Ereignis,* the "event of appropriation."

Art and Equipment

I will return to this engagement with the work's "work-material" at greater length below. Before doing so, however, I wish to note a second consequence of Heidegger's attempt to grasp the thingliness of the work beyond its determination as "formed matter": the counterpoint between artwork and equipment. If we understand basic thingliness as a "formless" mass, then nevertheless, Heidegger observes, this mass can only be given "form" if it gives itself to being "formed" in advance. He will reiterate this in "The Concept and Essence of *Phusis* in Aristotle's *Physics B, I.*" *Hule,* subsequently translated into "post-Greek thought" as *materia,* matter, is originally "the appropriate orderable" (P 214/351). If matter can be put to service only because it is itself serviceable, then we find more generally that "the intermingling of form and matter" depends on the piece of matter's "serviceability" (OBT 10/18). Heidegger thus concludes: "matter and form are determinations of beings which find their true home in the essential nature of equipment" (OBT 10/18). What is at issue in the counterpoint of artwork to equipment is, then, an attempt to get beyond these "in no way original determinations belonging to the thingliness of the mere thing" (OBT 10/18) in order to trace the way in which the first becomes manifest as a thing.

The contrast between art and equipment, or the "useful" more generally, is of course a motif that recurs throughout the history of aesthetics; yet Heidegger will argue that, since aesthetics itself tacitly, if unknowingly, accepts the ontology of equipmentality, it is unable to grasp the full salience of this opposition. He thus reproaches Nietzsche who, while shifting the focus of aesthetics from the reception to the creation of artworks, does "not unfold the essence of creation from what is to be created, namely, the work [but] . . . from the state of aesthetic behavior." As a result, in Nietzsche's aesthetics "the bringing-forth of the work does not receive an adequately delineated interpretation which would distinguish it from the bringing forth of utensils by way of handicraft" (Ni 117/117). The difference, that is, lies not in the modes of *making* employed by artist and craftsman respectively, but rather in the coming-forth of the things made; if both artist and craftsman were described in Ancient Greek thought as *technites,* this is because "both the setting-forth of works and the setting-forth of equipment happen in that bringing forth which allows beings, by assuming an appearance, to come forth into their presence" (OBT 35/48).

Far from disregarding the specificities of artistic technique, Heidegger's concern is to reframe the significance of technique. "To be sure," Heidegger says, "the sculptor uses [*gebraucht*] stone just as, in his own way, the mason uses it. But he does not use it up [*verbraucht*]" (OBT 25/36). The use of the sculptor is distinguished at the level not of technical proficiency, but of manifestation: "the painter, too, makes use of pigment; he uses it, however, in such a way that the colors are not used up but begin, rather, *for the first time,* to shine. To be sure, the poet, too, uses words, not, however, like ordinary speakers and writers who must use them up, but rather in such a way that the word *first* becomes and remains truly a word" (OBT 25/36; translation modified, my emphasis). When the craftsman uses up his or her work-material, the material subsequently "disappears into usefulness," becomes "inconspicuous" (OBT 39/53). The "use" that does not "use up," by contrast, resists utility not simply by refusing to be useful, but by insisting radically on the irreducible conspicuousness of things. Yet this resistance to utility does not thereby open on to an "aesthetic" realm where we appreciate the work "for its own sake"; rather, it serves as the basis for the work's being free to render manifest, for the first time, its own work-material, be it pigment, marble, or word. As we will see below, this means that the creation of the artwork, this "using up" is understood from out what Heidegger calls the "createdness" of the work: the way it advertises its thrust into the open, the fact that this particular artwork *is* rather than *is not.*

Once again Heidegger is engaged in critical dialogue with the history of aesthetics in order to reframe one of its central tropes in order to grasp the ontological significance of the artwork, but beyond this dialogue with aesthetics lies a dialogue with his own earlier work. The opposition of artwork and equipment constitutes a continuation of, and a corrective to, the analyses of the "ready-to-hand" (*das Zuhanden*) given in *Being and Time.* Here he had argued that we only first come to grasp the "world" as the context or horizon of "assignments" and "references" that render circumspective our dealings with ready-to-hand entities (such as hammers) intelligible, at those moments at which an assignment ceases, however momentarily, to function. At such moments, the individual piece of equipment becomes "intrusive" and "conspicuous," and, as a result of this intrusion and conspicuousness, "the context of equipment is lit up . . . as a totality constantly sighted beforehand in circumspection." It is, he continues, "with this totality" that "the world announces itself" as "something 'wherein' *Dasein* as an entity already was" (BT 75–76/105–6). When the being withdraws from the way it is grasped in our habitual dealings with the world, its reliability and serviceability are no longer taken for granted and so it attains a heightened conspicuousness, which brings us into an encounter not only with the structure of the world itself, but with our own place within it as being-in-the-world.

We hear an echo of this early in "The Origin of the Work of Art," when Heidegger comments of the "peasant shoes" of Van Gogh's painting: "Perhaps it is only in the picture that we notice all this about the shoes. The peasant woman, by contrast, merely wears them . . . she knows all this without observation or reflection" (OBT 14/23). The importance of the painting of the "peasant shoes," however, extends beyond making us notice the shoes; it does not simply uncover what is already there but rather opens up the space for this uncovering. If the painting has "let us know what the shoes, in truth, are" (OBT 15/24), this is not because it illuminates the essence of these shoes, but because "this being steps forward into the unconcealment of its being" (OBT 16/25). The being is "in truth" in a very literal sense: the artwork engenders the space of unconcealment in which the being depicted can disclose itself. The conspicuousness of broken equipment of *Being and Time* arises from a breakdown in the ready-to-hand to render manifest this readiness-to-hand as such. Like the broken equipment, the artwork becomes conspicuous when, used but not used up, it withdraws from utility. However, its conspicuousness is of an entirely different order. The broken equipment renders manifest a readiness-to-hand which, as an interpretation of beings, is itself left unquestioned. The artwork's resistance to equipmentality, by contrast, necessitates a thinking of thingliness irreducible to such readiness-to-hand and the form-matter distinction that Heidegger retrospectively suggests guides it. Given that Heidegger had described this distinction as "a conceptual mechanism that nothing can resist" (OBT 9/17), this is no mean feat.

Artworks, quite simply, open up an encounter with beings anterior to the equipmental interpretation of beings. Thus poetry will show us, he claims in the 1936 lecture on "Hölderlin and the Essence of Poetry," that "language is not merely a tool which man possesses among many others" but is that which "first grants the possibility of standing in the midst of the openness of beings" (EHP 55–56/35). Only because it has always already granted this openness can language become a tool to be possessed. When Hölderlin's prosaic versifying refuses to disappear into euphony, not only do the poem's words (e.g., *Denn*) *sound* in such a way that we would never hear when we use them in everyday discourse; sounding as though for the first time, they exceed their referential and pragmatic function.[12] Moreover, this first time is indicative of a transformation taking place within the word itself—and within the other media Heidegger mentions in "The Origin of the Work of Art": rock, metal, color, sound—by which the very parameters that frame our encounter with beings in the world are transformed. The sounding of the poem's words does not simply disclose the world of this encounter as something that precedes, but shapes the way this world comes to presence. The artwork's engagement with its medium is always an engagement with the limits of this medium; shifting the limits of what is intelligible within the medium, it shifts the limits of intelligibility as such. This limit is not simply semantic (and in this respect, it is striking that, for Heidegger, the sounding of Hölderlin's poem concerns the meaning of an individual word, *Denn*) but prosodic, the incursion of dissonance into euphonic singsong. The limit of language as medium is experienced as *noise*. If poetry is to exceed, and antecede, the conception of language as tool, and thereby attain the *aletheic* vocation through which it does not simply announce what is "in" the open, but can shape the open itself, then this will require an engagement with the limit and opacity of that language out of which arises.

That the Work Is

The artwork's truth, then, takes place as it shifts the limits of the open region through which beings disclose themselves in an intelligible manner. While situating this in the work's engagement with its medium, Heidegger is also concerned with how this shift is experienced by the work's audience. For, if the artwork advertises its own entry into appearance, then it is precisely the fact that this artwork appears as an existent thing that is striking. This "uncanny," "salient" fact "that this work *is* rather than is not" (OBT 39/53) strikes us so that, as "the work [is] transported into the openness of beings it itself opens up," it "carries us," its audience, "into this openness and, at the same time, out of the realm of the usual" (OBT 40/54). Only through experiencing the work's firstness, that is, can we come to inhabit the open space first opened up by this artwork, and thus open ourselves to the singular configuration the artwork gives to the modes in which beings enter into presence.

Here again, Heidegger is developing on a central motif in *Being and Time*. In this earlier work he asks what happens when it is not simply one assignment within an intelligible context that ceases to function, as is the case with broken equipment, but the context (i.e., the world) itself. As the world's meaningful texture is "sunk into insignificance," Dasein is confronted with the "'nothing' of the world" (BT 393/343). Yet how can this "nothing" be disclosed at all; how can utter insignificance be rendered meaningful? To explain this, Heidegger turns to the state-of-mind (*Befindlichkeit*) of anxiety (*Angst*). What separates anxiety from, say, fear, is that what we feel anxious about is not a particular being, but something quite indefinite, something "nothing and nowhere in the world." Earlier in *Being and Time* Heidegger had suggested that this nothing and nowhere mean that "*that in the face of which one has anxiety*" is quite simply "*the world as such*" (BT 231/186–87); here he offers a more radical interpretation: anxiety discloses not the world as the meaningful context of our engagement with other beings, but rather its breakdown into meaninglessness. The resultant disclosure does not, as is the case with circumspective understanding, grasp a being "as" such-and-such, but "brings one back to the pure 'that-it-is' [*Dass*] of one's ownmost individualized thrownness" (BT 394/343). What is disclosed is the sheer fact, and facticity, of our being-in-the-world, whose scope we cannot gauge but which pervades our every encounter with other entities. We are "being-*in*-the-world," at home in the world and "familiar" with the context of circumspective understanding, and yet, we are "in" the world uncannily: thrown into the world, we are "thrown into uncanniness [*Unheimlichkeit*]" (BT 394/343). And indeed, Heidegger suggests, uncanniness pervades anxiety as *Stimmung* (the mood or attunement) we have when we feel anxious. The *Dass* thus disclosed is at once the *Grund* (ground) of our openness to the world and, withdrawing from this openness and only showing itself as *nothing,* at the same time *Ab-grund* (abyss). The attuned disclosure furnished by anxiety renders thinkable that which by definition exceeds all thought. From the disclosure of our finitude within the world, ironically enough, comes the potential for thinking beyond this finitude; the attuned disclosure of the nothing is what secures Dasein's transcendence with relation to the world as a specifically *finite* transcendence.

In "The Origin of the Work of Art," the site of this finite transcendence is displaced from Dasein onto the artwork itself. It is, in the first instance, now the artwork that is brought face to face with the withdrawal from intelligibility. What Heidegger first approaches as a withdrawal from use or utility is in fact index of the work's attempt to engage with the concealing movement and opacity of the work-material itself, which Heidegger terms the "earth" (OBT 24/35). The earth, conceived of as "coming-forth concealing [*Hervorkommend-Bergende*]" (OBT 24/35), describes the movement by which the withdrawal that frames presence becomes discernable; when the earth is "set forth" in the work, it is not only the work-material that is rendered conspicuous, but this movement as such: its concealing movement, as it were, "comes forth." Once again, we find a finite being engaging with the withdrawal that conditions and limits it, and thereby shaping the modalities of its own finitude.

This is what will ultimately endow the artwork with its ontological significance: engaging with the opacity of its medium, the work will shape not only its own autodisclosure, but autodisclosure more widely, and thereby reframe the limits of possible experience. Before looking at this, however, I would like to focus on the way in which the work appears to its "preservers" echoes the account of the attuned disclosure of the "nothing" given in *Being and Time* and "What is Metaphysics?" In this 1929 lecture, Heidegger asks how the "nothing" can ground Dasein's transcendence, and at the same time attempts to shift his understanding of the "nothing" beyond the account of the insignificance of the world given in *Being and Time* and on to a nonbeing anterior to any determination of negativity. He says: "Only because the nothing is manifest in the ground of Dasein can the total strangeness of beings overwhelm us. Only when the strangeness of beings oppresses us does it arouse and evoke wonder. Only on the ground of wonder—the manifestness of the nothing—does the 'why?' loom before us" (P 95/18). The "nothing" instigates a search for grounds (asking "why?") because it engenders in us "wonder," what Aristotle called *thaumazein*.[13] As the world around us ceases to appear familiar, we ask the "basic metaphysical question": "why are there beings, and why not far rather Nothing?" (P 96/19). And so it transpires that the artwork, rendering manifest its own withdrawal, strikes its beholders with the "salient," "uncanny" fact "that this work is rather than is not," its *factum est* or, with a nod to his earlier account of Dasein's thrownness, the *Dass* of the work's createdness (OBT 39/53).

The account of *Stimmung* in *Being and Time* was part of an attempt to articulate a mode of disclosing the world that was anterior to circumspective understanding. Such disclosure, situated at the limits of explicability, would also be able to grasp Dasein's constitutive finitude. In this respect, experience became an inalienable moment in Dasein's coming to understand itself and the world it inhabits, but only if grasped in terms of its disclosure. "The Origin of the Work of Art" continues this insight, searching for, in Fynsk's phrase, "a recovery of human experience."[14] Again, what is at issue is the sheer "fact" of the work's bare existence, which advertises itself as something inexplicable and strange. And again, attending to this strangeness exacts a mode of experience-as-disclosure which will gauge the finitude that bounds all beings that appear "in being." Exhibiting the fact that it is rather than is not, the work becomes "strange" and "solitary"; it "stands within itself" and "seems to sever all ties to human beings," and in this strange, solitary subsistence it "thrusts" into the open (OBT 40/53). In this, it constitutes an "uncanny address" to those very humans with whom it severs its ties;[15] the "recovery of human experience" takes place by way of an encounter with the artwork as resolutely *non*-human. This uncanniness then extends to the audience's experience of the work's address. Carried "out of the realm of the usual," the audience will "submit to this displacement," and thus open itself to the truth of being the work brings about (OBT 40/54).

And here, the artwork has not only brought us face to face with the uncanny, the strange, and the inhuman, but also, advertising the fact of its existence, it advertises the possibility of its nonexistence: the fact that *it is rather than is not.* Just as in the experience of *Angst* in *Being and Time* and "What is Metaphysics?," we are brought into an encounter with the "nothing." If the artwork can effect such an encounter, this is by virtue of its own engagement with the nothing, taking place in its "use" of the earth of its "work-material." When the work "sets forth the earth" (OBT 24/35), it renders manifest the principle of its own withdrawal as the condition of its appearance, and thus traces the same relation of ground and abyss, *Grund* and *Ab-grund,* disclosed by Dasein in anxiety. And in both instances this inflects the firstness of the work: advertising its own existence, the work will "sound . . . as though for the first time"; and this firstness itself arises out of the artwork's engagement with, and of, the opacity and limits of medium.

Heidegger's thinking at this juncture has a significance beyond the problematic of finite transcendence, however. The account of the work's *Dass,* with its insistence on strangeness, its staging of our uncanny encounter with a work which appears hermetic, nonhuman, and uncommunicative, and its depiction of our sense of being overwhelmed and speechless in the face of the artwork, constitutes a revaluation of the broader category of "aesthetic experience." It has often been noted how Heidegger's thinking at this juncture bears striking resemblance to the theory of defamiliarization or enstrangement (*ostraniene*) outlined by Viktor Shklovsky.[16] And indeed, both thinkers are concerned with the role played by art, and in particular poetry, in the "recovery of human experience" identified above. For Shklovsky, "in order to return sensation to our limbs, in order to makes us feel objects, to make a stone feel stony, man has been given the tool of art."[17] If this invocation of the stoniness of a stone recalls Heidegger's account of earth, the description of art as a "tool" should give us pause; insofar as this tool is characterized by its capacity "to lead us to a knowledge of a thing through the organ of sight instead of recognition,"[18] the conception of the human body adhered to is one that will be challenged by Heidegger's own recovery of human experience, for which the category of an "organ of sight" abstracted from "recognition" is highly questionable. That the description of art as "tool" should coincide with the abstraction of bodily experience from cognition would simply confirm Heidegger in his view that formalism interprets things through an ontology of equipmentality.

This points to a far more fundamental difference in their thinking of the work's strangeness. For Shklovsky, the poem provides a "description [of an object] that changes its form without changing its essence"[19]—precisely the opposition that Heidegger seeks to undermine when he grasps being in terms of the modalities of autodisclosure. Heidegger's recovery of experience is not an awakening of subjective sensation but rather the insistence on experience as condition of our being able to trace the movement of beings into appearance. To separate this experience from the "essence" of the work would be to prevent in advance our experiencing the happening of truth brought about in and by the work. Indeed, it is Heidegger's contention that the work's uncanniness issues from the very structure of the truth of being. As he puts it in the *Contributions to Philosophy* of 1936–39: "in the unavoidable ordinariness of beings, be-ing [*Seyn*] is the most non-ordinary; and this estranging of be-ing is not the *manner* of its appearing but rather is be-ing itself" (C 163/230). If the artwork discloses the open *as* uncanny, in other words, this is because uncanniness is the mode in which beings come to stand within the open. The strangeness of the work characterizes not only its thrust into the openness of beings, and the uncanny dynamic both between the created work and its preservers, but also between the truth of being.

In the phenomenon of estrangement, form and essence are inextricable from one another; we can only grasp the truth of being as an "estranging of be-ing" if we experience it, and ourselves, as uncanny, estranged. And yet the converse is also true: if experience is closed off to such estrangement, then art is, as Hegel would have it, "a thing of the past." Thus Heidegger, in the "Afterword" to "The Origin of the Work of Art," added in 1956, will muse: "perhaps experience [*Erlebnis*] is the element in which art dies" (OBT 50/66). Like Hegel, Heidegger considers the death of art that moment when it loses its claim to proof the turn to form indicative of a greater malaise in which beauty is no longer considered a mode of beings' autodisclosure but merely as the object of a judgment of pleasure. This, he suggests, coincides with a shift in the concept of experience, from *Erfahrung,* a kind of *traversal* of the world we inhabit, to *Erlebnis,* the "lived experience" that Husserl and Dilthey situate in subjective consciousness.[20] If "lived experience" refers to the subjective processes through which we can make objective truth-judgments, the conditions of this truth are nevertheless excluded from the experience itself. Yet if we understand truth as unconcealment, and experience as our continual encounter with beings as they, and we, inhabit a space of unconcealment, then the very category of truth is rendered experiential. That the work should announce itself in its *Dass* arises from the transformation of the parameters of beings' autodisclosure by which the work becomes "the setting-itself-to-work of truth" (OBT 44/59).

"The Origin of the Work of Art" is thus in dialogue both with the aesthetic tradition as a whole and with Heidegger's earlier work, and aims to confront and overcome the lacunae of each. His critique of the work's "formal features," his analyses of the work's excess over utility, his attempt to reframe beauty in terms of beings' entry into appearance, and his "recovery of experience," all demonstrate an insistence on the importance of these moments within the work's capacity to open up an encounter with beings, and allow him to develop his own understanding of this encounter. This means that an "ontological" approach to the artwork is so far from disregarding "form" as to endow it with a heightened value within the artwork's *aletheic* vocation. Yet this leaves unanswered the question as to how precisely form can attain this transformative value, and it is to this problem that I will turn in the following section. As we will see, Heidegger continues to develop a thinking of form throughout "The Origin of the Work of Art," firstly through the earth of the artwork, and then through the work's figure or shape, its *Gestalt*. Insofar as earth inheres in the work-material of the artwork, its deployment in the artwork is quite clearly linked to what we often call artistic form. Indeed, Heidegger's concern is not simply artistic form, but, in the portrayal of earth as a coming-forth concealing movement, the metaphysical concept of form, *morphe*. Then, I will turn to his account of the artwork's *Gestalt*, its singular look, and his attempts to explain how it is that the work, in its deployment of its earthly medium, can in fact attain a fixed look at all. In both instances, what is at issue is the work's engendering its own first quality: the earth first shows itself as earth; the *Gestalt* first advertises its own figure. It is to these problems that I now turn.

Rethinking Form: *Gestalt*

Heidegger initially situates the earth in the work-material of the work; however, rather than equating earth with the "materiality" of this medium, he argues that it is characterized first and foremost by its movement of "coming-forth concealing." In the use of the artist's technique, the earth is "set back" (*zurückgestellt*) into itself, and thereby "set forth" (*hergestellt*) such that the work-material, for the first time, comes to show itself as itself. "Rock comes to bear and to rest and so first becomes rock; the metal comes to glitter and shimmer, the colors to shine, the sounds to ring, the word to say" (OBT 24/35). In this movement that sets back and sets forth, Heidegger argues, the earth finds itself in "strife" with the world—that is, the context of intelligibility through and in which beings show themselves. Insofar as this movement into and out of intelligibility arises out of the artist's use of medium, one can see why earth would furnish an account of artistic form; however, he also aligns this movement with the metaphysical concept of form (*morphe*). Earth, that is, becomes form in two senses. But there is a third thinking of form taking place in the lecture: the singular

Gestalt of the individual work, by which this movement itself becomes discernable. And this, we will see, arises out of the work's engagement with the limits of its medium, staging, as it were, this very engagement. Heidegger's rethinking of form is thus directed toward the artwork's transformative capacity, its claim to "say" truth as *aletheia*.

Coming-forth Concealing

Heidegger's account of earth has to confront a central problem, namely, how can earth, which only becomes conspicuous through its withdrawal, give itself to be thought at all? He notes: "The stone presses downwards and manifests its heaviness. But while this heaviness weighs down on us, at the same time, it denies us any penetration into it. If we attempt such penetration by smashing the rock, then it shows us its pieces but never anything inward, anything that has been opened up" (OBT 24–25/35). The earth's "coming-forth concealing," however, is not merely a "withdrawal from representation,"[21] or from the calculative thinking that aims to penetrate into the rock; if this were the case, then its withdrawal would be a feature of representational-calculative thinking rather than of earth itself. When, for example, Marc Froment-Meurice calls earth "a pseudonym for the without-name" that "resists all appropriation by meaning,"[22] he has implicitly posited in advance a conception of "meaning" whose *modus operandi* is to "appropriate." Heidegger's own account, whereby the artwork, using but not using up its work-material, "lets the earth be an earth" (OBT 24/35), and his demand that the "preservation" of the work stand within the openness of beings it brings about, is precisely an attempt to avoid this model of meaning, and rather to trace the earth's withdrawal as withdrawal (and not merely as "withdrawal from"). In this, the concern about how to trace earthly withdrawal develops on the earlier concern as to how we can interpret the thing without thereby assaulting it, and shape our thinking according to the thing's autodisclosure rather than bringing the thing to fit the shape accorded it in advance by an epistemological formula.

In this, the difficulty of relating what Heidegger terms the "strife" between world and earth to, for instance, the form-matter distinction, is central to the way Heidegger attempts to grasp "earth" as something to be thought. As Froment-Meurice warns, "it is always possible to make what Heidegger says with the names *world* and *earth* conform to the old difference between signifier and signified, form and content."[23] Although world and earth are presented in counterpoint to these "old" differences, something which has led Mark Sinclair to characterize the "discovery of earth" as a "*hylo-morphic repetition*," and Robert Bernasconi to argue that the "form-matter distinction . . . gives way to the strife between world and earth,"[24] Heidegger insists that the shape of their interaction is qualitatively different to any such opposition. As seen above, Heidegger's engagement with artistic "form" takes place through his analyses of the "work-material"; when, moreover, he says that the "element within the work . . . which looks like its thingliness when the work is taken as an object (according to the usual concepts of the thing), experienced from out of the work, is its character as earth" (OBT 42/57), this "thingliness" extends not only to the materiality of a thing but also to its formation.

If they are not analogous to "matter" and "form," might we characterize the strife between earth and world as equivalent to the opposition between materiality and phenomenality, in which materiality would structure all phenomenal experience, but abyssally, beyond all possible phenomenal grasp?[25] Insofar as the earth, in Michel Haar's phrase, "can be thought, at least *negatively,* as the dimension that in itself rebels against phenomenality,"[26] it could perhaps constitute a "nonmetaphysical" continuation of philosophical materialism.[27] However, Heidegger warns against looking for ontological significance in antiphenomenal "brute" matter when, in the lecture on Aristotle's *Physics,* he discusses the Sophist Antiphon's distinction between *to arruthmiston proton,* the "stable" and "elemental" which is untouched by temporality (P 204–5/337–38), and *ruthmos,* the temporal aspect of beings' entry into appearance. For Antiphon, to appear temporally is to be "less being" than to be independent of time; insofar as all appearance happens in time, the "most being" must be inapparent. Later in the lecture, Heidegger will develop this reading of *ruthmos* to consider the temporal movement through of beings' autodisclosure; for now we should note Heidegger's wry aside: "From the viewpoint of the history of being, the basis of 'materialism' as a metaphysical stance becomes apparent here" (P 205/338). Antiphon is postulating a sphere of truth behind appearance that remains stable precisely because it does not appear and is atemporal; Heidegger, by contrast, approaches truth as the movement of appearance itself, a movement that must be grasped in its temporality.

If the earth, "set back" into itself, rebels against phenomenality, this rebellion nevertheless takes place on a plane of phenomenality, as it is "set forth" into the openness of world. At the same time, this setting forth is engaged—and this is implicit in the very choice of the term *earth*—in the natural aspect of the work-material: stone, wood, and so forth. Indeed, the definition of earth as "that in which the arising of everything that arises is brought back . . . and sheltered" (OBT 24/35) recalls what in *Being and Time* he called "the nature that stirs and strives" (BT 100/70), and is now aligned with what "the Greeks called *phusis.*" However, central to the intimacy of earth to *phusis* is that this latter cannot be reduced to *natura,* the class of natural objects, but should be grasped as a mode of presencing: "everything that arises." This is developed in the 1939 Aristotle lecture: *phusis* is conceived of as that mode of presencing in which beings emerge into presence of their own accord; it is distinguished from *techne* insofar as beings in *phusis* possess their own principle of *kinesis* or "movedness," whereas those in *techne* have this principle imposed upon them (P 190/318). The "technique" of the artist, then, lies in not imposing a movedness upon the earth, but rather tracing the movedness inherent in the work's medium. Here we find artistic artifice and the earth of medium to be complementary, and even mutually dependent. The "sheltering" of the earth, then, becomes a countermovement to the emergence of *phusis;* and, as its countering movement, conditions the modalities of this emergence.

I suggest that we think of earth as something like an open E-string played on the violin: at once pitch, timbre, and the oscillations of the string reverberating on the soundboard, but at the same time the scraping of horsehair on catgut. This is not simply to oppose noise to music—the scraping of horsehair on catgut has its own timbre, which is indeed one expressive possibility for the music itself. Rather, the scraping and reverberations are central to music production, yet it is only as the scraping subsides that the reverberations can soar, thus allowing us to hear harmonic series or melodic lines. As the bow moves across the string, we hear its scraping subside and resurface, continually making way for, and then irrupting into, musical tone; again, the condition for the musical sounding is *noise.* This double movement of withdrawal and irruption into sound will become most palpable when the E string's timbre becomes the focal point for the music's harmonic and melodic themes, as, for example in the first subject of the opening movement of Beethoven's op. 47 Kreutzer Sonata, where the cadence lands on the chord over four strings in the mediant relative major key of C (CGCE), dwelling on the open E in a pause, before echoing through the rest that follows. The continual movement between scraping and reverberation is internalized into the musical texture and thus rendered manifest as the very shape and movement through which the musical note "first comes to sound." Hence something like an earth is freed, through the sonata's engagement with its medium—be it the materiality of violin and bow, the cadences of diatonic harmony, or the anticipation of the exposition that it heralds through the change of time signature and tempo (something that the paused cadences serve only to increase)—to be heard as the very condition of this medium.

Here we can see the intimate relation of the earth to artistic form. However, it is also part of Heidegger's attempt to rethink the metaphysical concept of form. In his 1939 Aristotle lecture, he identifies embedded within the Greek term *morphe* a double movement of presencing and absencing which shapes a being's "kinetic intelligibility."[28] Above we saw that *hule* ("matter") is determined in advance by the way in which it enters appearance (that is, by *morphe*); it is thus glossed as the "appropriate orderable." *Morphe,* however, is not simply the appropriating or ordering act of forming matter, the production of an appropriable material; rather, it is a "placing into the appearance [*Stellung in das Aussehen*]" (P 211/346), where "placing" describes not an act but the movedness by which *hule* enters into place (*Stelle*). Above I noted how even supposedly formless matter only presences according to a form: the "indeterminate form" of the "mere" thing or "brute" matter is still a form of sorts (OBT 9/17). But if *hule* first enters appearance as appropriable by taking the form of being-appropriable, then *morphe* and *hule* are not in binary opposition at all. Heidegger continues: "as the placing into the appearance, *morphe* surpasses the orderable (*hule*) insofar as *morphe* is the presencing of the appropriateness of that which is appropriate, and consequently, in terms of presencing, is more original" (P 220/358). In other words, *phusis* is not the interaction of *morphe* and *hule;* rather, "*morphe*—not just more than *hule,* but in fact alone and completely—is *phusis*" (P 222/360).

Heidegger wants to understand *morphe*'s "placing into the appearance" as specifically *kinetic.* If *morphe* alone describes the movement into appearance of beings in *phusis,* this also means that the "essence of *phusis* as *kinesis* is fulfilled only by the kind of movedness that *morphe* is" (P 224/363). The movedness *morphe* traces is double; as well as placing beings into appearance, it also places into appearance their lack or absence (*steresis*). Recalling the broken equipment of *Being and Time,* Heidegger says: "When something is missing, the missing *thing* is gone, to be sure, but the *goneness* itself, the lack itself, is what irritates and upsets us, and the 'lack' can do this only if the lack itself is 'there,' i.e., only if the lack *is,* i.e., constitutes a manner of being" (P 226/366). As a result, the "self-placing into the appearance always lets something be present in such a way that *in* the presencing an absencing simultaneously becomes present" (P 227/367). *Morphe* thus becomes "the presencing of an absencing" (P 227/367): it is both "coming forth" and "concealing," and, as concealing, it brings this concealment to come forth.

This "coming-forth concealing" movement is what "The Origin of the Work of Art" names *earth;* in both instances, what is at issue is the shaping of the limits not only of a being's autodisclosure, but of the "open" in which this disclosure takes place. Why should it be that the artwork in particular is able to "set" the earth "forth" into the world, that its treatment of medium should "let the earth be an earth"? Because, Heidegger suggests, the artwork internalizes into its own modes of meaning the "strife" between earth and world. The Kreutzer Sonata, for example, did this as the earth of the open E string came to sound within a particular context of timbre, cadence, and thematic structure, so that two aspects of the E string—its earthly withdrawal and its role within both the violin's tonal palette and the sonata's structure—are brought into contest. It is by setting the two into strife that the artwork can come to grasp earth not simply as work-material, but as a limiting movement, and thereby render it palpable.

The Contest between Measure and Limit

Earth, withdrawing from world, nevertheless comes to show itself within this world: this is the shape that Heidegger terms their *Streit* (strife). If Heidegger is resisting the equation of world and earth with other traditional oppositions—such as form and matter, phenomenality and materiality, culture and nature—then, in characterizing their interaction as a strife he also wishes to avoid any dialectical opposition. This might not seem clear from Heidegger's first thematization of the strife, where he says: "the opponents raise each other into the self-assertion of their natures," with "each opponent carry[ing] the other beyond itself" so as to set them into "the intimacy of simple belonging to one another" (OBT 27/38). Indeed, this could easily be interpreted as portraying two countering forces, dependent on one another to overcome themselves and reach their own natures, which, through interacting and counteracting, make up a unity. Yet it would be misleading to think of earth as "negating" world; rather, its withdrawal both serves as a limit to the world, and conditions the autodisclosure of beings within the world. Moreover, Heidegger does not want the "unity" of world and earth to defuse their opposing movements: if the work "instigates this strife," it is by virtue of its holding these two movements—toward withdrawal and toward openness—in a continual tension, "so that the strife remains a strife" (OBT 27/38). The movement Heidegger traces would not "sublate" earth as its limit, but rather shift this limit so that the earth's "coming-forth concealing" shows itself as such. The limit is not "cancelled" or "superseded" but reshaped.

In the *Introduction to Metaphysics*, Heidegger glosses the Greek term *polemos* as that which "sets the essential and the unessential, the high and the low, into their limits and makes them manifest" (IM 120/87), and the strife also is conceived as a setting-into-limit by which beings enter appearance. If the artwork's striving against the earth's concealing is an engagement with the limits of appearance, however, these limits are never static; rather, this strife should be understood as a *morphetic* "placing in the appearance." Here, Heidegger argues that what is finally placed into appearance is "*eidos,* and *eidos* must be understood in relation to *logos*" (P 210/345). That is, a being will attain a particular shape (*Gestalt, eidos*) only as the *logos* of human thinking "addresses a this and a that as this and that" (P 210/345) and thus "gathers" it into such a shape. If the shape through which a being discloses itself reflects the singular configuration of its being gathered in *logos,* then the movedness (or, in Young's preferred translation, "agitation") of the artwork is thematized as a "continually *self-surpassing* gathering" (OBT 27/38, my emphasis). That is, addressing beings "as" such-and-such within the work, the work at the same time exceeds the very "as"-structure of this address: the work is continually more than, and irreducible to, its "gathering" *logos,* and this excess becomes the very basis of its movedness. In Cézanne's *Portrait du jardinier Vallier,* for example, even as we see the figure of the gardener, the movement of the brushstrokes renders this figure unstable, entering into and receding from appearance as the painting composes and recomposes itself.[29]

The artwork's own shape, its *Gestalt,* would involve a kind of *logos* that draws this excess into presence while allowing it to exceed such presence; we find ourselves in the paradoxical situation where the excess the artwork engenders is nevertheless situated not beyond the work, in an "over and above" of its content, but deep in the core of its texture. The artwork continually "strives" to grasp an excess that, lying in the very medium out of which it is fashioned, conditions its own gathering into presence. In the work's struggle with the limits of its medium, the earth, which, "bearing and rising up, strives to preserve its closedness" (OBT 38/51), is captured and traced within the world from which it would withdraw—both within the world of the work, and within the work as a being in the world. This tension between bringing-into-the-open and receding-into-closedness Heidegger names "*Riß,*" a term that incorporates both "rift" and "design," both a mode of the strife and the way it sketches itself (OBT 38/51). This *Riß* "does not allow the contestants to break apart. It brings the contest between measure and limit into a shared outline [*Umriß*]" (OBT 38/51). The artwork would embody this outline in which the opposing movements of gathering and self-surpassing are held together in a continual tension, a tension that pervades the work's engagement with the limits of its medium.

Here we find the intersection of the artwork's formal techniques by which it can grasp the opacity of this medium, with the ontological vocation of the artwork, now thematized through the term *Riß*. *Riß* holds together the ontological and formal through a dense working of its cognates: as well as providing the *Auf-riß* (outline sketch) as which, and the *Umriß* (outline) in which, the contest between measure and limit is rendered manifest, it effects the *Durch-riß* (rupture) of the figure from its surroundings, and points to the *Grundriß* (fundamental design) that shapes this strife in advance (OBT 38/51). *Riß,* then, describes the precise movement by which the work renders manifest its striving entry into appearance, and at the same time the technique by which the artist, in Dürer's phrase, will "wrest [*reißen*] the work from 'nature'" (OBT 43/58). Yet *Riß* has a further ontological significance: as some of the most powerful readings of "The Origin of the Work of Art" have observed, it serves as the institution of difference as such—of ontological difference itself, but also of the conflictual difference of world and earth, and that differential process by which beings can distinguish themselves from other beings and from the horizon of the world in which they appear. Haar thus terms *Riß* the "rending stroke [*trait-déchirant*]," "the most profound tracing of the world-earth relation," whereas for Fynsk it is "a scission and . . . the tracing of an outline" that "draws out, and gathers into a unity through a kind of differential traction, the fundamental traits (*Grundzüge*) of the happening of truth."[30] Fynsk's insistence on "unity" is crucial: the entry into the phenomenal world requires not only this differential traction, but also the opening up of a space of mutual belonging through which beings are "joined" together within the open. Rather than beings entering presence as a morass of unintelligible matter, or else as highly individuated monads shut off from one another, their autodisclosure must involve the structures of intelligibility that allow us to identify them as beings. It is this "structure" or "adjoinment" (*Gefüge*), as well as an ontological origin of difference as such, that the artwork renders manifest.[31]

At stake in the work's "wresting" of its work-material from stone, pigment and word, then, is the differential-gathering movement that makes up the intelligibility of worldly experience, and it is this that Heidegger is trying to grasp when looking at the contest between the "measure" through which the work deploys its medium—that is, the repertoire of means and techniques an art form has at its disposal for bringing its work-material into a particular meaningful configuration—and that which, lying latent within the medium, exceeds the measure the art form seeks to effect. In each instance, measure is in contest with what exceeds its own limits—that which artistic technique cannot grasp, to which the formal conventions of the time are blind. These constraints, be they self-imposed or a result of a historical blindness, themselves render possible particular configurations or modes of articulation: as the work explores and contests such constraints, it at the same time reflects on them and transforms them; thus its measure comes to sketch and to render manifest the contest in which it continually finds itself. This is as much at work in the painterly perspective of cinquecento Florentine painting, which continually probes and questions its own illusory techniques, as it is in Manet's dismantling of perspective through pointedly incongruous spatial relations of figures, or Cézanne's attempt to evoke depth through shading and texture rather than through linear perspective; it is as much at work in the metrical conventions of the heroic line in eighteenth-century English verse, where placing a caesura after the eighth syllable of the line attains a powerful expressive effect, at once release and destabilization, through its introducing a prosodic weight against the overarching cadence of the line itself, as in the radical dissonance of the "prosaic" opening of Hölderlin's "Germanien," or the typographical explosion of Mallarmé's *Un coup de dés*. In the cadence from the Kreutzer sonata mentioned above, it would be the way that the open E string is at once part of the cadence, but in its noise becomes uncontainable within the cadence itself: the sonata's "outline" involves both cadence and excess of the cadence, holding them in a tension that reverberates even after the last oscillations have subsided into silence.

In this, the work, as long as it remains a work and at work, *continually and without cease says and performs its own entry into appearance*. It is thus that it announces the *Dass* of its createdness: at each moment that it advertises its entry into appearance, it also advertises the indelible fact that it exists. Moreover, the work's engagement with limit, through which it performs this entry into appearance, reaches to the very condition of its autodisclosure: contesting the limits of its medium, the work not only "manifests its limits as limits,"[32] but comes to shape the contours of this limit. Hölderlin's prosodic dissonance not only shifts the way we hear the word *Denn* as it comes to sound, but also the coming to sound of the word *Denn* as such, and indeed the sounding of language as a whole. This is what constitutes the *aletheic* capacity of the artwork: if the artwork, through an engagement with its own earthly limit, can shape the parameters of its own autodisclosure, then it may also shape the parameters of autodisclosure *as such*. When the work's gathering continually surpasses itself, it is precisely this limit that is surpassed, and at this moment, something that was hitherto beyond the bounds of world enters into appearance—*for the first time*. Contesting its own limit, the work offers to experience a different shaping or configuration of the open than had hitherto been possible or thinkable.

The work thus becomes the exemplary site for finite transcendence: it is a "projective saying" that "allows [the] open to happen in such a way . . . that now, for the first time, in the midst of beings, it brings them to shine and sound" (OBT 45/60). This happens as the work sets the tensions underlying its own intelligibility—the entry of pigment into figuration, of noise into music, verbal matter into meaningful sign—back into the very pigment, noise and verbal matter out of which it came, thereby rendering manifest pigment, figuration, and the tension between the two. This tension is then "fixed in place" (OBT 38/52) in, and by, the work's *Gestalt*.

Gestalt

The term *Gestalt* (shape) is a crucial one for Heidegger's thinking during the 1930s, holding together, as Bernhard Radloff notes in his book-length study of the term, two strands of thought. Firstly, it continues the problematic of how beings can first disclose themselves within a world; that Heidegger should now term this disclosure a *Gestalt*, Radloff demonstrates, would appear to allude to the Gestalt psychology of Christian von Ehrenfels, for whom cognition functions not through processing sense-data, but rather through picking up on the shapes through which objects are given to consciousness.[33] Yet (and here Radloff discerns the influence of Ernst Jünger) Heidegger also sees such *Gestalt* as having a specifically historical character. If for Jünger modern man takes his *Gestalt* from the total mobilization that forms him, Heidegger sees the *Gestalt* of beings' autodisclosure as arising out of a particular configuration of the history of being whereby humans are attuned in a specific way to the openness of beings.[34]

This might imply an equivocation in the term *Gestalt* itself, describing both the individual shape through which the being discloses itself, and the configuration of the open region in which beings would, in Radloff's phrase, "take gestalt." We encounter both senses of the term in Heidegger's discussion, in "The Origin of the Work of Art," of the temple at Paestum. On the one hand, the temple-work "encloses the figure [*Gestalt*] of the god" (OBT 20/31), and this figure, rendering the god visible, structures the relations that "win for the essence of man the shape [*Gestalt*] of its destiny" (OBT 21/31). On the other hand, and conversely, it is only on the basis of the truth disclosed by the god that the statue can first become a "figure." As Heidegger's account of the *Gestalt* of the artwork progresses later in the lecture, however, his concern is increasingly with the individual figure, and in particular, the way in which this figure might shape the parameters of its own autodisclosure. In this sense, Heidegger's thinking of *Gestalt* continues his concern with the limits of phenomenality, something he makes clear in the *Introduction to Metaphysics:* "Whatever places itself into and thereby enacts its limit, and thus stands, has form [*Gestalt*]" (IM 63/46).[35] As we have seen, the artwork enacts its limit as it holds together in tension the opposing movements of limiting and opening within its own self-surpassing gathering.

The "shape" of this *Gestalt,* then, is "shaped" out of the work-material, but also shapes its own entry into appearance as it "sets" (*stellt*) itself into a particular configuration of limits. In this respect, *Gestalt* serves as the culmination of a long meditation on *Stellen* (placing and placement) that takes place throughout "The Origin of the Work of Art" by way of a dense play on verb cognates and etymology. The interpretation of art as the *Vorstellung* (representation) or *Darstellung* (presentation) of a preexistent object or idea is dependent on an anterior *offene Stelle* (open place); the work can "set up a world" (*eine Welt aufstellen*) and thus give shape to this *offene Stelle* only as it "sets itself back" (*sich zurückstellt*) into its work-material and thereby comes to "set forth the earth" (*die Erde her-stellen*).[36] The earth's concealment takes place either as *Versagen* (refusal) or as *Verstellen* (obstruction, dissembling, or disfigurement) in which it does appear, but shows itself in a distorted way (OBT 30/42).[37] When the strife between the *Aufstellung* of world and the *Herstellung* of earth is "fixed in place" (*festgestellt*) in the *Gestalt,* Heidegger remarks: "What we here call 'figure' is always to be thought out of *that particular* placing [*stellen*] and placement [*Ge-stell*] as which the *work* comes to presence when it sets itself up and sets itself forth [*insofern es sich auf- und herstellt*]" (OBT 38/52).[38] And that "particular placing" through which the work "comes to presence," finally, is *morphe,* the "placing into the appearance [*Stellung in das Aussehen*]" (P 211/346). If the work comes to presence as a particular placing and placement, then this also necessitates an artistic technique that uses the earth without using it up, and thus "brings it forth" into the open; the act of creation is to be understood not as the act of a "sovereign subject" (OBT 48/63), but from out of createdness as a mode of presencing, that is, the entry into appearance that the work continually says and performs.

In this, the thingliness of the artwork is to be grasped by recourse to its work-character: at once the strife between earth and world and the work's own striving. The work is necessarily continually in motion for as long as it remains at work—the "self-surpassing gathering" of the work's movedness (its "striving") thus transpires to be the mode in which the strife of world and earth is "fixed in place." And, in looking at how the *Gestalt* gathers this movement into itself, we find Heidegger add one final dimension to this movedness: "What is here called figure [*Gestalt*] is the structure [*Gefüge*] as which the rift joins itself [*der Riß sich fügt*]. This joined rift is the jointure [*Fuge*] of the shining of truth" (OBT 38/52).

In "jointure," Heidegger aligns the appearance of truth with one of the most complex and programmatic forms of classical music. In a fugue, one motif (the subject) is developed polyphonically, undergoing a series of inversions and modulations, changes of register and timbre, but always guided and bounded by a strict forward motion. Each time the subject returns in a new melodic strand (a voice), undergoing inversions and modulations, it is at once linked to and differentiated from every other voice within the polyphony; moreover, each voice, as it enters into the fugue's polyphonic fabric, advertises its own entry into audibility and at the same time advertises it as an entry *out of absence*. It is notable in this regard that the subjects of most of Bach's fugues took extended upbeats as their starting point, as though to perform its movement from silence toward the cadence that would signal its arrival. And, within the fugue's broader structure, the subject's movement from absence into presence, and its recurrence in differing forms, cuts against the forward propulsion of the fugue as a whole, so as to create a highly wrought temporal frame. Without this forward propulsion the counterpoint of these different voices would lose its intricacy; without the counterpoint, the forward propulsion loses its urgency. The movedness of the work, then, demonstrates beings' entry into appearance to be guided by a specifically fugal rhythm.

How are we to understand such rhythm, or better, rhythmicity? Insofar as it pertains to the artwork as such, it cannot be restricted to, say, the tempo of a piece of music or the prosody of a poem. Rather, it will lie in the very texture of manifestation of the work's *Gestalt*. In Cézanne's portrait, for example, we might observe the way in which, the arching of the gardener's shoulders and the thickly applied downward brushstrokes of blacks and dark greens that make up his coat and waistcoat serve to create an extraordinary sense of *weight*. Set firmly at the center of the composition, this weight becomes a kind of formal organizing principle for the painting, drawing the various other textural movements toward a focal point. An addition to being a formal feature, this weight serves as a means of characterization of the painting's subject: as the focal point of the portrait is displaced from Vallier's face, the painting emphasizes his humility and fatigue, but at the same time, as he assumes the painting's compositional weight he comes to be endowed with a pathos of dignity and understated strength. Characterization and composition reflect back on one another, Vallier's pose and indeed his person serving as countermovement to the inward gravitation of the composition. On the one hand, the painting's weight would thus lead us to encounter a heaviness that cannot quite be contained by the painting itself; it is at once a heaviness of pigment, and yet its heaviness exceeds the pigment itself. And on the other, its deployment of pigment renders the painting more palpable and in the same gesture opens up a space beyond its palpable aspect—a space, that is, in which depiction can take place. It is, I would argue, precisely this complex of movements between presence and absence, luminosity and opacity, that Heidegger is alluding to when he speaks of the work's "self-surpassing gathering," and which he tries to thematize as *Riß*.

The site of this complex of movements, the painting itself becomes strikingly, uncannily *still*. And indeed, Heidegger characterizes the agitation of the work as its "self-subsistence," its "closed, unitary repose of self-support" (OBT 26/37). If this might seem to imply "the opposite of motion," Heidegger immediately counters: "Only what is in motion can rest. . . . Where rest includes motion, there can exist a repose which is an inner concentration of motion, hence a highest state of agitation" (OBT 26/37). When, late in his career, Heidegger devotes an ekphrastic poem to Cézanne's portrait, it is precisely this singular stillness that he finds most salient:

Das nachdenksam Gelassens, das inständig
Stille der Gestalt des alten Gärtners
Vallier . . . (GA13 223)

(The reflecting released, the standing-within
Stillness of the figure of old gardener
Vallier . . .)

This "inständig / Stille der Gestalt" directly echoes the account, over three decades earlier, of the artwork as a whole. Heidegger evokes a stillness born of, and borne by, movement, in which the movement itself is figured, becomes figure. Here also Heidegger is eliding any rigid separation of the painting's composition from its characterization of the subject of the portrait, both in its "releasement" and in the "figures" of gardener and painting as a whole. Again, what is at issue is the painting's "inner concentration," something analogous to the weight Cézanne's painting engages, at once the focal point of the work's "agitated" crisscrossing of movements and textures, and for precisely this reason its point of greatest stillness. The work thus becomes a "unity": the various movements taking place within it cohere not simply into the figure of Vallier himself, but into the singular figure that this work is. In the term *Gestalt,* then, lies at once an attempt to describe the unity of a singular work, and to describe individual *Gestalts* within the work as a whole: compositional details, moments, gestures, asides, inflections that serve as points of coherence and intensity, and that render the work most powerfully "at work."

Heidegger's radical revaluation of form leads him both to grasp the earth as the coming-forth concealing situated in the work's medium, and to see the "fixing in place" of the *Gestalt* as the way in which this movement is traced in a singular way by an individual work. If this offers a profoundly new way of attending to artworks, then Heidegger's most concerted focus is the ontological vocation of these works. Once again, form and ontology cannot be extricated from one another: both concern the movement into appearance through which beings come to show themselves in the open, and the artwork's "formal" use of medium quite simply is its claim to truth, that is, to transform the limits of this open. Heidegger's great insight here, I would suggest, lies in the focus on the movedness of the work, which then gives on to a "fugal" account of the way that the work is joined into a unity.

The Rhythmicity of the Artwork

Heidegger's account of the artwork involves a deep engagement with its movedness, which is grasped variously as the "self-surpassing gathering" of the work, the coming forth concealing of the earth, the *morphetic* "placing in the appearance" that is fixed in place in the work's *Gestalt,* and the "joining" movement by which *Riß* comes to trace itself in this *Gestalt.* In this last instance, Heidegger starts to explore the cognates of the verb *fügen*, a verb that will in later texts be increasingly aligned with rhythm. Variously translated as "to structure" and "to compose," but also "to join," and providing the nouns *Gefüge* (structure), *Fügung* (structuring, but also adjoinment), and *Fug* (order) as well as *Fuge*—which, as mentioned above, not only denotes jointure but also alludes to the musical form of the fugue— *fügen* is depicted as a structuring movement that joins beings together in such a way that they disclose themselves intelligibly and thereby enter into presence. Crucially for Heidegger, such structure or jointure serves as an irreducibly *temporal* condition bounding the presencing of beings. In this, it develops the engagement with limits we find in "The Origin of the Work of Art" so as to grasp the movedness of such presencing; yet at the same time, it involves a far more concerted encounter with poetic rhythm, that is, prosody and the "measures" through which this prosody is set to work. In this final section, I wish to sketch both the directions that Heidegger takes this insight into the movedness of the work as a kind of "jointure," and the directions that it opens up for poetics more generally.

Fugal Jointures

The concept of *ruthmos* plays a central facilitating role in Heidegger's reading of Aristotle's *Physics,* and in particular his interpretation of *morphe* as the "placing into the appearance" characteristic of all beings in *phusis.* *Ruthmos,* he suggests, is to be translated as "articulating, impressing, fitting, and forming": *Gliederung, Prägung, Fügung, und Verfassung* (P 204/337). Articulation, like *Riß,* entails both difference and jointure, such that a self-differentiating being must also sketch out the hinges by which it is bound in relation to those beings around it—less the self-expression of a subject than the articulation of a joint between two bones; and this will be crucial to Heidegger's thinking of language, as I will argue in Chapter 2. For now, however, I wish to pursue Heidegger's choice of *Fügung* (translated by Sheehan as "fitting"). For here he anticipates the claim, in a reading of Stefan George's "Das Wort" given twenty years later: "Rhythm, *ruthmos,*[39] does not mean flux and flowing, but rather structure [*Fügung*]" (OL 149/230). I will return to the reading of George below; for the time being I wish to note that Heidegger's initial concern in the discussion of *ruthmos* in the Aristotle lecture is Antiphon's claim that the *proton arruthmiston*— that which is untouched by *ruthmos* and thus by the temporality of appearance—is what is "most being" (even if, for precisely this reason, what is "most being" will never enter presence). Aristotle, Heidegger argues, inverts this in order to grasp "being" as the temporal structure by which beings enter into appearance.

One might then expect *ruthmos* to become intrinsic to Aristotle's analysis of the presencing of *phusis,* whereby "both interpretations of *phusis* [in terms of *morphe* and in terms of *ruthmos*] are given equal rank, and this offers the possibility of constructing a double concept of *phusis*" (P 209/343). However, Aristotle in fact supplants the distinction between the *proton arruthmiston* and *ruthmos* with the *hule-morphe* distinction, and, Heidegger suggests, this is crucial to his being able to grasp the *kinesis* by which beings come to presence: "The *hule-morphe* distinction is not simply another formula for *arruthmiston-ruthmos.* Rather, it lifts the question of *phusis* onto an entirely new level where precisely the unasked question about the *kinesis*-character of *phusis* gets answered, and where *phusis* for the first time is adequately conceived as *ousia*" (P 209/343–44). It is, precisely, because Aristotle grasps the articulating and fitting of *ruthmos* as a "placing in the appearance" that he can both ask and answer the "unasked question about the *kinesis*-character of *phusis.*" What is termed *ruthmos* might describe the shape of beings' movement into appearance, but not the principle of movedness itself as a mode of placing. What seems to be at issue is the counterpoint between *stellen* and *fügen*, something Heidegger confronts when describing the artwork's *Gestalt* as "the structure [*Gefüge*] as which the rift joins itself [*sich fügt*]" (OBT 38/53), where *fügen* would belong to the *Riß* itself, and *stellen* to the artistic activity by which earth is "set back" (*zurückgestellt*) into its work-material and thus "set forth" (*hergestellt*). But this would also mean that, far from *ruthmos* being dropped, and the double concept being of *phusis* being dismissed entirely, Heidegger is trying to sketch a mode of thinking that would be able to trace the *ruthmos* of beings' entry into appearance, and this is what *morphe* facilitates.

We encounter a similar train of thought in Heidegger's gloss of the term *dike* in his 1946 lecture on "Anaximander's Saying." In place of the standard translations of *dike* as "penalty" or "damages," Heidegger turns to another cognate of *fügen*: "*dike*, thought out of being as presencing, is the ordering, joining order [*fugend-fügende Fug*]" (OBT 269/329, translation modified). In order for beings to show themselves in presence—that is, in an intelligible manner such that they can be grasped as "present"—they must be joined in such a way that they are intelligible. The "ordering, joining order" would describe this intelligible structure. Yet if we are to think "jointure" and "order" out of "being as presencing," then this requires attending to the specifically *temporal* dimension of presencing: the relations between presencing and absencing as two competing movements. As with the account of the artwork, beings come to presence insofar as they inhabit a limit (*peras*) that is itself characterized by movedness. Here, however, this limit is explicitly temporal: it is "the 'between' of a twofold absence" (OBT 272/333), such that *Fuge* "adjoins [*verfügt*] . . . all that presences [*die Anwesende*] between a twofold absence (arrival and departure)" (OBT 277/339). *Jointure* thus describes the temporal movement into limit, and the configuration of beings within this limit; it is the way in which beings enter into the presence (*ta eonta*) of their boundary (*peras*)—a boundary that is both the parameters of the open the being inhabits, and the temporal finitude of its presence in the open. Heidegger continues: "The jointure of the while confines and bounds what presences as such a thing" (OBT 277/339).

The "while" would thus characterize the temporal dimension of beings' appearance, and in this respect is contrasting to mere "continuation." But this does not mean that continuation is rejected outright by Anaximander; rather, Heidegger sees Anaximander's fragment to stage a contest between these two conceptions of time. As an entity attempts to persist in presence, to "continue," it "concerns itself no longer with the other things that are present" and so "stands in dis-jointure [*in der Un-Fuge*]": it presences "without and against the jointure of the while" (OBT 268–69/328–29). Such continuation anticipates what Plato conceptualizes as "constant presence." This "metaphysical" interpretation of presencing as constant presence is, then, already latent in Anaximander's fragment; but for Anaximander, Heidegger argues, dis-jointure becomes the mode in which the being in fact "gives jointure." In other words, the being's resistance to its temporal finitude becomes the mode through which it inhabits time as a finite being.

The jointure of a being's autodisclosure lies in its capacity to retain a unity within the fluctuations of its temporal appearance, rather than remaining only as "sheer persistence" (OBT 269/329). Time, then, must be thought out of the double absence that bounds it, and in this Heidegger is gesturing toward *Being and Time*'s critique of the model of temporality, prevalent since Aristotle, of time as a series of "nows" (BT 474/412), and in its account an originary temporality made up of three "temporal ecstases," having-been, presencing, and futurity, which structure the way in which Dasein can first understand itself as being-in-the-world (BT 377/329). Heidegger's analysis of the jointure in "Anaximander's Saying," however, moves beyond this account of originary, ecstatic temporality by pointing to an intimate relation between such jointure and the *logos* that "gathers" into a "tarrying presence" (OBT 278/340). In the *logos,* the rhythmicity of the "while" will come to exist within language itself. In Chapter 2 I will note that this coincides with Heidegger's coming to conceive of *Sprache* (language) as a "way-making" movement (*Be-wëgung*) from the openness of beings into *Sprechen* (verbal comportment]; but we do not need to see the intricacies of this conception of language to realize the potentially enormous consequences that this conception of jointure, inscribed at once in the rhythmic fabric of experienced time and the speaking of language, can have for poetics. For this implies that we can grasp a poem's measure not by recourse to an external framework of time (what Meschonnic once called the "tick tock on the cheek of the metronomic metrician"[40]) but rather by tracing a temporality immanent within language; and at the same time, this temporality, or rhythmicity, rather than being a paralinguistic effect cut off from a poem's meaning, becomes the very process by which the poem means.

This would not be the first time that the discipline of poetics would identify in Heidegger's thinking such a possibility. One can, for example, think of the *Stilkritiker* of 1940s and 1950s, many of whom saw in Heidegger's account of ecstatic temporality the possibility for an overhauled thinking of poetic rhythm. Perhaps the most powerful insight made by these thinkers lies in Carl Jünger's axiom that, in poetry, "time and rhythm are one,"[41] which precisely rules out any attempt to measure the prosodic movement of a poem by recourse to supposedly objective models of time. We can also note Beda Allemann's invocation of Heidegger's "unsurpassed temporal analysis of Dasein" as forming the basis for a thinking of rhythm,[42] and Emil Staiger's claims that the task of poetics "would consist in acquiring the hardwon insights of *Being and Time,* in the spirit of the Hölderlin studies and of the *Essence of Truth,* and then in building a bridge from ontological to aesthetic scholarship."[43] Heidegger's own lukewarm response to these thinkers is well documented;[44] and indeed, his turn to the artwork first arises as he tries to address what he considers lacunae in his earlier accounts of the finite transcendence of being-in-the-world, something of which the originary "ecstatic" temporality was a central feature. If Heidegger's thinking is eventually to furnish a radical account of rhythm, we should attend to the way in which these later writings on poetry move beyond his earlier accounts of temporality, and aim to grasp this jointure as something engendered by the rhythmic movement of poetry itself.

One such example comes in his discussion of the relation between the "site of Trakl's poetry" and the individual poems that make up his oeuvre, in the lecture on "Language in the Poem" (OL 160/38). Here he suggests that we encounter an "animating wave [*bewegende Woge*]" as the poetic site enters into a singular poetic instance. He argues: "From the site of the poem [*Gedicht*] there rises the wave that in each instance moves his Saying as poetic saying. But that wave, far from leaving the site behind, in its rise causes all the movement of Saying to flow back to its ever more hidden source. The site of the poem, as the source of the animating wave, holds within it the veiled essence of what—to metaphysical-aesthetic representation—can at best appear as rhythm" (OL 160/38, translation modified). The "veiled essence" of rhythm lies in the "source" of the wave—in, that is, the very impetus into movement through which the poetic site articulates itself in an individual poem; in this, it echoes the movedness (or, in Young's translation, "agitation") that, in "The Origin of the Work of Art," characterized the artwork's engagement with the limits of its medium. What is taking place here is the movement from a gathering *logos* into the poet's enunciation, and this movement is subsequently reconstructed by "metaphysical-aesthetic representation" as "rhythm" (i.e., the suprasegmentals of speech, prosody). The rhythmic jointure of *Fuge* pertains not only to the autodisclosure of beings but also to language itself: beings are "joined" into an intelligible whole, while at the same time having their reciprocal difference sketched out. As David Farrell Krell notes, this rhythm lies in the "peculiar binding power of language," a power that lies "beyond the mere linkage of syllables, or even of words and things, a binding power beyond both 'naming' and 'predicating,'"[45] and to be found rather in the oscillation (*Schwingung*) between presence and absence language effects. When Heidegger turns to "rhythm," what he has in mind is this oscillation.

Below, I will discuss the relation between this "metaphysical-aesthetic representation" of rhythm and the rhythmicity taking place within the jointures of experience and *logos*. For now, we should note that here, as in "The Origin of the Work of Art," what is at issue is the poem's movedness. This has two aspects: the poem, like all artworks, arises out of the movedness of the strife of world and earth, of the countermovements of presencing and absencing; and, tracing these movements in its *Gestalt*, it comes to be marked by a singular movedness of its own: the "self-surpassing gathering." To follow the figure that Heidegger gives in "Language in the Poem," it is not only "animated" by its "wave," but animates in its turn. Even as Heidegger's later writings build on and in some cases diverge from the analyses and assertions of "The Origin of the Work of Art," they continue its central problematic. Firstly, they aim to grasp a mode through which the poem will render manifest its own inherent movedness, as though for the first time, and thereby join beings in a singular rhythm; secondly, they try to attend to those moments when the poem, as it were, sets such movedness into motion, so that its rhythm will shape the modalities of this jointure.

Rhythm and Measure

Yet what of the status of the metaphysical-aesthetic conception of rhythm, of the relation between the prosodic patterning of Trakl's verse and the setting-into-relation of beings' autodisclosure? Krell's analysis of "Language in the Poem" focuses on Heidegger's rejection of prosody, arguing that his account of rhythm "has essentially nothing to do with the conformity of spoken or written language to inherited standards of measure and versification. It does have to do with the intrinsic motion and animation of language as such."[46] Krell's use of the word *essentially* here is telling; he takes Heidegger to be distinguishing the ontological dimension of the poem's rhythm, situated in "language as such," from the ontic features of actual poems' prosodic patterning. While this appears to be borne out by Heidegger's laconic dismissal of the meter of Trakl's "Ein Winterabend": "Meter and rhyme pattern can be defined accurately according to the schemes of metrics and poetics" (PLT 193/18), I have argued that to read him thus would be to return him to the opposition between form and essence that he continually endeavors to undermine. More broadly, it would be to read "ontological difference" in such a way that the ontological, being essentially untouched by the ontic, becomes a hypostatized transcendental postulate, rather than describing the movement by which beings come to presence, and thus to show themselves as "being." The ontological dimension of rhythm concerns precisely this movement; and as such cannot be abstracted from the modes in which an individual work, as the being that it is, enters into presence. If the sounding of Hölderlin's "Germanien," lying within language as such, is anterior to the sound-sense opposition that grounds metrical patterning—what Krell calls "mere linkage of syllables"[47]—this does not entail that such sounding foregoes prosody altogether; as noted above, the "apparent prose" by which this sounding is first heard is itself a prosodic effect, the dissonance of its incursion into verse a "limit" to verse's "measure." This certainly complicates our understanding of the value of verse features, but for this very reason does not reject it.

And this means that Heidegger's account of rhythm *does* have *essentially* something to do with standards of versification after all: it is only through such standards that we can first come to experience the animation guiding language itself. It does so, however, with the proviso that we listen to what is at work within the very texture of the versification—and in particular that, rather than treating versification as mere form, and as formalizing the various intonation contours and cadential shapes verse makes use of, we should hear the versification free these contours and shapes to render manifest their constitutive role in a poem's *aletheic* movement. This is a rebuttal of a particularly rigid approach to meter, and the mode of reading that sustains it, but not of the prosodic rhythms of poetry; nor, in fact, does it require that we approach these rhythms with complete disregard toward the "inherited standards of measure and versification" through which these rhythms are treated in verse. To put it another way: the "contest between measure and limit" requires some conception of measure if the work is to contest and thereby reconfigure its limits.

This reading might appear to contradict Heidegger's own assertion that rhythm (that is, prosody) is merely the way in which this *aletheic* "animating wave" appears "at best" to "metaphysical-aesthetic representation." Yet, I would argue, Heidegger's statement also entails the opposite: if, from within a "metaphysical-aesthetic" epoch in which one facet of poetic technique involves the patterning of syllables, we are to grasp this animating wave that conditions beings' entry into appearance, then we must do so precisely by looking to rhythm, for it is here that the poem will exceed the purely formal determinations of its measure. "Metaphysical-aesthetic" it might be, but, both in Trakl's "animating wave" and Hölderlin's prosodic dissonance, versification serves as a crucial means through which the originary rhythmicity of presence and absence can disclose itself in human speech—at least so long as human speech speaks within an epoch of metaphysics. Just as Heidegger's dismissals of form and aesthetics in fact amount to a recuperation of their central categories within the wider project of the thinking of being, the dismissal of the "metaphysical-aesthetic representation" of rhythm is part of a negotiation between a poem's prosodic movement and the oscillations between presence and absence that condition this movement, but toward which this movement gestures. And, as with Heidegger's analyses of form, this necessitates a radical revaluation of such versification, so that it is no longer *mere* versification, is no longer exhausted by its generic and technical analysis, but is attended to as it opens up the experience of a movement that will overflow its notation in a scanned metrical line, but which movement is not therefore unrelated to a scanned metrical line.

This is not to say, however, that Heidegger does not aim to think the rhythmicity of poetry beyond the categories of prosody and versification, as can be seen when, in his later writings on poetry, he offers a thinking of measure far removed from the measures of versification. In his 1950 reading of Trakl's poem "Ein Winterabend," he looks at the "dif-ference" (*Ent-scheidung*) between world and thing as that which "measures out, apportions, world and thing, each to its own," and thus "metes out the measure of their presence" (PLT 200/26). A year later, in ". . . poetically man dwells . . . ," he speaks of a measure that "gauges the between" of earth and sky and hence opens up a "dimension" or "clearing" within which beings enter appearance (PLT 218–19/195). In both instances, measure is concerned with the unity by which the "fourfold" of earth, sky, mortals, and divinities can be bound together in "harmony"; what is peculiar to this measure is that, from within the world, it can engender such a binding (or, one is tempted to extrapolate, *jointure*). In the latter of the essays, Heidegger alludes almost immediately to the measures of versification: Hölderlin's "measure-taking," he says, "has its own *metron*, and thus its own metric" (PLT 219/196), as though to supplant measure in its "metaphysical-aesthetic" sense. Here, Heidegger argues, "the nature of the 'poetic' [lies] in the taking of the measure through which the measure-taking of the breadth human being is accomplished"; poetry, enacting this measure-taking, becomes a "naming" of the "measure" itself (PLT 220/196, translation modified).

As Chapter 4 will show, Heidegger's reading of this "measure" is in fact heavily dependent on the versification of the particular fragment of Hölderlin that he reads. Here I would like to note that, while the measure Heidegger situates beyond prosodic meter does not continue his thinking of the animation of the artwork and of language, it nevertheless retains the insistence, made in "The Origin of the Work of Art," that a measure must be open to that which surpasses it, and that it can only gather into presence when engaging with a movement of absencing. Thus measure will be a measure-taking of a difference (what Heidegger here thematizes as difference and as the "between") that both conditions and yet exceeds thinking, so as to grasp this difference without subsuming it into the "same." And, insofar as this difference characterizes human "dwelling," it is being conceived temporally; this notion of measure is understood as rhythmic in the broadened sense Heidegger has given the term. The thinking of measure is necessarily a thinking of limit; in measuring, the poem necessarily will encounter its limits in their irreducible difference, an encounter that permits the work to articulate a measurement that would bring these limits into view.

These two references to "measure" (*Maß*) continue the same project that, fifteen years earlier, had situated the sounding of Hölderlin's use of the word *Denn* in the moment at which a poem's *Versmaß* tries to accommodate that which exceeds it. In the later lectures Heidegger dismisses the notion of any link between these two kinds of measure; yet the point of intersection between the two is central to his discussion, in the *Introduction to Metaphysics,* written at the same time as "The Origin of the Work of Art" and a year after his lecture series on "Germanien," of the first choral ode from Sophocles's *Antigone,* and its portrayal of man as the "most uncanny" (*das Unheimlichste*). Man's uncanniness is predicated on his being torn from the earth that would otherwise be "home." He continues: "The ode . . . sings of breaking forth upon the groundless waves, of giving up firm land. This breakaway does not take place upon the cheerful smoothness of gleaming water but amid the winter storm. The saying of this breakaway is situated in the law of motion of the word- and verse-structure [*das Bewegungsgesetz der Wort- und Versfügung*], just as the *chorei* in verse 336 is placed at the point where the meter [*Versmaß*] shifts" (IM 164/118; translation modified). A few minutes earlier, as though to emphasize the word and verse-structure, and render audible this moment where "the meter shifts," Heidegger had read the ode aloud in the Greek (IM 156/112). It is immediately striking that the metrical shift is considered to transform utterly the very content of the ode's "saying"—it does not simply emphasize or qualify the saying's meaning by drawing our attention to the way it is said, nor does it constitute a formal effect to heighten our attentiveness or "echo" its sense, but rather quite fundamentally changes what the word *chorei* "says." Quite simply, without this metrical shift we would not be able to see that Sophocles is at this precise juncture depicting man as the most uncanny. In the opening translation, *chorei* is given as *kreutz* (rendered by Polt and Fried as "cruises," IM 156/112), but after attending to its metrical position, Heidegger can continue: "[Man] gives up [gibt . . . auf] the place, he heads out [rückt . . . aus]—and ventures to enter [wagt sich] the superior power of the sea's placeless flood. The word stands like a pillar in the construction of these verses" (IM 164/118). Standing "like a pillar," the word is at once bounded by, and yet exceeds, its "law of motion." It is, in other words, uncannily situated—just as is the human being it describes—and this uncanniness lies in its balancing its metrical weight with the ontological weight of its movedness. The shift at once inaugurates the ode's "law of motion" and is subject to this law; it initially advertises itself as a metrical feature, but immediately reaches beyond its local metrical function to render manifest the law governing this function. Both through Heidegger's simile and through the role it plays within the movedness of the lines at this juncture of the ode, this passage brings to mind the temple in "The Origin of the Work of Art," whose self-subsistence lies in its standing there in a repose that structures the relations around it. In both, what we encounter is an "inner concentration of motion" which, far from being the absence of movedness, is in fact its nodal point: the point at which the movement into presence articulates itself prosodically. The metrical shift of *chorei* is thus the irruption of this originary movedness into the poem's own measure—and conversely, the poem's measure forges, through its metrical shift, a space into which this movedness can irrupt. This moment in the ode thus constitutes what Heidegger would call a *Gestalt*: a moment of coherence where the series of countermovements—metrical, tropological, and grammatical—intersect in agitated stillness. At such a moment, however, we not only become open to the "law of motion" underlying such stillness, and of which such stillness is a cipher; the condition of man as the "most uncanny," *for the first time,* comes to shine and sound. From the metrical shift thus issues a broader shift in the parameters of the open; in the use of its prosodic medium, the poem allows us to see a truth that had hitherto remained beyond our grasp.

At the same time as he is working through the question of the movedness of the work that will be so central to "The Origin of the Work of Art," then, Heidegger is trying to grasp the relation between this movedness and the prosodic movement of individual poems. And it is this same concern that will motivate his discussion, in the 1958 lecture on George entitled "Das Wort," of George's poem "In stillste ruh": "Rhythm, *ruthmos,* does not mean flux and flowing, but rather structure [*Fügung*]. Rhythm is what is at rest, what structures [*fügt*] the movement of dance and song, and thus lets it rest within itself. Rhythm bestows rest. In the song we just heard, the structure shows itself if we pay heed to the one fugue [*Fuge*] which sings to us" (OL 149/230, translation modified). Again, central to the account of the poem's rhythm and animation is *rest;* rhythm is "at rest," but it also "bestows rest"; "rest" is both a feature of rhythm as structure/adjoinment, and is what this structuring-joining rhythm engenders. As was the case in "The Origin of the Work of Art," Heidegger argues that, far from being the absence of movement, such rest renders movement possible; it gathers the dance and song's movement "within itself," into what he termed the artwork's "closed, unitary repose" (OBT 26/37). "Such rest is," Heidegger specifies in the earlier work, "a state of extreme movedness": only when we "grasp the movement of the happening in the work-being of the work as a unity" can we "come . . . into proximity with [its] repose" (OBT 26/37, translation modified). To "grasp the movement of this happening," however, requires that we distinguish the poem's "structuring" or "adjoining" rhythm from the "flux and flowing" of a series of discrete "nows." If this gestures toward what "Anaximander's Saying" termed the "disjointure" of "sheer persistence," we now see it is a contribution, specifically, to the way of measuring the prosodic movement of poetry. Only as we see the poem organizing its own movement around its adjoining stillness can we come to hear its *fugue;* this fugue, moreover, holding the poem together into a unitary stillness, is index of the coherence and inner concentration of the poem's *Gestalt.*

Heidegger situates this "fugue" in a trope that develops throughout the poem: "secure soul and sudden sight, stem and storm, sea and shell" (OL 149/231), and the syncopations it effects against each metrical line and against the three-stanza structure of the poem as a whole. Even if the rhythm is "at rest" and "bestows rest," even if it is eventually structure, adjoinment, or jointure, that is, it only first engendered as the patterning of individual words and themes within the taut frame of George's lyric sets up a highly fraught push and pull. The ontological adjoinment does not lie behind the poem, then, but performs its jointure as the poem engages with the rhythmicity of its medium. This medium, moreover, is rhythmic not simply through its stanza form and meter, but also (and, for Heidegger's reading, ostensibly) through its use of trope and syntax—indeed, the rhythmic jointure we "hear" in this poem takes place only as these different elements enter into dialogue with one another, condition one another, and thus open up a space in which the *Stille* lying within this jointure, at once stillness and silence, can trace its inner movement and thus, for the first time, come to *sound.*

■

With this in mind, let us return to the problem broached at the beginning of the chapter: the relation between *Poesie,* an individual linguistic work, and *Dichtung,* the poetic more generally which, characterized through its bringing beings to shine and sound, Heidegger calls the "essence" of all artworks. We have seen that the rhythm or rhythmicity of *Dichtung* extends beyond the technical employment of prosody, extends, even, beyond the "linguistic work" as a whole, to touch upon the "inner concentration" of the work through which the various countermovements are joined together and structured in agitated stillness. Yet this rhythmicity cannot be extracted from the actual artwork to constitute a purely "essential" rhythmicity: in each case, it arises out of a "use" of medium, be it Cézanne's heavy downward strokes and the countermovement they exact, Beethoven's cadences, or Hölderlin's prosodic dissonance. Moreover, as this rhythm, as jointure, poetry's "dynamization" of its verbal medium complicates and deepens the rhythmicity latent in all earthly work-material, and thereby comes to embody that movement which Heidegger will attribute to the "gathering" of *logos.*[48] The poem thus renders audible the movement happening within language itself as it comes to sound. As Heidegger puts it in "The Origin of the Work of Art," "since language is the happening in which for man beings first disclose themselves to him each time as beings, *Poesie* . . . is the most primordial form of *Dichtung* in the essential sense" (OBT 46/61). In the next chapter, then, I will pursue the question of movedness as it takes place within language itself, and its relation to what Heidegger terms "the naming power of the word" (OBT 24/35).

But what we have also seen is that Heidegger's thinking, even when presenting, not to mention valorizing, itself as a peremptory dismissal of poetics, in fact constitutes, and necessitates, a prolonged engagement with the central categories of this latter, even at those junctures in which poetics would lie within a "metaphysical-aesthetic" tradition. The focus on the firstness of the artwork is less the rejection of a work's formal features than a reconfiguration of their meaning. Form, quite simply, is never *mere* form, but rather concerns the way the artwork exhibits its own entry into appearance, and in so doing opens up a space for the encounter with beings. The work's thrust is thought both in terms of its form and in terms of truth as *aletheia* because the two are one and the same. Fixing in one being the movement that characterizes all entry into appearance, such that it takes place in, and as, the work's *Gestalt,* the artwork shapes a thinking to come. And as the following chapters will show, Heidegger's prolonged engagement with poetry and poetics constitutes an unceasing attempt to set such a thinking on its way.

2

The Naming Power of the Word

In "The Origin of the Work of Art," Heidegger situates the earth in the "work-material" of the artwork: "the massiveness and heaviness of the stone, . . . the firmness and flexibility of the wood, . . . the lightening and darkening of color . . . the ringing of sound, and the naming power of the word" (OBT 24/35). That Heidegger should place "the word" last is a rhetorical gesture toward poetry's status in the pantheon of the arts. It is both that art form to which "architecture, the visual arts, and music must all be referred back" (OBT 45/60), and also, by virtue of its linguistic character, something of an anomaly.[1] Whereas architecture, sculpture, painting and music are all "set back" into the *qualia* of their thingliness, a "naming power" is less straightforwardly tangible, and, insofar as it implies a named, it appears to contradict the antimimetic thrust of the lecture as a whole. How can a "naming power" come to constitute poetry's "thingly substructure" (OBT 17/27)?

Following on from the movement Heidegger characterized as earth, one might sketch a tentative first response to this question. The "naming power" would withdraw from the "naming" itself, and through this withdrawal become the power that renders naming as such possible. This echoes the characterization given by Bruns: "Language is the earth out of which poetry emerges and into which it withdraws; but it is more . . . Heidegger wants to link language up with truth as *a-letheia*."[2] That is, withdrawal, as an engagement with limits, serves to frame the open region itself, and is thus an integral moment in the event of truth. And yet herein lies a fun-

61

damental difficulty. Bruns's talk of "linking up" implies a prior separation of the two. The question as to how to grasp these two moments as one and the same is a central challenge to understanding Heidegger's thinking not only of the language of poetry, but of language more broadly.

This is the question the current chapter seeks to address. Late in "The Origin of the Work of Art," Heidegger argues that we need "the right concept of language [*die rechten Begriffes von der Sprache*]" (OBT 45/60). This "right concept" has two aspects. Firstly, verbal language should be seen not simply in terms of those "sense-giving acts that furnish the word-sound with a sense" (WCT 129/133), but should extend to those aspects of language, often termed "paralanguage," which are meaningful without necessarily having a determinate signification. Yet language is also a "projective saying," which "allows [the] open to happen in such a way . . . that now, for the first time, in the midst of beings, it brings them to shine and sound" (OBT 45/60). By virtue of its "naming power," language can, "in the midst of beings," reach beyond these beings and transform the way in which they come to presence: it "nominates beings *to* their being and *from out of* that being" (OBT 46/60–61)—something of increasing significance for his later work. Heidegger's task is thus dual: to give an account of the originary articulation that renders possible language as such, and which in his later work he terms *Sagen* (saying); and to delineate a model of verbal language, or *Sprechen* (speech), that can attend to the openness it inhabits. It is in the point of transition or threshold between these two levels of articulation that Heidegger situates what he terms "naming."

Responding to this dual exigency, naming becomes central to Heidegger's account of how poems mean. Much has been said of the "turn" that Heidegger's thinking undergoes in the 1930s, of which the increasing concern with language is a central feature.[3] I, however, want to stress the continuity in his thinking, especially regarding this relation between verbal language and the originary openness that renders it possible. In the first section, I will examine the ways in which, throughout his work, Heidegger resists the reduction of verbal language to reference, focusing rather on verbal language as a "whole" (*Ganze*) of the different meaningful practices that make up linguistic openness. This involves on the one hand a critique of the conception of linguistic meaning in terms of the verbal sign, and on the other a radical rethinking of the meaningful structure of verbal sound. The second section will develop this latter issue, looking at how Heidegger's engagement with the bodily aspects of language not only pertains to verbal language and its paralinguistic features, but also to this originary openness. First I look at the discussions of *Gebärde* (gesture) and *Wink* (hint) in his later work; I then refer this back to the role played by "voice" in *Being and Time*. Here we will see two conceptions of voice at work: the intonation, modulation, and tempo that characterize "'poetical' discourse," and the silent call of the "voice of conscience." What I propose is that Heidegger's later account of naming will try to reconcile these two different conceptions of voice, and does so through its discussion of a "peal of stillness" (*Geläut der Stille*) through which "language speaks" (PLT 205/30). It is to this "peal of stillness," and its relation to the sounding of verbal language, that I shall turn in the final section.

The Right Concept of Language

Heidegger's "right concept of language" is delineated in contradistinction to "the usual account," according to which "language is a kind of communication" divided into a nonsensuous, prelinguistic content on the one hand, and the sensuous tokens that comprise the "aural and written expression of what is to-be-communicated" on the other (OBT 45/60). Communication, he ripostes, "is not what language, in the first instance, does. Rather, it brings beings as beings, for the first time, into the open" (OBT 46/60). The critique of what is here deemed the "usual account" is an abiding feature of his work from his earliest discussions of language in the 1920s onwards. Heidegger continually tries to sketch an account of verbal language that resists reduction into reference, be it symbolic or by signification,[4] or expression, but which, as he puts it in his lecture course *History of the Concept of Time*, comprises a whole of discourse (*Rede*) (HCT 264/364).[5] Yet the claim that language "brings beings . . . into the open" constitutes a new development in his thinking on language, one which is intimately related to the increasing importance of poetry in his later work. Whereas in his earlier writings he sees verbal language as articulating the originary intelligibility, or "discoveredness," through which beings show themselves within a world, he is now suggesting that verbal articulation can in fact engender this intelligibility. It is this mode of verbal articulation that he thematizes as naming.

Logos: *Verbal Language and the Intelligibility of the World*

The critique of language as reference recurs throughout Heidegger's oeuvre. In *History of the Concept of Time* and *Being and Time*, he argues that to reduce discourse simply to its determinations as reference or expression would be to overlook the diverse modes of meaning taking place in all "discoursing." In his 1925 lecture series, he proposes "four structural moments which belong essentially to language itself": the "about which," the "discursive what" (the "said as such"), the "communication," and the "manifestation" (HCT 263/363). In Jan Aler's succinct formulation: "(1) I say (2) something (3) to someone (4) about something."[6] Discourse, Heidegger argues, constitutes the whole of these four "structural moments"; these moments, moreover, constitute not a lexical and syntactical system but a verbal comportment that we continually live—that is, it is an *existential*. To approach language simply via its referential, expressive, or communicative character would "allude to only *one* phenomenal character in language itself and one-sidedly take it as a basis for an essential definition" (HCT 264/364).[7] This critique of language as reference, expression, or communication is reiterated in the introductory observations to his 1950 lecture "Language," where he identifies three assumptions behind the idea that speaking is the "activation of the organ for sounding and hearing" (PLT 190/14). Firstly, *Sprechen* (speech) is the expression of an internal content through an external medium to an external source; secondly, it is an activity of man, what Humboldt called *energeia*, and thus to be understood in terms of human agency rather than by recourse to its *Sprachwesen* (linguistic nature); thirdly, "human expression is always a presentation and representation of the real and the unreal" (PLT 190/14), whose reference is secured through the correctness of such (re)presentation.

While this latter analysis is consistent with Heidegger's understanding of language as a "discursive whole," it nevertheless diverges sharply from the conception of this whole as an *existential,* as can be seen in his opposition of language as human activity (*energeia*) to "linguistic essence": the speaking of language, Heidegger will argue, is "nothing human" (PLT 205/30, translation modified), something I will turn to at the end of this chapter. For the time being let us note how this rejection of the model of language as reference or expression entails a radical revaluation of "paralanguage," the "variables" of "pitch, loudness, tempo, timbre and voice quality," which have been termed "non-linguistic aspects of speaking."[8] Rather than constituting additional features to a language determined semantically, intonation, gesture, silence, and others would in fact serve as the condition for any such semantic determination.[9] It is here, indeed, that Heidegger's thinking first accords a privilege to poetry in grasping the meaningful fabric of worldly experience, and the ontological dimension that makes this experience possible.

Calling into question any hard and fast separation of paralanguage from language also complicates the opposition of conceptual-linguistic cognition to supposedly prelinguistic phenomenal experience. Instead of trying to situate a moment at which experience enters into language,

Heidegger in *Being and Time* offers various strata of meaning which increase in linguistic definition. For the world to be "discovered" (*entdeckt, erschloßen*) requires that it be "intelligible" (*verständlich*) in advance. Our understanding (*Verstand*) subsequently "interprets" (*legt . . . aus*) this discoveredness in such a way that it becomes "meaningful" (*bedeutsam*). In "meaningfulness" (*Bedeutsamkeit*), "there lurks the ontological condition which makes it possible for Dasein, as something which understands and interprets, to disclose such things as 'meanings' [*Bedeutungen*]; upon these, in turn, is founded the being of words and of language" (BT 87/121; translation modified).[10] To these "meanings," Heidegger says, "words accrue" (BT 204/161), and we enter *Rede* ("discourse" or verbal comportment), *Verlautbarung* (utterance), and eventually *Sprache* (language) itself as a lexico-syntactic system. Yet even after the institution of this lexico-semantic system, language functions primarily as mode for our circumspective dealings with the ready-to-hand: predication, which Heidegger also terms the "apophantic 'as'" (BT 201/158), is a derivative mode of the "*existential-*hermeneutic 'as'" through which beings can first be addressed in verbal comportment, but which does not itself furnish conceptual assertions of beings that are "present-at-hand" (*vorhanden*).

This is not, Heidegger argues, an epistemological model of meaning-production, with a teleological movement from the basic discoveredness of the world to verbal predication; rather, these different levels of meaning are at work alongside one another, as can be seen in the employment of the term *logos*. "The Greeks," Heidegger informs us, "had no word for 'language'; they understood this phenomenon 'in the first instance' as discourse" (BT 209/165); and yet *logos* does not pertain exclusively to verbal comportment. In a brief discussion of Aristotle's *zoion logon ekhon*, he says: "Man shows himself as the entity which talks. This does not signify that the possibility of vocal utterance is peculiar to him, but rather that he is the entity which is such as to discover the world and Dasein itself" (BT 208–9/165). Man becomes the "entity which talks" by virtue of a discoveredness that precedes and renders possible *logos;* yet it is only in this *logos* that "an entity is manifest," only "with a view to this entity" that "words are put together [*zusammengesetzt*] in *one* verbal whole" (BT 201/159). This gives a paradoxical situation according to which *logos* engenders, through its putting together, the very discoveredness in which the "view" to this entity is first given to it.

This focus on *logos* as "putting" beings "together" anticipates Heidegger's later translation of *logos* not as discourse but as "gathering," or, as he puts it in his 1939 Aristotle lecture: "To bring together into a unity and to bring forth this unity as gathered [*versammelt*]" (P 213/348–49). In this later work the gathering of *logos* concerns not verbal articulation but the intelligibility that first renders possible such articulation. "Of itself," Heidegger insists, "*legein* has nothing to do with saying and with language," but pertains to "the original and fundamental relation to beings" through which beings come to show themselves (P 213–14/350). In the earlier work, *logos* described how already intelligible beings are put together into verbal language; now it becomes that movement through which beings first become intelligible in such a way that they can be thus put together. In both instances, however, the central concern is the movement from this originary intelligibility in which beings show themselves into verbal language itself.

It is this movement that Heidegger will, in the 1958 lecture on "The Way to Language," identify in the archaic Swabian word *Bewëgung*, translated by Hertz as "way-making." What Heidegger is concerned with is how *Sagen* (saying), the originary *logos,* can enter human *Sprechen* (speech) (OL 130/261). To say that "language speaks" (*die Sprache spricht*) (OL 124/254), then, is more than simply an instance of tautological thinking;[11] in the "speaking" of language, the originary *logos* attains verbal articulation. Heidegger's concern in this lecture is twofold. Firstly, he wishes to ask how verbal language can first trace the originary openness of *logos,* or *Sagan,* how human speech can hold within it something of language in its "linguistic essence"; probing this question will allow him to grasp this linguistic essence on its own terms, so that language is not simply understood in terms of human activity. But secondly, he asks if human verbal comportment might in fact shape the originary intelligibility that renders it possible? Can, that is, "speech" itself provide an impetus for the movement, "language," through which it comes to be spoken?

In this respect, logos traces a double movement: the originary intelligibility moves into verbal language and conversely, this verbal language shapes the intelligibility it inhabits, it "nominates beings *to* their being and *from out of* that being" (OBT 46/60–1), as he put it in "The Origin of the Work of Art." Here again we can note a continuity in his thinking from *Being and Time* to his later work. In the earlier work, Heidegger had argued that discursive articulation is not simply a question of providing meanings with lexical tokens; these lexemes must themselves become meaningful. Above, I cited from a passage that I now quote in its entirety: "The meaningful whole [*Bedeutungsganze*] of intelligibility is *put into words* [*Wörter*]. To meanings, words accrue [*Den Bedeutungen wachsen Worte zu*]. But word-things do not get supplied with meanings" (BT 204/161; translation modified). Meanings are brought into verbal comportment through a reciprocal growth; its "accrual," as Aler notes, refers at once to the "unfolding" of the linguistic meaning out of discoveredness, "as if it were to differentiate itself and begin to flourish," and to "the process of the growth of the words" themselves.[12] In this latter growth, we see *Wörter*, "separate lexical items or vocables," transformed into *Worte*, "phrases and expressions as *used* in language,"[13] whereby words cease to be determined simply semantically (*Wörter*), but engage the full breadth of their meaningfulness (*Worte*): they cease to be mere "language" and become "discourse." If it is in *logos* that "the words [*Wörter*] are put together in *one* verbal whole" (BT 201/159), then this entails not simply a gathering of meaning into words, but a gathering of words as lexical units into a "whole" that engages all dimensions of verbal meaning. It would be the very animation of language.

While the meaning of *logos* changes in Heidegger's thinking, then, the shape of thought remains the same. Heidegger is concerned throughout with verbal language not as a lexico-syntactic system but as verbal meaning more broadly, anterior to any relation of correspondence between word and thing. However, he also wants to give an account of originary intelligibility that would first render such language possible. In *Being and Time*, *logos* refers to the discourse that articulates an already open human experience; in his later writings it is deployed to describe the originary gathering movement that brings about such openness; for both, it is only by grasping verbal language in its wholeness that we can first encounter the gathering movement underlying it. As we will see below, this is the problematic motivating his analyses of "naming."

"Meaning is never a sign"

There has been much critical dispute regarding the place of language in *Being and Time*'s account of circumspective understanding, and whether Heidegger can be said to belong to the "linguistic turn" of twentieth-century philosophy. Charles Guignon's ambivalence in this regard is emblematic. He portrays Heidegger as "torn between two incompatible views of the nature of language":[14] an "instrumentalist view," "grounded in some prior grasp of the nonsemantic significance of the contexts in which we find ourselves," and a "constitutive view" for which language is "a *medium* in which man dwells."[15] Cristina Lafont tries to hold these two views in tension when she summarizes the conception of language in *Being and Time* in the dictum, "sense determines reference."[16] On this account, individual linguistic meanings are for Heidegger dependent on language as such, understood as a frame grounding the coherence of worldly experience. She specifies: "what *lies prior to the statement is not anything prelinguistic, but rather language itself.* Language understood as an 'articulated whole of significance' . . . first supplies Dasein with the intelligibility it requires in order to be able to express a statement at all."[17]

Striking in Lafont's account of the "language" prior to the "statement" is the implication that Heidegger's ultimate interest is how we are able to "express a statement," despite his insistence that statement is merely a "derivative" mode of interpretation (BT 195/154). Similarly, Guignon, ascribing to the pre- or nonlinguistic a "nonsemantic significance," takes the significance of language to be semantic; if language is taken as a discursive whole, however, it is pervaded through and through by "nonsemantic significance." That is, Heidegger's concern in *Being and Time* is not to effect a transition from nonlinguistic into linguistic meaning, or to demonstrate that worldly experience is always already linguistic; rather, it is with how we come to articulate, in verbal comportment, the discoveredness of the world. And this supposes that the various strata of meaning enumerated above are part of a continuum in which the entry into verbal language can take different forms.

Central to the claim that the Heidegger of *Being and Time* follows the "linguistic turn" is the role of "signs" in his analysis of the "Worldhood of the World" (BT 76–89/107–14). The intelligibility of being-in-the-world shows itself through a series of assignments or references (*Verweisungen*) that are implicit in Dasein's circumspective dealings with the world. While Lafont takes this to mean that the world is "symbolically structured,"[18] it is striking that Heidegger's examples of such "signs" ignore any specifically "symbolic," let alone "linguistic," dimension, comprising, in *Being and Time,* "signposts, boundary-stones, the ball for the mariner's storm-warning, signals, banners, signs of mourning, and the like" (BT 77/108).[19] Speaking, in *History of the Concept of Time,* of the "meanings" (*Bedeutungen*) that are articulated in language, he is at pains to resist the conflation of verbal language and of signification: "every sign *means* [bedeutet], which is to say that it has the mode of being of meaningfulness. Meaning, however, is never a sign" (HCT 204/279; translation modified).[20] Instead of taking this to prove that the nonverbal signs through which Dasein encounters the world are grounded in language, I would suggest that he is concerned, precisely, with a meaningfulness that, while pervading both verbal comportment and ready-to-hand assignments, cannot be reduced to either.

Many commentators have attempted to align Heidegger's account of language to the Saussurean distinction between *langue* and *parole*. Françoise Dastur, for instance, suggests that the conception of language at work in *Being and Time* is situated "within the horizon of *signification,* that is to say out of the difference between the moment of articulation of meaning, discourse (*Rede*), and that of its verbal exteriorization, language (*Sprache*),"[21] and Giorgio Agamben extends this analogy to touch upon the very structure of ontological difference: "The opening of the *ontological* dimension (being, world) corresponds to the pure taking place of language as originary event, while the *ontic* dimension (entities, things) corresponds to that which, in this opening, is said and signified. The transcendence of being with respect to the entity, of the world with respect to the thing, is above all, a transcendence of the event of *langue* with respect to *parole*."[22] Lafont, by contrast, notes a fundamental discrepancy between Saussure's and Heidegger's accounts of this relation: whereas the *langue-parole* distinction aims only to "mark . . . the *methodological* difference between two perspectives of the reflection on language," Heidegger attempts "to establish a *founding* relationship between the two aspects of language."[23] However, if Heidegger does indeed try to "found" language as a lexico-syntactic system on discourse, this bears little resemblance to Saussure's own distinction. Firstly, *discourse,* far from being the sum of possible meanings, is, as an *existential,* the lived reality of verbal comportment, far closer to what Saussure termed *parole.* It might then be tempting to suggest that Heidegger inverts the Saussurean distinction; yet his challenge to this distinction goes far deeper, as it calls into question the very framework of the dyadic linguistic sign. In the relation between discourse and language, the basic unit of meaning is not anything verbal, but rather being-in-the-world itself.[24] Moreover, in understanding the word as a dyadic sign, one has already made certain assumptions about how this word *means,* and has in particular effected the reduction from the whole of discourse to one of its phenomenal moments, and with it the demotion of paralanguage from this structure of meaning (to say nothing of that other methodological claim made by Saussure: that the sonorous dimension of the sign is "arbitrary").[25] Later, in *What is Called Thinking?,* Heidegger will make this explicit: when we consider the "constituent of the word" to be "signification," we in advance posit a dichotomy between a signification that "cannot be perceived by the senses" and "the purely sensuous aspect of the word-sound [*Wortlaut*]," which, "conceived as mere resonance [*Schall*], is an abstraction" (WCT 130/134). To hear this sensuous aspect requires that we abstract ourselves from the "sphere of what is spoken"; but it is precisely "the sphere of what is spoken" that Heidegger wishes to inhabit.

Heidegger develops this analysis of the verbal sign in his lectures "The Way to Language" and "The Essence of Language," both of which treat the same passage from Aristotle's *De interpretatione,* which states that "letters are the signs of sounds, the sounds are the signs of mental experiences, and these are signs of things" (OL 97/204). Aristotle, Heidegger argues, offers a tripartite model of the verbal sign: it is at once *semeia* (the showing), *sum-*

bola (the linking), and *homoiomata* (the likening); of these three, *semeia,* "showing in the sense of letting-appear [*Erscheinenlassen*]," has privileged status, as it facilitates the "architectonic" structure that fixes the levels of sign (OL 115/245; in other words, letters "show" the sounds they signify, and so on). Aristotle's account of *semeia* is of especial interest to Heidegger as it lies at the point of transition between two conceptions of linguistic meaning, with the notion of "showing" being supplanted by the conventional relation between sign (*Zeichen*) and signified (*Bezeichnetem*) (OL 115/245).[26] In this particular passage the two conceptions are in tension, even if Aristotle's text is part of a historical progression that will eventually see the latter subsume the former entirely, something Heidegger makes explicit in an aside: "The transformation of the sign from something that shows to something that designates has its roots in the change of the nature of truth" (OL 115/245).[27]

If the sign-signified relation assumes in advance a model of truth as *adaequatio intellectus et rei,* and if *aletheia* is originary to any determination of correctness, then it follows that "*the essential being of language is Saying as Showing* [die Zeige]. Its showing character [*Zeigen*] is not based on signs of any kind; rather, all signs arise from a showing within whose realm and for whose purposes they can be signs" (OL 123/254). Heidegger's reading of *semeia* has led some commentators to conceive of showing as a "direct," "pure" or "natural" sign, as opposed to a "signifying" or "artificial" sign.[28] In this case, it would seem as though Heidegger, even as he attempts to escape the framework of signification, is caught back within it. Froment-Meurice notes that such a "pure" or "direct" sign is unable furnish an "'intact' origin of saying as showing delivered from all supplementarity of the sign."[29] For the identity of the "direct sign" with what it "shows" would still be predicated on the difference between the "sign" and the "shown": as the sign stands for what is shown, it supplements it. But then, if Heidegger is attempting to escape the framework of signification, it is not clear why showing would be any kind of sign, "pure" or otherwise. Indeed, if one assumes "showing" to be some kind of sign in advance, it is hardly surprising that signification will transpire to be an ineluctable condition of all language. What we need to do is ask what kind of an "'intact' origin" Heidegger is in fact trying to grasp, and how it can be that this "origin" should open up a space for signification while exceeding, and preceding, the conception of ontic reference as sign.

We encounter an analogous problem when showing is said to afford access to "the immediacy of the thing" or "unmediated revelations."[30] De Man warns that such unmediated revelations would be fatally undermined by Heidegger's own "metaphorical" discussions of "hiding and revealing":

as with Froment-Meurice's critique, we find that the chain of linguistic representation—here understood in terms of metaphor rather than significa-tion—will resist any immediate union of word and referent. Yet discussions of "direct signs" and the mediation-immediacy nexus are notable in their absence from Heidegger's vocabulary,[31] and I would suggest it is because such concerns are alien to the shape of his thinking. This does not mean that a characterization of "the true nature of language" in terms of its vocation "to reveal Being to us" is false,[32] but it certainly limits the way in which this "revelation" should be understood. If the "revelation" of being were of the order of correspondent to referent, signifier to signified, then *being* would be transformed into *a being*; rather, language must engender the space in which beings can come to disclose themselves in their being. Only as it shapes the modes of such auto-disclosure can language "reveal" being. In this, the saying of language becomes "showing" not as it "points" (Heidegger is here employing the term *Zeigen* in the full breadth of its connotations) to a preexistent referent already present in an open region, be it an individual being or being as such, but as it points *toward* "letting-appear," it guides thinking toward the openness in which this being would give itself to be thought, and at the same time guides the being toward that openness in which it can be encountered.

Bringing into Name

Given the claim that signs are derived from an anterior showing, it might come as a surprise that Heidegger should on two occasions elaborate on the "showing character" of language through discussions of Hölderlin's use of the word "sign." In his lecture series on the hymn "Der Ister," he glosses the phrase "a sign is needed [*Ein Zeichen braucht es*]"; in *What is Called Thinking?*, he refers to a line from a draft (Heidegger calls it a "project" (*Entwurf*), WCT 10/11) version of the hymn "Mnemosyne": "We are a sign that is not read." In the "Ister" lectures, Heidegger warns against any temptation to "replace the name 'sign' by the influential term 'symbol'"; the sign's showing, rather, "is of such a kind as to first let appear that which is to be shown" (IH 149/185). The "sign" comes to stand for the figure of the poet, who "is the one who points [*der Hinzeigende*], thus something that shows [*ein Zeigendes*], and is thereby a 'sign' [*ein 'Zeichen'*]—not a thing-like sign, not some sign-thing, which is what we mistakenly take to be the specific nature proper to a 'sign' [. . . but] can, in saying, let appear that which is to be said only because it has before this already been shone upon by that which thus appears as what is to be poetized" (IH 151/189). The phrase "a sign is needed" draws attention both to the relation between the naming through which speech can render manifest the intelligibility of "world," and also to the poet's "vocation" of effecting such a speech. Here we should note two things. Firstly, the poet's saying is the response to a "need" (*Brauch*): this anticipates Heidegger's later assertion that "language needs and uses [*braucht*] human speech" (OL 125/256). And secondly, the showing of the Hölderlinian sign only takes place through an engagement with the limits of what shows itself: "The sign shows—and in showing, it makes manifest, yet in such a way that it simultaneously conceals" (IH 165/202). It is this that is emphasized in the reading of "We are sign that is not read" (where what was previously the poet's vocation is now a human condition): "To the extent that man *is* drawing that way, he *points* toward what withdraws. *As* he is pointing that way, man *is* the pointer. . . . Something which in itself, by its essence, is pointing, we call a sign. As he draws toward what withdraws, man is a sign" (WCT 9–10/11). If man becomes a sign by entering into relation with what withdraws, then this withdrawal itself refuses to be "signed": "The sign stays without interpretation [*Das Zeichen bleibt ohne Deutung*]" (WCT 10/11). In order for man to become a sign, he must inhabit the very limits of meaning, that is, engage with the modalities of non-presence.

The sign articulated in these two instances would describe something akin to what others would thematize in terms of mediation: how a verbal icon can bring an entity to be thought. Indeed, when for Hölderlin the poet becomes sign, it is because he stands in a "between" that separates the divine from the human. However, rather than mediating between divine and human, Heidegger argues, the poet would embody their reciprocal difference, internalized into his own uncanny vocation. Only thus can the poet bring the divine to appear. In his thinking on the verbal icon also, Heidegger focuses on such "letting appear." The word does not "stand for" the entity or "signify" it; rather, it *draws* the entity by drawing *toward* it, and in the same gesture drawing toward its withdrawal. The sign—man, language—brings into presence only as it engages with the absencing movement that frames it, but which it by definition cannot grasp without distorting.

Later on in *What is Called Thinking?* Heidegger returns to this question, but now in order to outline a conception of language as naming. Instead of approaching "the relation between name and thing as the coordination of two objects," word and referent, we should look at how the name holds what we wish to think in presence. "By naming," he continues, "we call on what presences to arrive" (WCT 120/124). The naming is neither reference to what is already present, nor is it a conjuring trick making beings magically appear. Rather, it is a verbal comportment that, by attending to beings' autodisclosure, can shape their entry into presence, and determine the way in which they remain in presence and give themselves to thought. It is in this sense that language can be "projective"; it "reveals" being only as it "projects" an openness within which beings can show themselves in, and be encountered in, their being.

The "call" does not refer to something already present, but is rather an "anticipatory reaching out" (WCT 117/121), and in this it is not unlike a performative. This point is made by Derrida in specific reference to the modes of naming we encounter in Heidegger's own "text," which he describes as "the performance or, in a very open sense of this word, the performative of writing by which Heidegger names . . . Neither neologism nor meta-writing in the gesture that *there is* here."[33] When Heidegger argues that the "saying" of language "lets beings appear in their 'it is'" (OL 155/237), what is at issue is precisely the claim that such and such a being *is,* and that, claiming that this being *is* in fact conditions the modes in which it discloses itself as a being. Language does not create the being, nor is such performativity a mere stylistic or rhetorical feature of language usage: in its "anticipatory reading out," this performance determines the parameters of the open in which the thing named can appear. Naming, in its "anticipatory reaching out," determines the parameters of the open in which the thing can appear. Its engagement with withdrawal is central to gauge the limits of its saying, and thus of the open itself; at the same time, it *gathers* this being into presence by grasping it in a particular configuration through which it can appear and remain apparent. In the lecture of George's "Das Wort," Heidegger terms this *Be-dingnis,* translated by Stambaugh as "bethinging," but which also retains the verb *bedingen,* "to condition" (OL 151/232). *Bedingung* is "the word's rule": that "which makes the thing be a thing. The word begins to shine as the gathering which first brings what presences into presence" (OL 155/237).

But how is a being to enter thus into presence? Here we might recall the analyses of *Fuge* and *Riss* in the previous chapter. The *Riss* functions as that which both joins and differentiates, tracing the artwork as a coherent unity by way of a double movement, at once differentiating it from beings as a whole and joining its disparate elements into coherence. Heidegger conceives of the gathering of language as effecting a similar movement: as it draws a being into presence, it gathers this being into a singular configuration through which it discloses itself, yet does so by bringing it to stand apart from other beings, and from the world in which it appears. Discussing the motif of "pain" in his 1950 lecture on Trakl's "Ein Winterabend," Heidegger argues that "it separates, yet so that at the same time it draws everything to itself, gathers it to itself" (PLT 202/27). In this double movement, pain in Trakl's poem "names" what Heidegger terms "the join-ing of the rift" (*die Fuge des Rißes*). Pain would thus touch upon—and *name*—the very mode through which language itself names. Trakl's line reads: "Pain turned the threshold to stone," and yet, Heidegger argues, in its joining-separating movement pain *is* a threshold. That is, it would stake out a joining difference both between man and the beings that enter into presence, and between things and world, but at the same time a joining difference between the originary gathering of *logos* and the human speech through which this gathering articulates itself.

Allen suggests we think of this double gesture of drawing together and pushing apart as a "cleaving" of language.[34] In the following pages I will employ the term *articulation,* a term already used by Heidegger (*Glie-derung*) in *Being and Time* as the movement of dividing-out and joining together central to interpreting a being "as" such and such a being (BT 195/153; Heidegger argues that this articulation is anterior to its meaning as subjective expression). While this is not given great emphasis in *Being and Time,* it eventually comes to be crucial for Heidegger's conception of naming. Verbal articulation calls beings into presence through a double gesture: it sets beings apart, from us, from one another, and from the world they inhabit, and at the same time opens up a shared space in which they can appear. What Heidegger here terms "difference" is an originary setting-into-relation that both differentiates and joins; in both senses of the term, it *articulates*—not only the speaker and the beings the speaker calls into presence, but ultimately language itself. It thus becomes, Heidegger will conclude, "the relation of all relations" (OL 107/215).

■

Although Heidegger considers saying to be anterior to human speech, it is speech that calls and therefore, in each instance, brings a being into pres-ence as the being it is. This means that before Heidegger can attempt to explain the basis of the "rule" by which speech can first draw beings into presence, before he can sketch the relation, within language, of "saying" and "speech," he must first have provided an account of speech itself—that is, of verbal language ("speech" in this instance not being restricted to oral utterance)—in accordance with the "call" it would effect. As I have argued, this involves approaching language through its whole, and thereby resisting a precipitate division of language as a lexico-syntactic system from paral-anguage. The next section will look at how gesture and vocal inflection are particularly crucial to Heidegger's conception of naming; the articulation of language thus becomes inextricably linked to the articulation of the hu-man body. And in the final section we will see that Heidegger conceives of this dual articulation as a *sounding*, whereby the entry into verbal utterance and the entry into bodily experience take place concomitantly.

The Bodily Articulation of Language

Heidegger's focus on verbal language as a discursive whole involves a radical revaluation of those non- or extrareferential aspects of verbal language often termed *paralanguage*, and indeed seems to call into question the very demotion of such features to a paralinguistic plane. This section focuses on two aspects of verbal comportment often deemed paralinguistic that are central to Heidegger's understanding of naming as a means of bringing beings into presence: gesture (both rhetorical and physical gestures) and vocal inflection (both cadences and nonverbal exclamations). Heidegger's revaluation of paralanguage not only calls into question a precipitate equation of linguistic meaning with reference; those aspects of utterance that arise from the human body become the mode through which we encounter language in what Heidegger terms its "*linguistic* essence." In this, we find a retrieval of the Aristotelian *zoion logon ekhon,* in which the *zoion* and *logon* become mutually dependent and mutually conditioning.

Gesturing and Hinting

Ironically enough, Heidegger's retrieval of Aristotle's *zoion logon ekhon* proceeds by way of a critique of another moment in Aristotle, namely his account of verbal sound. We have already seen that Heidegger's exposition of originary saying as showing proceeds through a reading of Aristotle's *De interpretatione,* according to which writing shows speech, which in turn shows mental experiences, which themselves show things. In another reading of this passage, given in the third and final of the 1957–58 lectures that constitute "The Nature of Language," he picks out another consequence of Aristotle's model of *semeia.* While the conventional relation between sign and signified treats verbal sound as meaningless in itself, he counters: "It is just as much a property of language to sound and ring and vibrate, to hover and to tremble, as it is for the spoken words of language to carry a meaning" (OL 98/205). Reiterating the claim from *Being and Time* that "it requires a very artificial frame of mind to 'hear' a 'pure noise'" (BT 207/164), Heidegger argues that these two properties cannot be thought in isolation from one another. Bodily experience is primarily meaningful; only afterward does it become "sense data." Verbal language hovers and trembles; only afterward can it be "explained physiologically as a production of sounds" (OL 98/205). To split a word into its nonsensuous referential function and its sensuous token is an abstraction from a meaningful experience that comprises the openness of both bodily and linguistic-discursive comportment.

This relation between bodily and linguistic openness is made perhaps most explicit in Heidegger's discussion of gesture. Thus, in *What is Called Thinking?*, when Heidegger states: "Apes, for example, have organs that can grasp [*Greiforgane*], but they do not have hands" (WCT 16/18), he justifies this by noting how "the hand's gestures run everywhere through language." The hand no longer grasps, but, suffused with *logos,* it becomes, as he puts it in his "Dialogue on Language" two years later, the "gathering of a bearing" (OL 18/107): in its gesture it sets about a movement that will first permit humans to comport themselves toward beings, and the human body becomes the site of this comportment.

In and through gesture, man and beings are brought into an open relation in which beings first show themselves and man can first comport himself toward these beings. Gesture serves as a kind of reciprocal attuning of man and world, and has a similar position between language and body. "Thinking . . . guides and sustains every gesture of the hand" (WCT 23/26); yet, in chiasmic intersection, gesture can guide and sustain thinking. In his "Dialogue on Language" with Professor Tomio Tezuka, he (the "Inquirer") and Tezuka (the "Japanese") discuss the "Europeanization" of Japanese thinking and art, and the "Japanese" gives Akira Kurosawa's film *Rashomon* as one example of Japanese art that has been "Europeanized" (OL 16/104). "But," Heidegger's "Inquirer" enquires, "are there not subdued gestures?" This enquiry leads him to be admonished by his interlocutor for his blindness toward the "inconspicuities" of genuine gesture. The Japanese gesture, in which "the hand is suffused and borne by a call calling from afar and calling still farther onward, because stillness has brought it" (OL 16/104) is, the Inquirer notes, "a gesture with which a European will hardly be satisfied" (OL 18/107). A European himself, Heidegger's "Inquirer," one might infer, is attesting, albeit obliquely, to his own dissatisfaction, effectively admitting to being unable to hear the "call" preserved in this gesture, and thereby the happening of world it inaugurates. Indeed, this miscomprehension is mutual: the Japanese in turn laments that "the essence of what your language calls 'gesture' is hard to say" (OL 18/107).

Gesture would thereby articulate something that has already been released into a (culturally specific) open. Yet, perhaps paradoxically, it is at this precise juncture that "gesture" affords, and indeed becomes, a kind of "naming." Despite having had the world that comes to show itself in the Japanese's gesture withheld from him, and having heard the Japanese admit his incomprehension regarding the "essence" of "gesture" in his own language (German, but also the language of European "metaphysics"), the Inquirer continues undeterred: "And yet, the word 'gesture' helps us experience truly what is here to be said," and the Japanese concurs: "Ultimately, it coincides with what I have in mind" (OL 18/107). We might, not unreasonably, discern in this exchange something of the bathetic ceremonial politeness remarked upon by Hans Ulrich Gumbrecht, and perhaps even ask whether Heidegger's after-the-event redrafting of this exchange is not somewhat tendentious and conciliatory—even embarrassing.[35] However, this would be to overlook the centrality of this nonadequation of Heidegger's thinking to that of his interlocutor, and vice versa, in the formulation of their shared "definition" of gesture as "the gathering of a bearing." What Inquirer and Japanese have touched upon in their dialogue is not the "essence" of gesture as such (an adequation, or *adaequatio*, of a different sort); rather, the dialogue seeks to render something thinkable within the shared space it opens up. Just as the dialogue, with its conciliations and ceremony, is intrinsically gestural, so is the naming it affords.

In this, the hand's gesture accords with a gesture which not only is implicated in language, but which takes place within words: the *Wink* (hint or wink). Moments later in the dialogue, Heidegger speaks about his formulation, the "house of being" (OL 22/114), which "only gives a hint into the essence of language" (OL 24/114, translation modified). This *Wink* (the German word, *Wink,* while broader in reference than the English one, can also allude to gesturing with a single eyelid) would render thinkable this essence of language, not by pointing to it as a preexisting referent but by hinting toward it, by engendering a new way of thinking about language and the mode in which it comes to presence. In this, the *Wink* will bring into thinkability something that beforehand remained unthinkable, absent, and it is for its inaugurating gesture that Heidegger will tentatively suggest that it might constitute (*wäre*—Heidegger here remains firmly within the *Konjunktiv*) the "fundamental trait [*Grundzug*] of the word" (OL 24/114, translation modified). The hint, like gesture more broadly, sends language *on its way,* and does so as it engages language at the limits of the thinkable.

Let us look more closely at how this "hint" *means.* If it is gestural, it is also, speaking of a "house of being," verbal. Similarly, the phrase constitutes an ontological "naming," but also employs the ontic reference of the words "house" and "being." "House of being" might not correspond to any specific referent, but it is nevertheless a phrase with a referential meaning, and this reference would seem crucial to its capacity to hint at a thinking to come. As Chapter 3 will emphasize, such moments of apparent "aberration" from "normal" meaning are crucial to Heidegger's attempt to open up spaces for thinking that are occluded by conventional word usage and philosophical terminology. But for now we must pose a far more narrow question: how is it that such a word or phrase, when encountered within a lexico-syntactic system, can effect a *naming* that both exceeds its position in this system, and indeed is then taken to be anterior to it, and even to ground the possibility of such a system?[36]

This question is taken up by Jean-Luc Nancy. Nancy asks in what way we can consider *Wink* as a "sign," linguistic or otherwise. Approaching the *Wink* from the perspective of signification, we might identify in *Wink* "a sign of awaiting, or of putting expectation in the position of a sign."[37] Nancy's focus on the temporal and kinetic aspect of this opening is crucial; *Wink* not only "awaits" but "mobilizes," possessed of a "motility" that sets signifying in motion. And, it transpires, this motility lies at the very core of the signifying movement of language, a movement whose continual deferrals of significatory closure Nancy aligns with what Derrida has named *différance:* "We must await its interpretation, but that waiting is, in itself, already a mobilization, and its mobility or motility is more important than its final interpretation."[38]

From the perspective of signification, Nancy argues, the *Wink* is radically indeterminate; it "departs from the established order of communication and signification by opening up a zone of allusion and suggestion, a free space for invitation, address, seduction, or waywardness." Yet, if the *Wink,* from the perspective of signification, is characterized by its "waywardness" or indeterminacy, then might such waywardness belong less to the *Wink* itself than to the perspective of signification through which we conceptualize it? If its excess over and withdrawal from signification are intimately related to its mobilization of a signifying movement, then one would assume that the mobilization cannot subsequently be grasped from within the signifying movement it has mobilized. Nancy notes this problem when arguing that "there is, in the *Wink,* or in *winken . . .* an energy that its sign per se does not possess," which "energy" is "an active power that arises at the moment of the signifying act and that, in terms of sense, goes beyond it and gives way to it at the same time."[39] However, Nancy here sees the excess of the *Wink*'s "energy" as arising *through* a signifying act, and in this he seems not only to be inverting Heidegger's thought, but, in so doing, overlooking its radical implications. Firstly, insofar as this is a "signifying act," he would be returning language from its "linguistic essence" to a human activity; its energy would in this respect be startlingly close to Humboldt's *energeia*—an energy that animates the act and gets lost in the signification. Secondly, and most problematically for our purposes, the excess over signification is taken to belong to the structure of signification itself. But even if this excess over signification is activated by words that signify, the excess would subsequently undermine the very framework of the sign, and point to a level of meaning anterior to that of signification. *Wink* might show itself to us through signs, but that does not mean that it is to be understood simply in terms of its uncontainability with regard to this framework. What signification sees as "waywardness" would in fact indicate the originary openness that makes something like signification possible.

We can see this difficulty from the opposite direction, by attending to the bodily dimension of this *Wink*. When Nancy suggests that "the wink . . . makes the eye into a signaling, not a seeing, organ,"[40] his point is that the openness of visual experience is always already suffused by language. While this is certainly what Heidegger wishes to argue, he would also argue that this entails that we recognize the signaling/seeing opposition to be a false choice. Indeed, as we will see in Chapter 3, the notion that the eye is an "organ" at all is something that its bodily-linguistic openness renders questionable. The *Wink* in Heidegger serves, from within an ontic bodily and verbal comportment, to open up the space through which such comportment can take place, not by becoming a "pure sign," but by engaging those aspects of verbal and bodily meaning that not only exceed signification, but to which the schema of signification is blind. It is here that naming continually functions as a mode of gesture—and, moreover, here that Heidegger has recourse to poetry.

Poetry at the Limits of Discourse

Nancy's reading, then, is not radical enough to grasp the ultimate stakes of the Heideggerian *Wink*. Firstly, *Wink* collapses the dichotomy between linguistic and bodily openness, and refuses to consign those bodily, non-signifying aspects of speech to mere paralinguistic effects; secondly, *Wink* points toward an openness that exceeds and antecedes signification. That these two moments should coincide is far from accidental. Only because verbal language, in its engagement of bodily modes of meaning, is continually greater than its referential (or signifying) function, can it grasp a level of openness anterior to verbal comportment.

And indeed, this double concern, between the meaningfulness of non-referential, bodily features of verbal language, and the ontological space in which verbal language can first take place, is what motivates Heidegger's first discussion of poetry, or more precisely "'poetical' discourse," in *Being and Time:* "Being-in and its state-of-mind are made known in discourse and indicated in language by intonation, modulation, the tempo of talk, the 'way of speaking.' In 'poetical' discourse, the communication of the existential possibilities of one's state-of-mind can become an aim in itself, and this amounts to a disclosing of existence" (BT 162/205).[41] Situating "'poetical' discourse" in features like "intonation," "modulation," and "tempo," Heidegger further claims that these features, far from being extraneous or accessory to discourse, are integral to the ways in which discourse can "make known" and "indicate," what Françoise Dastur terms "the *life* of the language."[42] Yet Dastur takes this to mean that Heidegger's account of "'poetical' discourse" is "conceived merely in its form, and deduced from one of the moments of discourse, instead of itself grounding discourse,"[43] something which Heidegger himself, insisting on the meaningful discursivity of supposed paralanguage, Heidegger would dispute. Indeed, he is already resisting the false choice between "formal" and "ontological" dimensions of poetry that I examined in Chapter 1.

By engaging a manifestational dimension of language that reaches beyond reference, Heidegger's brief invocation of poetry is crucial to his analysis of language as a discursive whole. Yet its fleeting presence at this juncture is also unsettling for Heidegger's account of discourse, and indeed appears to be introduced initially in order to address a lacuna within the architectonic of *Being and Time* as a whole. Heidegger asserts that "state-of-mind and understanding are characterized equiprimordially by *discourse*" (BT 133/172), and later in the work deduces (one is tempted to call it a "quasi-transcendental deduction") these three *existentials* from the three ecstases of Dasein's originary temporality: having-been, making-present, and futurity (BT 384/335). This lacuna is in fact emphasized when, in a marginal note added decades later, Heidegger feels obliged to remind himself that "thrownness is essential to language."[44] As we have seen, Heidegger takes language and discourse to *articulate* the discoveredness effected in interpretation. And yet Dasein's thrownness is disclosed when its "mood brings Dasein before the 'that-it-is' of its 'there' [*das Dass seines Da*], which, as such, stares it in the face with the inexorability of an enigma" (BT 175/136). The word *Dass* serves as verbal articulation for something in the face of which we are rendered inarticulate, the demonstrative indicating a failure of predication, that is, our inability to say what *Dass* actually denotes. As our thrownness withdraws from discursive understanding, it irrupts into our experience with language, and inflects the very fabric our discourse. This is not simply, Heidegger suggests, a semantic property of the word *Dass,* or the speech act it implies; rather, it is something continually at work throughout our verbal comportment. And the mode by which this predicament—of the non-discursive irrupting into discourse—is most potently articulated, he argues, is "'poetical' discourse."[45]

This attempt to think *Stimmung* and language together contains a double exigency. On the one hand, *Stimmung* is "falsified" both when its disclosure is "measur[ed] against the apodictic certainty of a theoretical cognition of something," and when it is "banished to the sanctuary of the irrational" (BT 175/136). On the other, to say that language is "equiprimordial" with and inflected by *Stimmung* does not reduce it to subjective expression. Steven Crowell has shown the centrality, in Heidegger's writings in the 1920s, of the "anti-psychologistic thesis that the judgment is 'significative content,' neither the psychical act nor the grammatical structure but 'valid meaning.'"[46] It is this resistance to equating meaning with a "psychical act" that Heidegger has in mind when he claims, "communication is never anything like a conveying of experiences [*Erlebnisse*] . . . from the interior of one subject into the interior of another" (BT 162/205), but is grounded on co-understanding and co–state-of-mind. In other words, people can communicate not because of any immanent psychological law, nor because of an objective standard of language, but because they inhabit, and are shaped by, the same world. "'Poetical' discourse" makes use of and heightens the meaningful valency of vocal inflection in order to disclose the "attuned" being-in that characterizes our shared habitation of the world into which we are always already thrown.

This insight will have far-reaching implications for Heidegger's thinking on language. As noted above, the articulation of *Stimmung* takes place at the limits of discursivity: when "'poetical' discourse" internalizes *Stimmung* into discourse, *Stimmung* comes to show itself as a limit within the fabric of discourse itself.[47] In Chapter 1, we saw that Heidegger's turn to discuss the artwork and poetry arises out of a need to think beyond the lacunae and aporiai of his earlier work; now we see that poetry is, in this earlier work, the site at which some of these lacunae and aporiai first become apparent.

Stimmung *and* Stimme

This is not the only time when *Stimme* (voice) serves as a crucial aporia for *Being and Time*. In the introduction, Heidegger distinguishes between *phone* and *logos*. In a "fully concrete" instance of *logos, logos* becomes *phone meta phantasias:* "an utterance in which something is sighted in each case" (BT 56/33). *Phone* is simply one concrete mode of *logos;* the "sighting" of *logos* is explicitly separated from the phonic dimension of its utterance. This continues a discussion of the relation of verbal sound to linguistic articulation in *History of the Concept of Time*, which concludes: "Phonetic speaking and acoustical hearing are in their being founded in discoursing and hearing as mode of being of being-in-the-world and being-with" (HCT 266/366). However, the voices of *Being and Time* are not so easily contained, as is evidenced by two voices that interject at crucial moments: "the voice of the friend whom every Dasein carries with it" (BT 206/163) and the "voice of conscience" (BT 313/268). Much has been said about the first of these voices, and especially how it offers a point of contact between Heidegger's "fundamental ontology" and an ethics of responsibility toward an "other";[48] I, by contrast, will focus on the voice of conscience, not for its own ethical dimension, but rather for the structure of linguistic articulation it implies, and the complex relation of *phone* and *logos* taking place within it. Then we will see how these two strands of Heidegger's thinking on voice, "'poetical' discourse" and the "voice of conscience," come to intersect in his later work.

If *Gewissen* initially means conscience as a moral awareness, Heidegger also wishes to play on the cognates of *wissen* (to know) more generally: it "gives us something to understand; it *discloses*" (BT 314/269); for the purposes of *Being and Time,* this call gives us to understand nothing less than the basis of our own being-in-the-world. When we are called to by our consciences, Heidegger suggests, we interpret it as an imputation of guilt, which leads him to transcribe the content of the "call" as the judgment "Guilty!" (*Schuldig!*) (BT 326/281). But insofar as "Guilty!" is a predicate of our being ("*I am* guilty"), we should move beyond its ontic definition to ask what its ontological significance might be; the imputation "Guilty!," in other words, "must . . . be detached from relationship to any law or 'ought' such that by failing to comply with it one loads himself with guilt" (BT 328/283). Instead of worrying about its moral content, or even its subjective affect, we should refer guilt back to the basic relationality of Dasein to the world it inhabits—and to itself.

In this respect, it is significant that the German noun *Schuld* has a far broader connotative field of indebtedness or lack; and this for Heidegger is the call's distinctive feature. Its semantic content is, "taken strictly, nothing. The call asserts nothing, gives no information about world-events, has nothing to tell" (BT 318/273). And this "nothing" of assertion points to the "formally existential idea" of "being-the-basis for a being which has been defined by a 'not' [*'Nicht'*]" (BT 329/283), that is, a being whose transcendence is grounded in an encounter with the "nothing." Moreover, this *Nicht,* if gestured toward by the semantic field of "Guilty," is most powerfully experienced in the call's structure: "The call comes *from* me and yet *from beyond me*" (BT 320/275), inhabiting "something like an *alien* voice" (BT 321/277, emphasis in original). It discloses by opening up a scission within Dasein itself, as Dasein internalizes this "nothing" into its own mode of self-relation: it calls from itself to itself "by way of *nothing* at all." Disclosing this nothing through its structure, the call touches upon the central feature of human being-in-the-world: "The caller is Dasein in its uncanniness: primordial, thrown being-in-the-world as the 'not-at-home'—the bare 'that' in the 'nothing' of the world" (321/277; translation modified).[49]

Once again, we find an attuned disclosure of that which exceeds discourse: the call articulates the sheer fact that Dasein "is its own *Dass*" (BT 330/284). It thus furnishes a mode of *Stimme* that can articulate *Stimmung*—and thereby becomes integral to the institution of Dasein's finite transcendence. And it does so through its excess of *phone* over *logos:* voice, rather than being the bodily production of discourse, becomes the mode through which the nondiscursive irrupts into discourse. Voice might be thematized by *Being and Time* in terms of a concrete instance of *phone meta phantasias,* yet we subsequently find that it is *phone,* in the form of the "call of conscience," which renders possible the "sighting" of *phantasias*—and even *logos* as such. As voice brings discourse to reach beyond the condition of its own intelligibility, it becomes the basis of Dasein's finite transcendence.

It is because of the focus on the structure of the call that Aler describes the voice of conscience as "wordless."[50] Yet it nevertheless *does* take place in words, namely the word *guilty,* and the connotative field of this word is crucial to the disclosure the voice of conscience effects. What we find, however, is that the word's *mode* of meaning never becomes a referential content, but internalizes the nothing of its disclosive structure into a "nothing" that imputes "guilt" as a lack to be made up. The indeterminacy of its referential content might remind us of the *Wink* discussed above, as it means by pointing toward rather than through denoting; hence the tendency to treat it as "wordless." Yet this semantic indeterminacy issues from a far more pervasive indeterminacy: the "nothing" at the core of Dasein's uncanny being-in-the-world. And if Aler argues that the voice thus "shed[s] light on the prelingual and extralingual aspects of man's understanding in the ontological characterization of speech,"[51] it appears that these voices rather "shed light on" the problematic separation of language from any prelingual or extralingual sphere—not by rendering the prelingual or extralingual *linguistic,* but rather by showing how language is continually inflected, and ultimately formed, by features that do not fit within a lexico-syntactic system.

As "Guilty!" refuses to be reduced to a signifying content, the voice of conscience's excess of *phone* over *logos* points to an excess of discourse over reference. Yet we should also note that the *vocal* excess of *phone* is not, as it were, a *phonic* excess. The voice of conscience, Heidegger tells us, is a "silent voice" (BT 321/276), its "call discourses in the uncanny mode of *keeping silent*" (BT 322/277). The vocality that exceeds discourse, in which *Stimmung* is brought to *Stimme,* belongs to a voice divested of vocal sound. And in this respect, the voice of conscience would appear to be incompatible with that other attempt to set the two into relation: the "intonation, modulation [and] tempo" of "'poetical' discourse."

•

There are, then, in *Being and Time* two attempts to hear *Stimmung* in a *Stimme.* Although both aim to explain the way in which thrownness can be essential to language—and indeed in doing so both become central moments in holding together the wider architectonic of the work and unsettle this architectonic—their respective conceptions of "voice" diverge profoundly, one insisting on the disclosive power of the phenomenality of voice, and the other appealing to the "authentic" speech of silence. It is this antinomy that Heidegger seeks to address, over two decades later, when he turns to the "sounding" of poetry. For, on the one hand, in the poem we hear "language speak as the peal of stillness [*das Geläut der Stille*]"; our access to "linguistic essence" is given by way of a silence become palpable. And at the same time, the poem is concerned with its modes of "sounding" (PLT 206/31). In this, we can see how the two moments at which Heidegger hears *Stimmung* within *Stimme*—the voice of conscience's withdrawal from phenomenality into silence and "nullity" and the vocal expressiveness of poetry—coincide. Crucial to this are his analyses of the earth as a "coming-forth concealing," both *sounding* and *silence* simultaneously. It is here also that we come to see how the bodily articulation of language is crucial to Heidegger's attempt to grasp "the naming power of the word."

Sounding/Silence

So far I have focused largely on Heidegger's account of verbal language, rather than the originary articulation that would render such verbal language possible. This is for the most part because naming itself takes place in verbal language: it uses language as a verbal "whole" in order to address beings and call them into presence in such a way that they will disclose themselves. This engages not only performative dimensions of language, but also the bodily gesture and vocal inflection. If Heidegger considers this as a whole of discourse irreducible to reference, voice nevertheless exceeds such discourse, and, as we will see, this excess attains increasing importance in his thinking on language from 1950 onwards. Thematized in terms of the "earth" of language, this excess becomes crucial to its "naming power";

however, it also points toward a "linguistic essence" (*Sprachwesen*) that, belonging purely to language rather than to human activity, lies beyond the reach of verbal language and renders it possible. Naming must attend to this "linguistic essence" if it is to effect its own articulation; inversely, Heidegger suggests, such naming is central to "linguistic essence" fulfilling its own movement.

The Opacity of Verbal Matter

If the "earth" of language is its "naming power," then, Heidegger suggests, the manner in which this "naming power" is "brought forth" in the poem will be in some way akin to the "bearing and resting" of stone, the "shining" of color, and the "ringing" of sound (OBT 24/35). It is therefore unsurprising that, trying to grasp the earthiness of language, many of the most powerful recent readings of Heidegger have situated the "earth" of language in what Haar calls the "opacity of verbal matter": "The sounds of spoken language, its rhythm, its accents, its timbre, its resonance, its pace, as well as its written characters" which, "through their material weight . . . escape signification and withdraw from the clarity of sense and from the transparency of the world."[52]

However, to "escape signification" will not in and of itself entail a withdrawal from sense and world: as we have seen, Heidegger sees sense and world to be constructed by a series of meaningful practices and gestures that are irreducible to signification, and which inhere in the nonsignifying aspects of language. This points to a far more general difficulty in grasping the earth in language, namely that earthly withdrawal cannot simply be equated with those aspects of language that do not signify, nor conceived simply in terms of a binary opposition between verbal opacity and semantic clarity. Froment-Meurice tries to move beyond this opposition when he situates the "terrestrial [earthly]" in "speech [*parole*]" in its "sonority, musicality, but also the geographic and even geological character of every language 'speaking' of the land," as opposed to "the side of sense (. . . reduced to simple signification)." But this begs the question—why should we accept this parenthetical reduction of sense to "simple signification" in the first place?[53] Moreover, if the earth of language lies in its "sonority," then while it might withdraw from signification, it will hardly withdraw from the world of experience: after all, it remains audible. If the opacity of verbal matter is opaque to all phenomenal presence as such, then, to the extent that it inheres in the sonority of language, it must also withdraw from sound. It must be opaque to our hearing as well as to our deciphering of signifiers. The invocation of musicality is even more problematic:

music, as a formalization of sound, does have some role within a signifying structure—harmonic series, rhythm, phrasing, instrumentation, timbre, and so on. But his suggestion of the "geographical" and "geological" strikes me as a powerful point of entry; below I will argue that Heidegger situates this geography in the opacity of the human body as it is pervaded by "earth's flow and growth" (OL 98/205).

First, however, I will return to the paradox mentioned at the beginning of this chapter: that the thingly opacity of earth should be conceived of as a "naming power." My suggestion is that we should understand this opacity within Heidegger's thinking of limit as that which bounds and conditions presence. When Heidegger situates the "earth" in the "naming power of the word," he wishes to argue that, withdrawing from presence, the word shapes this presence, and thus shapes the possibilities of naming itself: its opacity of meaning becomes the very opening of meaning. And this requires a far broader and more rigorous understanding of linguistic opacity, and the relation between such opacity and sonority.

"The Origin of the Work of Art" itself is silent on the question as to how such a naming power might inhere in the sonority of language; however, the 1939 lecture series on Herder's *On the Origins of Languages,* published under the title *On the Essence of Language,* aims to articulate a conception of language as a "sounding" that would elide the opposition of sensuous token to nonsensuous reference, and with it physical opacity to semantic clarity. The published version of the lecture series is made up for the most part of lecture notes, and constitutes less an overarching account of language than a thinking through of some of Heidegger's most abiding concerns, and for precisely this reason it provides an illuminating depiction of Heidegger attempting to confront these concerns. Throughout these notes, he returns to Herder's claim that the sounds of language are heard not in the ear but in the "soul," which Heidegger takes to mean that, instead of sounds being "added to meaning, rather the meaning *sounds*" (EL 94/111). As a result, "'sounding' is at first *a self-showing as a being, an appearing, that lets appear*" (EL 96/111). It is the site of openness, in which we set ourselves into relation with the world around us. This involves distinguishing between the sounding of language that "means" and "lets appear" and the sonority of the word, *Wortlaut* (word-sound) or *Lautgebilde* (the word's "sound-form"), where the former is abstracted (or, in Heidegger's more extreme, and, given the political context, troubling terminology, "degenerated") into a "present-at-hand" sensuous token whose function is to transmit the meaning of a referential sign (EL 38/34). Indeed, Heidegger goes so far as to claim that "sounding [is] not essentially related to the tone [*Ton*] and sound [*Schall*]" (EL 107/125), but rather to the originary articulation of *logos,* which is now characterized not as a silent call, or as the silent "saying" of his later writings, but as a "gathering sounding" (*sammelnde Lauten*) (EL 29/35).

Heidegger's onus on the sounding of language here is striking: not only is this seen as the way *verbal* language is experienced, anterior to the sound-sense split, but the originary *logos* also becomes a mode of sounding. But how can we *hear* this "gathering sounding" in verbal language? To see this, I will turn to another aspect of this sounding: "sounding," he proposes, has "the character of strife (earth—world)" (EL 28/34), and, a few pages later, sounding is the "happening of the strife of earth *and* world" (EL 45/54). On the one hand, this "character of strife" can point to its structure of articulation: it both binds beings together and differentiates them. However, also central to the strife between earth and world is an engagement with the limits of phenomenality: as we saw in Chapter 1, the strife of earth and world serves to bring the earth's own concealing movement—that which bounds the limits of phenomenal experience—to show itself within the phenomenal world. *Sounding,* one can surmise, would be precisely that moment at which the limits of verbal language are themselves articulated linguistically.

However, Heidegger goes further: verbal sound is the "*preserving keeping—earth of the world*" (EL 93/109), that is, it retains the movement of the earth within its sound, even when the earth itself has once again withdrawn into self-seclusion. In the sounding of language, earth enters the phenomenal world in such a way as to become audible, and so inhabits the *Wortlaut* even as the *Wortlaut* blots it out. But it can do this only because the sounding of language, tracing the earth's coming-forth concealing movement, brings such sonority to confront its own silence. To complete the sentence cited above: "sounding [is] not essentially related to the tone and sound, but *to the openness and clearing* of being and, that is, to the silence and the rending of the silence in the strife of world and earth" (EL 107/125). Heidegger's claim that the openness and clearing of being should be "silence" might at first seem a continuation of the strain in *Being and Time* for which "authentic" discourse is silent (BT 208/164–65); yet what is at issue here is less a pathos of authenticity than an insistence on the excess of this clearing over phenomenal experience. The clearing must be anterior to any verbal articulation: insofar as language comes to sound only when it enters human discourse, a clearing that precedes and conditions human openness must be silent—at least to human ears. And, as we have seen, the earth of language, insofar as it traces a movement of coming-forth concealing, must withdraw not only from signification but also from sonority. In "The Origin of the Work of Art" the strife of earth and world engages a double movement of presencing and absencing so as to shape the parameters of our encounter with beings; here Heidegger is transferring this pattern onto language, with the strife now shaping the possibility of language to name and thereby to bring beings into presence. Sounding, as it were, can only come to sound as it engages with this double silence. In this, it is audible as a "peal ↑ of stillness [*Geläut* ↑ *der Stille*]" (EL 78/90), the arrow pointing upwards indicating the movement of this peal into sounding, embodying the "coming-forth" of the earth into phenomenal experience.

To situate earth simply in the materiality of verbal language, then, where its opacity refers to a resistance of its written or oral marks to signification, would be to conceive of language—and indeed of world and earth—according to the relation between signifier and signified that Heidegger's thinking on language wishes to overcome. The "opacity of verbal matter" must withdraw not simply from "signification," "sense," and "the transparency of the world," but also from the very sonority—"rhythm, accents, timbre, resonance"—in which we would situate it, and it is this paradox that motivates Heidegger's formulation of the "peal of stillness" which will become a guideword in his later attempts to characterize the "speaking" of language. In the claim that the naming of language takes place as a sounding, its earthly "naming power" would refer to the engagement with the silence that withdraws from and shapes the limits of this sounding and thus fixes the limits of the sayable. What Heidegger is attempting to grasp is how the sounding of verbal language arises out of the double silence that structures it, so that what we hear in this sounding is precisely this withdrawal as it "comes forth" into verbal language, so that the silent "peal" is preserved within language as it sounds.

The Peal of Stillness

This invocation of the "peal of stillness" constitutes a major advance for Heidegger's thinking, as it allows him to resolve a tension between the two accounts of voice found in *Being and Time,* the sonorous expressivity of "'poetical' discourse" and the silent "voice of conscience." Both focused on the excess of voice over discourse, yet where poetical discourse identified a sonorous excess, the voice of conscience was experienced phenomenally as silence. In the "peal of stillness" it is precisely this silent excess that constitutes a sounding; insofar as it engages the "earth" of verbal matter, the sounding withdraws from discursivity, but in so doing brings this withdrawal to "sound." The engagement of phenomenality and withdrawal in Heidegger's account of earth as naming power reconciles these two conceptions of voice, and with it, their respective ways of inhabiting the limits of their own discursivity.

The "peal of stillness," which finds its first, tentative formulation in these lecture notes, will become a crucial motif for Heidegger's writings on language in the 1950s. When Heidegger asserts that "language speaks as the peal of stillness," his concern is double: first, he wishes to characterize the way a "silent" language anterior to reference can be experienced; second, he wishes to grasp the movement by which this originary language enters verbal articulation. In both instances, the way we conceive of verbal sound is crucial, as this becomes the mode by which this "peal" is experienced. In "The Way to Language," the culmination of his thinking on language of the period, and perhaps the most succinct statement on language he makes, he sums it up thus: "The phonetic-acoustic-physiological explanation of sounding does not experience their origin in the peal of stillness, even less so how sounding is thereby brought to voice and determined [*die hierdurch erbrachte Be-stimmung des Lautens*]" (OL 122–23/252, translation modified). There are two striking things about this passage; firstly, one can note how, through his insertion of a hyphen into *Bestimmung*, he wishes to suggest that the determination of verbal language takes place not merely as semantic clarity but as a bringing-to-voice. This means that semantics is inextricably bound up with the human body: indeed, Heidegger links the "phonetic" explanation of verbal sound as a sensuous token with the "physiological" explanation of sound production through the vocal cords. Secondly, this "bringing to voice" is concerned with the movement into language of two peals of stillness: the silence of a "linguistic essence" beyond all human activity, and therefore beyond the limits of the audible, and a silence that stems from out of the opacity of the human body itself.

The first of these two silences is first probed in the 1950 lecture "Language," a reading of Trakl's "Ein Winterabend." In that lecture he argues that silence, *Stille* (the German word also has the connotations of motionlessness we find in the English *stillness*), is by no means the "soundless" (*das Lautlose*), that is, the absence of sound, but lies anterior to any soundsoundless opposition (PLT 204/29). This argumentation echoes his discussion of the "self-subsistence" and "rest" that characterizes the movedness of the artwork. This involved a "repose which is an inner concentration of motion, hence a highest state of agitation [*Bewegtheit*]" (OBT 26/37), which later leads him to portray "rhythm" as "what is at rest, what structures [*fügt*] the movement of dance and song, and thus lets it rest within itself" (OL 149/230). Here we find that "rest has its essence in the fact that it stills. As the stilling of stillness, rest, conceived strictly, is always more in motion than all motion and always more restlessly active than any agitation [*Regung*]" (PLT 204/29, translation modified). Once again, *Stille* is conceived of as a mode of gathering, specifically as the "difference" that both binds beings together and sets them apart, and which, as an originary setting-into-motion, cannot itself be grasped as motion. The Saying which effects such motion would be silent/still both by virtue of lying anterior to verbal language and by virtue of its excess over verbal language. When we hear a "peal of stillness," what we are hearing in part is this excess from within the framework that is being exceeded.

How can such silence actually come to sound, if it exceeds the very framework of the sonorous/soundless opposition? On the one hand, the "peal of stillness is nothing human" (PLT 205/30, translation modified); on the other, it sounds within human speech. We find an analogous double bind in "The Way to Language" and its attempt to identify a "linguistic essence" irreducible to "the mere product of our speaking activity" (OL 125/256). Heidegger situates this in the movement from an originary articulation into verbal articulation; and yet it "needs and uses [*braucht*] human speech" (PLT 205/30, OL 125/256) if this movement is to be consummated. This "need/use" (*Brauch*) becomes the point of contact through which the originary articulation of linguistic essence enters verbal articulation. This means that the "peal of stillness," when it sounds, is necessarily distorted, or, to use a term Heidegger employs elsewhere, "disfigured" (*verstellt*). Coming to sound, "be it speech or writing, the silence is broken" (PLT 206/31). Arising from out of this silence, the sounding of language loses the silence that is its source: drawn into presence, it has been torn from the withdrawing movement proper to it. And yet what we hear in the sounding of speech as a "broken silence" nevertheless retains a trace of its provenance. In this respect, the "broken silence" in fact would, after all, retain within the sounding of human speech the peal that renders this sounding possible, but which such sounding "breaks," just as, in the lecture notes on *The Essence of Language*, "sounding" (*die Lautung*) echoed the "peal" (*Geläut*). But, as Fynsk has noted, insofar as language "needs" human speech, the breaking of its silence becomes a condition for this silence. Not only, then, does its silence speak through—and as—*noise*; noise becomes an integral feature to the silence of linguistic essence itself.[54] It is this "broken silence," moreover, that "shapes the mortal speech that sounds in verses and sentences" (PLT 206/31); poetry becomes a privileged site for hearing the way that "broken silence" shapes speech because it attends to the limits of its own sonority, and thereby probes the moments at which this "broken silence" shapes the poem's speech.

Here, the movement from the "peal of stillness," via a "broken silence," into the "sounding" of language, is portrayed as between two different levels of articulation: an originary saying and verbal language. However, it also involves an engagement with the physical production of verbal sound, and this is Heidegger's focus in his 1957–58 lectures on "The Nature of Language." As noted above, Heidegger takes issue with the notion that verbal sound is merely sound production, pointing to "the property of language to sound and ring and vibrate, to hover and to tremble." He then probes this relation between language and the body in which it sounds, rings, vibrates, hovers, and trembles: "body and mouth are part of the earth's flow and growth in which we mortals flourish" (OL 98/205). By this juncture in Heidegger's thought, earth is no longer being conceived as in strife with world, but rather one of the "fourfold" that makes up the world: it is in opposition with "sky/heaven" (*Himmel*), while on a second axis, deities (*Göttern*) are opposed to mortals. This has a subtle shift of emphasis; although still characterized by its coming-forth concealing movement, earth is now thematized much more in terms of what is "sheltered" by it and "emerges" from out of it. To see how precisely "earth's flow and growth" becomes at once bodily and linguistic, Heidegger calls upon some passages from Hölderlin, notably the description of language as "the mouth's flower." In Chapter 3, I will probe this passage in greater detail, as we see Heidegger discuss the metaphoricity of this phrase (and the simile, which Heidegger also cites, of "words like flowers"). For now, let us remain with what the phrase "the mouth's flower" would bring to sound. In this phrase, Heidegger continues, we hear "the sound of language rising up earthwise. From whence? From a saying in which happens the letting-appear of world. The sound rings out in the resounding assembly call which, open to the open, lets world appear in things. . . . The sounding, the earthly of language is held with the harmony [*Stimmen*] that, playing together in chorus the regions of the world's structure, attunes them toward one another [*einstimmt*]" (OL 101/208, translation modified). This sounding arises both out of the "earth" of the flowering mouth and throat, and out of the "saying" which first brings world to appear. In this respect, the "sounding of language" is something like the point of intersection of both movements—of saying into speech and of the earth of the body into a language that rings, vibrates, hovers, and trembles. Yet Heidegger is in fact making a far stronger claim: that these two constitute one and the same movement. The earth of the body engenders the open space in which we encounter ourselves and the world around us; at the same time, "saying" offers a "harmony" that attunes beings toward one another, thus setting them into relation and holding them within the world. We encounter an articulation at once bodily and linguistic, whose sounding arises out of the earth of this body, and even, as it *sounds,* preserves this earth in momentary presence. When

Froment-Meurice suggests that there is something "geographical" or "geological" in the earth, I suggest that we situate it in the human body itself.

This might elicit protests that Heidegger is indulging in the most flagrant phonocentrism. Such a charge, however, would be precipitate: Heidegger's conception of sounding aims to think the bodily in language far beyond any simplistic privileging of speech over writing, as evidenced by the marginal notes he adds to the 1960 editions of "The Origin of the Work of Art" and "The Way of Language": "Language and Body (Sound and Script)," and "Sounding and Bodying—Body and Script" (OBT 47; GA12 249). Placing "sounding" and "script" at opposing poles of a chiasmus, as Fynsk has noted, means not only that "the articulation of language opens in and through the human body," but also that any such bodily articulation of language will comprehend both speech *and* writing.[55] Indeed, as we will see in Chapter 3, this conception of sounding is deployed in order to question the division of bodily experience into auditory, tactile, visual, and so on.

At the crux of Derrida's critique of phonocentrism is his analysis of how the absolute presence of voice to the speaking subject that Husserl attempts to secure through the motif of "hearing-oneself-speak" is ultimately undermined through irreducible difference.[56] Yet this would mean that Heidegger's account of sounding offers a significant advance for deconstructive theory. As language is grasped in terms of the "earthwise" "rising up" of voice in throat, it withdraws from the very articulation it renders possible. The body becomes the site for language only as it becomes opaque to it—becomes, indeed, opaque to itself. The intersection of language and body happens, in other words, at the breakdown of bodily self-presence, which is at the same time the breakdown of a transparent *logos*. In this, the earth in the body is geo*graphy* in the sense that it effects a movement akin to what Derrida termed *writing*. What is at issue in this silence is precisely how the human body itself, far from securing self-presence, becomes the site of an opacity that shapes our experience of presence as such and endows the limits of presence with an aporetic phenomenal weight. Heidegger depicts language's originary articulation as a "soundless calling gathering [*lautlos rufende Versammeln*]" (OL 107/214): its binding power, and its capacity, in "calling," to engage with absence, are such that they exceed our experience of the phenomenality of language.

The Movement that Is Language

To say that "language speaks" is to say that the originary articulation of *Sagen* attains verbal articulation in the "sounding word" of human speech.

But how can human speech first bring such an originary articulation—an articulation that exceeds all speech—to sound? Heidegger asserts that verbal naming can only call beings into presence if it has "listened" to the peal of stillness. The capacity to *name* thus requires a listening to the movement traced by language itself; all human speech becomes *Nachsagen,* saying-after (OL 125/255). Trakl's "Ein Winterabend" provides one example of this: naming world and things, it would attend to the very "dif-ferential" articulation that guides its own naming. As noted above, Heidegger conceives of naming as a "call"; here, however, he inverts this: naming can only *call* if it is itself first *called* to language by language. Here, as so often, Heidegger's argumentation proceeds by way of a series of cognates: we can speak (*sprechen*) only if we co-respond (*ent-sprechen*) to language, which co-respondence lies anterior to the correspondence (*Entsprechen*) of word to referent and indeed opens up the space in which such correspondence can take place (OL 135/267). And so, how is such co-respondence first possible? Here Heidegger employs two more cognates: we can "give voice" (*be-stimmen*) to language only because we are "attuned" (*gestimmt*) toward it and can thus hear it; we can "hear" (*hören*) language only because we "belong" (*gehören*) to it. Verbal articulation can only take place because beings have always already articulated themselves (and because we are always articulated among them, and articulate ourselves in relation to them).

Ultimately, Heidegger wishes to ask what engenders such belonging, and this question motivates much of "The Way to Language." Heidegger approaches this as a problem that inheres within the linguistic essence of language: in other words, the movement from the originary *Sagen* (saying) into *Sprechen* (verbal speech) should be understood as characteristic of the internal dynamics of language itself, rather than of our language usage. Many critics have worried about Heidegger's tendency to elevate language into some kind of mystical entity; such an elevation of language, more-over, would be self-defeating for Heidegger's project, as, transformed into "a being" language would be denuded of ontological significance. To grasp this ontological significance, Heidegger wishes, one needs to move beyond language as such as a function of human speaking (as he had done in the *existential* of discourse in *Being and Time*), to approach the possibilities and constraints of this speaking, and for this one must search for what it is in language that constrains and renders possible our language usage.

"The Way to Language" is organized around the "guide word," "to bring language to language as language" (OL 112/242, translation modified). At first, Heidegger portrays this as a challenge for thinking: how can we say something about language when our means to do so are themselves linguistic? At the same time, these means are part of a human activity, so we run the risk of blinding ourselves to what "language as language" might actually be in its *linguistic* essence. Insofar as this linguistic essence is characterized by both the originary saying and verbal speech, however, and must in some way bind saying and speech together, we could also see in the guide word a deeper significance: the "bringing" by which saying enters speech might offer the key to what kind of movement language itself is. What, then, is language such that it can bring language to language as language?

This leads Heidegger to try to sketch the "unifying element" between saying and speech. If saying and speech might appear as a kind of "ontological difference," then this unifying element would be what shapes this difference, and in this Heidegger is following a similar line of questioning as encountered in his discussions of the artwork's *Gestalt* in Chapter 1, which would bind the work's treatment of its ontic medium to its ontological engagement with the double movement of presencing and absencing. It is therefore of little surprise that Heidegger should introduce at this juncture the same series of cognates—*reissen, fügen, zeichnen, zügen*—that he had worked through in "The Origin of the Work of Art": the "design" (*Aufriss*) incorporates "the whole of the traits of that drawing which joins together the open, unlocked freedom of language [*das Ganz der Züge derjenigen Zeichnung, die das Aufgeschlossene, Freie der Sprache durchfügt*]" (OL 122/251–52). Again, one can recall Derrida's observation that *Aufriss* "incises [*entame*] ontological difference itself": Heidegger is starting out with an opposition that resembles ontological difference, but the unifying element he sketches, providing an outline of the relation and setting it in motion (in this, Derrida's term is particularly apt, as these two moments accord to the two senses of the French *entamer*), would subsequently cut against any hard-and-fast distinction between ontological and ontic realms. In this, the collapse of ontological difference is not the breakdown of Heidegger's thinking but rather a crucial stage in his argumentation.

Initially, Heidegger approaches this "unifying element" at the level of speech itself. When we speak we come up against two modes of the "unspoken": "something not yet spoken" and "what must remain unspoken in the sense that it is beyond the reach of speaking" (OL 120/251). Only by speaking do we discover which kind of "unspoken" is at issue; we attend to the absence in order to differentiate between a surmountable limit and limit as such: only through an engagement with the limits of the speakable do we get to hear, and subsequently speak, the originary saying. It is this attending to the unspoken that characterizes what Heidegger had termed "co-responding" to the call of language; and language's "linguistic essence" becomes the way in which speaking is bound to, and shaped by, these two modes of absence. It is in this respect that verbal language as a human activity becomes a function of language, rather than the reverse.

This means that our speaking is always joined to an anterior saying, which "shows" insofar as it opens up the space within which we can address beings and bring them into presence with our speaking. Heidegger continues: "The design [*Aufriss*] is the drawing [*Zeichnung*] of linguistic essence [*Sprachwesens*], the adjoinment [*Gefüge*] of a showing [*Zeigens*] in which are joined [*verfügt*] the speakers and their speaking, the spoken and its unspoken out of the to-be-spoken" (OL 121/252, translation modified). The "speakers"—that is, us—have been drawn into linguistic essence itself, which is "pervaded by all the modes of saying and of the said, in which all presencing and absencing announces, grants, or refuses itself [*sich ansagt, zusagt oder versagt*]" (OL 122/253). This is what allows us to "hear" this saying: to "let its soundless voice come to us, and then demand, reach out, and call for the sound that is already kept in store for us" (OL 124/255, translation modified). Speech, listening to the "call" of language, will transform our relation to this unspoken, that which is beyond the reach of speaking becoming the "to-be-spoken." And in so doing, it will transform the saying itself, shifting the limits of what it brings into the open.

The name that Heidegger gives to the diversity and totality of the relations within language's linguistic essence between saying and speech is *die Sage* (also translated by Hertz, rather confusingly, as "Saying"; for the sake of avoiding ambiguity, I will leave it in its German original). Joining and separating saying and speech, *Sage* too is a form of articulation—only now articulating not the beings it brings into presencing, but the different levels of its articulation. This, then, will describe the linguistic essence by which language can be brought to language as language; it will also characterize the specific movedness of such bringing. But how can *Sage* bind *Sagen* to *Sprechen*, he asks: "Is *Sage* separated from our speaking, something to which we first must build a bridge? Or is *Sage* the stream of stillness which in forming them binds its own two banks—the *Sagen* and our *Nachsagen*?" (OL 124–25/255). That Heidegger should employ the figure of a "stream of stillness" might at first seem yet one more flight into the pastoral mode. And yet, this figure proves illustrative for exactly the kind of relation he is trying to outline. A stream is always in flux, something which gives to the figure "stream of stillness" the same sense of paradox that characterized the movedness of the artwork, and in Heidegger's translations of *ruthmos*, where stillness is reframed as an "inner concentration of movement," where its stillness lies in its binding power, which sets into motion the relations around it. Moreover, this inner concentration of movement would contrast with the stasis of the two banks (again, one can read this as a comment on the need to get beyond the framework of ontological difference). Finally, the stream not only separates and joins the two banks, it will also erode them and thereby shape, slowly but inexorably, the contours of their relation.

At this point Heidegger takes one further step back. *Sage* can only bind the two together if they are appropriate for, and appropriable by, one another. If *Sagen* is *Zeigen* (a showing), insofar as it points toward the openness in which we can encounter beings, then *Sage* is also a showing—*die Zeige*—pointing *Sagen* and *Sprechen* toward each other. Before, he had asked how humans can hear the silent peal of language, and this lay in the linguistic essence of *Sage* that bound the two together; now he asks how *Sage* can so bind the two. If we were to follow the figure of the stream binding together its two banks, we would now ask: what sets the stream into motion? It is at this moment that Heidegger invokes that key term of his later thinking, *Ereignis,* the "event of appropriation"; it is also here that we understand what is meant by asking after the *way* to language. Heidegger has not simply been asking how we can encounter the linguistic essence of language, but also how this essence, in its "way-making movement" (*Be-wëgung*), can set on its way is portrayed. This double movement would frame the ways in which we become appropriate for language, and language for us.

For here Heidegger points out that, if our speaking is a function of linguistic essence, then language is dependent on us in order to be set on its way. It is in speaking that mankind, as the *zoion logon ekhon,* becomes "proper"; we encounter language through "the sounding of the word" because this is how language enters our experience (OL 129/260). But this sounding of the word is also part of language's "linguistic essence," meaning that just as we are drawn into linguistic essence, so language "needs and uses" (*braucht*) our speech. This is not simply a question of bringing an originary openness to be spoken, but rather for language to fulfill itself: "man is used and needed [*gebraucht*] for bringing soundless *Sage* to the sound [*Verlauten*] of language [*Sprache*]" (OL 129/260), even if such need cannot be reduced to "the making or . . . command of our speech activity" (OL 125/256). And here, Heidegger asks no longer how *Sagen* and *Sprechen* are appropriate for one another, but how *Sprache,* language itself, can be appropriate for *Sage,* and how, inversely, *Sage* can be appropriated into *Sprache.* The "formula" (*Wegformel*) with which Heidegger had started, "to bring language as language to language," is now given its final interpretation: "The way-making movement [*Be-wëgung*] brings language (linguistic essence) as language (*Sage*) into language (the sounding word)" (OL 130/261).

But for *Sage* to come into language requires that language provide the impetus for this "way-making movement": not only is it the endpoint of the movement that language is, but it stands within this movement as the need/use that first sets it into motion. When "showing *Sage* moves [*bewëgt*] language [*Sprache*] into human speech," it is because "*Sage* needs to be sounded in the word" (OL 134/266). The sounding of language will not only co-respond to the silence of *Sage*, but will shape its silence: shaping the silence, moreover, it can transform the very movement that language is. In the sounding of language we experience once again its naming power.

■

Language's need for, and use of, human speaking, introduces yet one further stage of anteriority into Heidegger's argumentation: speaking can become appropriate for, and appropriated by, language, and language can be set into motion, only because language needs this speaking in order to become itself (this is an *Eigene* central to Heidegger's conception of *er-eignen*). Above I mentioned that humans can give voice (*be-stimmen*) to language only if they are "attuned" (*gestimmt*) to it; here we find that language can appropriate human speech only because of the impulse provided by its need for and use of the sounding word, with *Brauch* portrayed as something like the attunement of language itself. It is thus that language can be termed an "appropriating needful way-making" (*er-eignend-brauchende Be-wëgung*] (OL 130/261). However, at this juncture we also see Heidegger to be conceiving of the relation between linguistic essence and verbal language as radically reversible: in this need for the sounding word, the originary gathering of language is dependent on verbal language.

This returns us to a recurrent theme in Heidegger's writing on language: in *Being and Time* "discourse" shapes the very discoveredness out of which it issued; in "Origin" the "projective saying" of poetry will "name" beings in such a way that they enter the open "for the first time," what in "Words" Heidegger calls *Be-dingnis*, where the word "lets beings appear in their 'it is'" (OL 155/237). And crucially, this verbal language is not conceived of as a lexico-syntactic system, but as the "sounding word." Just as in *Being and Time* it was voice which, engaging the limits of discourse, could disclose the basic fact of Dasein's being-in-the-world, in "The Nature of Language" it was as a "broken silence" that the "peal of stillness" came to be heard, a peal that, in "The Nature of Language," Heidegger situated in the double movement of silence into sounding: from out of an originary *logos* and from the opacity of the human body, the rising-up of language out of throat and into voice. Despite the transformations that Heidegger's thinking undergoes over a period of over three decades, one insight endures: if verbal language is to attend to, and shape, the openness out of which it arises, it will do so only as it *sounds*.

In the most complete account of *Brauch* in Heidegger's thinking of language, Christopher Fynsk goes so far as to situate this "need/use" not simply in the sounding of language, but in the human body itself.[57] I would like to make a slightly different observation, although one that overlaps substantially with Fynsk's compelling reading. We have seen that Heidegger, in his late work, conceives of language as a double movement from silence into sounding: from out of the silent saying (*Sagen*) of *logos* and from out of the opacity of the body. In this, bodily and linguistic opacity are thematized together. But this also means that it is only by attending to the bodily opacity out of which language sounds can we bring the silent *logos* to sound; or, within the reversibility of Heidegger's argumentation, we could equally say: only by attending to this bodily opacity will we respond to language's need and set in motion the movement that language itself is. In "The Way to Language," Heidegger's concern is not with how verbal language might do this, but rather with what the linguistic essence of language might be such that this can happen at all; yet in the other lectures of *On the Way to Language* he is clear: the kind of language that might attend to the movement of *Sage* so as to bring *Sagen* into the sounding word, is *poetry*. If poetry becomes privileged here, it will be by virtue of its capacity to engage with the opacity of the human body, where it traces its own movement into sounding in such a way that this movement is internalized into the very fabric of its sounding.

In this respect, Heidegger is reiterating the central claims of "The Origin of the Work of Art": firstly, that poetry is a *projective saying* which brings beings to show themselves in an open region; and secondly, that in order to become projective in this sense poetry must engage with the earth of its work-material, what Heidegger in "The Origin of the Work of Art" called its "naming power." But this also has repercussions for *thinking*. If we are to attend to poetry's projective saying, then we must situate this saying in the poem's engagement with the opacity of its work-material as a bodily-linguistic opacity. That is, to grasp the "broken silence" poetry renders audible, thinking must listen to these points of breakage, which will surface according to the singularity of each poem. It remains to be seen whether Heidegger's own readings manage to live up to the exigencies demanded by his own insight. In the next chapter I will show how the question of the bodily articulation of language motivates his wide-ranging critique of metaphor and figurative language, before going on, in Chapter 4, to discuss his reading practices in detail.

Before doing so, however, I would like to make one final observation. When Heidegger asks why *Ereignis* should speak as *Sage*, the analogy he gives is telling: it is the *mode* in which *Ereignis* speaks—"not so much in the sense of *modus* or fashion, but as the melodic mode (*melos*), the song which, singing, says" (OL 135/266). This echoes a comment from the short lecture on George's "Das Wort," from the same period: "Singing is the gathering of saying in song" (OL 148/229). The latter of these observations shows the coherence between his critique of the scission of sound and sense in accounts of verbal language and his refusal to separate the artwork into its meaningful content and its formal features. The split of song into words and music would echo a broader abstraction of paralanguage from linguistic meaning, especially as in poetry the song's "music" would be made up of verbal sound rather than sung melody and instrumental accompaniment; the song's "saying" would not be mere content, but rather the gathering movement that brings beings to disclose themselves, and here again Heidegger insists that this must issue from language as a discursive whole, so that its "saying" takes place as a bodily articulation. And at the same time, the "singing" of poetry is not a superimposition of music as an addition or ornament to what the song would say; rather, the music becomes the mode through which saying can take place. But what is striking is that the movement by which the originary *logos* and the sounding word become appropriate for one another is now conceived of as *melodic*. Here one might see an analogy with another melody: that which sets this movement in motion, and where silent saying and sounding world are "attuned" to one another. In "The Nature of Language" Heidegger argues that in the voice, "the sounding, the earthly of language is held with the harmony [*Stimmen*] that, playing together in chorus the regions of the world's structure, attunes them toward one another [*einstimmt*]" (OL 101/208, translation modified); this "harmony" is not simply a metaphor, but rather issues from the mode by which this sounding is attuned and voiced. Following this hint—which, within the dynamics of Heidegger's thinking at this juncture, remains just that, a hint—we might propose that any reading that attends to poetry so as to hear its points of breakage and voicing will of necessity become a *melodics*. But what this melodics might look like, remains to be seen.

3

Heidegger's Figures

Given the prominence Heidegger accords to poetry throughout a *Gesamt-ausgabe* that now extends to 102 volumes, his discussions of figurative language are, at first glance, most conspicuous for their scarcity. Metaphor in particular is dismissed over four lapidary and categorical pronouncements. If this might be taken to demonstrate that Heidegger was simply uninterested in questions of metaphor, and of figurative language more generally,[1] one should nevertheless note that these pronouncements lie at the crux of his attempts both to think the *aletheic* capacity of artworks, and to "undergo an experience with language" (OL 57/159). It is in this respect unsurprising that the question of metaphor in Heidegger should have become the subject of much polemic, extending beyond Heidegger scholarship to broach wider issues of the idiom in which philosophy is written, and the concept and value of metaphor for poetics.

The centrality of metaphor to much of Heidegger's thinking can be seen in the reasons he gives, however laconic, for rejecting it. In his 1941 lecture series on Hölderlin's hymn "Andenken," he claims that "the key to all 'poetics,' the doctrine of 'images' in poetry, of 'metaphor,' cannot open any single door in the realm of Hölderlinian hymnal poetry" (GA52 40). In the following year, lecturing on another of Hölderlin's hymns, "Der Ister," he similarly argues that "symbolic images" such as "allegory and symbol, simile and metaphor, example and insignia" all lie within the "metaphysical" determination of the artwork, and are thus closed off to what is happening in Hölderlin's poetic "naming" (IH 16–17/17–19). More than a decade later, in *The Principle of Reason,* he claims that "there is the meta-phorical only within metaphysics" (PR 48/89, translation modified); and his final contribution to the topic is in the triple lecture on "The Nature of Language," where, in response to Gottfried Benn's quip that Hölderlin's "metaphorical" (more precisely, it is a simile) "words like flowers" turns poetry into a "herbarium," he warns: "we stay bogged down in metaphys-ics if we were to take the name Hölderlin gives here to 'words like flowers' as being a metaphor" (OL 100/207).

All four pronouncements consign metaphor, and the "symbolic images" (*Sinnbilder*) of which it is one instance, to the realm of metaphysics, and much of the ensuing debate has focused on whether metaphor is indeed metaphysical. Yet such sweeping use of the term *metaphysics*—a grandiose but peremptory gesture subordinating a rhetorical category to the history of the forgetting of being—hides a far more precise, and original, think-ing at work.[2] As I will argue throughout this chapter, to reduce Heideg-ger's thinking at this juncture to a putative "overcoming" of metaphysics tends to occlude much of the import of what is being thought. Heidegger argues that metaphor—in keeping with its etymological root of *meta-pherein,* "transposition" or "carrying-over" (in German *Über-tragung*)—is dependent on a preexisting and unquestioned division between sensuous and nonsensuous realms, and more specifically a conception of language as network of sensuous tokens whose meaning is governed by nonsensu-ous, conventional reference. The denunciations of metaphor thus become points of entry into the question of how to conceive of language's naming without lapsing into this opposition.

This chapter is an attempt to analyze in greater detail what is at stake in Heidegger's denunciation of metaphor. As my starting point I take the simple observation that, in both the *Principle of Reason* and "The Nature of Language," the question of metaphor arises out of a discussion of what Heidegger terms the physiological determination of the human body. In the former, he attempts to hear the "intonation" of an axiom, which in turn exacts of us a "hearing that brings into view" whose seeing and view-ing are irreducible to the conception of eyes and ears as receptive organs; the latter is concerned with the production of sounds in vocalization, once again resisting a reduction of "tones of speech" to "purely phonetic data" whose bodily dimension lies exclusively in the vocal cords (OL 98/205). The central claim of this chapter is that the intersection of these two critiques—of "metaphysical" metaphor and "physiological" body—is by no means coincidental. Rather, the denunciation of metaphor develops Heidegger's broader critique of the sound-sense dualism of a model of the conventional sign, and his attempt to grasp the entry into language as a bodily articulation. In short, in his discussions of metaphor, Heidegger is concerned with thinking alongside one another the *zoion* and *logon* of the *zoion logon ekhon,* the animality and discursivity of human openness.

In this, Heidegger's pronouncements on metaphor and figurative language exact a revaluation both of the idiom in which philosophy takes place, and of the critical task of reading and attending to individual figures and tropes in poetry, and this chapter will address these issues in turn. The first section follows Heidegger's suggestion that the recourse to metaphor serves as a means of explaining, and explaining away, a thinking or idiom that is taken by a preexisting norm of thought to be aberrant. This is particularly relevant to the reception of Heidegger's own text as being itself metaphorical. I will then aim to show how in the question of metaphor intersect two strands of Heidegger's thought: on the one hand, the attempt to grasp the naming of language as sounding; on the other, a nonmimetic account of art meaning that guides his analysis of the artwork's setting forth of its earthly medium, which I examined in Chapter 1. These two concerns not only intersect over the question of figurative language as *Sinnbild* or *Über-tragung* but also develop what "The Origin of the Work of Art" termed the artwork's *Gestalt,* which, as we have already seen, would translate into English, ironically enough, as "figure." It is here that the poem can render possible the thinking of an openness at once bodily and linguistic.

The Metaphoricity of Heidegger's Text

Throughout his writing, Heidegger confronts his reader with a highly idiosyncratic philosophical idiom that demands that this reader reflect on the question of idiom more generally, and nowhere does this seem more glaring than when he takes issue with metaphor—a figure of style for which one might sense Heidegger's to have something of a predilection. As Jean Greisch puts it, metaphor "functions richly throughout his discourse, and works it in profundity, more so perhaps than in any previous philosophical discourse";[3] it would seem strange, then, perhaps even perverse, for Heidegger to denigrate metaphor with such insistence. Derrida speaks for many when he notes that "the metaphoric power of the Heideggerian text is richer, more determinant than his thesis on metaphor. The metaphoricity of Heidegger's text would overflow what he says thematically, in the mode of simplificatory denunciation, of the so-called 'metaphysical' concept of metaphor."[4] This shared observation leads in two possible directions. If Heidegger's metaphoricity "overflows" his thesis on metaphor, might it not also in fact undermine it? In which case, Heidegger, at the very juncture where he seeks to distance himself from "metaphysics," is in fact returned to its domain. If implicit in Derrida's comment, this line of thinking is developed more avowedly by J. Hillis Miller and Giuseppe Stellardi.[5] Alternatively one might ask whether Heidegger's contribution to the question of metaphor in fact allows for a salvaged, "nonmetaphysical," concept of metaphor, which we can situate both in his readings of the "basic words" found in texts by Hölderlin, George and Trakl, and also in his own linguistic performance. This is the direction Greisch takes, and Paul Ricoeur and Gerald Casenave have also attempted to find in Heidegger's work the possibility of such a concept of metaphor. Metaphor, in this salvaged sense, comes to serve as a means of overcoming the very sensuous-nonsensuous opposition that Heidegger suggests structures it in advance.[6] That Heidegger's "text" *is* metaphorical—on this, both parties seem in agreement.

Metaphor and Metaphysics

Heidegger's critique of metaphor, however, is not simply concerned with the norms and limits of philosophical discourse. Three of the pronouncements listed above in fact discuss not the language of philosophy but poetry, and more specifically how we are to read a poem so as to "submit" to the displacements it effects on our worldly experience, rather than having it "captured by familiarity" (OBT 41–42/53). The critique of "symbolic images" thus develops that of form which I examined in Chapter 1. Metaphor, for Heidegger, as part of "the doctrine of images," becomes no less than "the key to all 'poetics'" (GA52 40), whose ability to provide an exhaustive study of, say, "the camel in Arabic literature" (GA39 16) comes at the expense of a pervasive deafness to the coming-to-sound that the poems that make up this "literature" might otherwise effect. Thus, discussing the "nighting pond" of Trakl's "Ghostly Twilight," he says: "The starry sky is portrayed in the poetic image of the nighting pond. But the night sky, in the truth of its essence, is this pond. By contrast, what we otherwise call night remains rather a mere image, the pale and empty counterfeit of night's essence" (OL 169/48). Once the "nighting pond" is approached as a "poetic image," it is reduced to a "pale and empty counterfeit." Again recalling the critique of "form," the image becomes ornamental to an "essence" determined in advance. That the poem might in fact shape and transform this "essence" is dismissed out of hand. In this respect, the concern with images in poetry and in philosophical discourse are intertwined. If metaphor blocks off in advance the possibility that the poem's saying might allow for a thinking of essence that exceeds the "metaphysical" account of being, then surely a thinking of being must equally divest itself of the metaphorical.

This leads Joseph Kockelmans to suggest that thinking does allow a place for metaphor as a feature of "ontic discourse," but insists that there can be no metaphor "in discourse that focuses on the ontological condition of all ontic discourse."[7] I have already suggested that Heidegger's thinking in fact calls into question so neat a separation between these two levels of discourse; nevertheless, Kockelmans's framing the question of metaphor in terms of ontological difference, and the ways, in particular, that words can "genuinely reflect the thinking of Being,"[8] goes some way to explaining why the issue of metaphor in Heidegger has provoked such passionate debate. "The metaphoricity of Heidegger's text," that is to say, could well be taken to demonstrate an incursion of the "ontic" into Heidegger's attempt to forge an ontologically originary language; such metaphoricity, signifying a blindness on Heidegger's part to the internal logic of his text's own figurative operations, would thus show these operations to undermine the very separation between ontological and ontic that is taken to motivate the denunciation of metaphor itself. For de Man, Heidegger's recourse to a vocabulary of "hiding and revealing" demonstrates "the play of differences and the play of misleading elements that are involved in the pattern of metaphor" taking place within what Heidegger himself would like to consider a rarefied ontological language of "unmediated revelations."[9] Hillis Miller, in a more polemical bent, argues: "Heidegger's trick is to affirm that analogies or figurative displacements are identities. He must forget, and lead us to forget, that they are figurative substitutions if he wants to claim he has purified his language of all rhetoric or figuration and can write as an absolute literalist."[10] Far from having suppressed "figuration" in his work, Miller continues, Heidegger simply denies "the necessary rhetoricity of language." This "rhetoricity" subsequently returns to undermine Heidegger's attempts to establish a mode of saying "proper" to being,[11] something echoed when Stellardi, who adds to such polemic a keen melodramatic flourish, writes, "Heidegger's text is overrun by metaphor. It does not control it: Expeled, metaphor comes back, uninvited, all the time, which would explain the occasional reaction, at times almost violent, of the author and master."[12] Yet such accounts ignore the sheer range of verbal artifice that Heidegger quite knowingly employs, whether in phrases like "language is the house of being" and "the neighborhood of thinking and poetry," or in the tautologies "world worlds" and "language speaks" (*die Sprache spricht*).[13] Indeed, we saw in Chapter 2 how such artifice pervades the hints and gestures through which the naming of language can attain its ontological vocation. One might wonder why, when calling Heidegger a "literalist," it does not occur to Miller to consider Heidegger's own discussion of the word *literal*. What does Heidegger mean, for example, when, in the "Letter on Humanism," he informs us that "bringing to language" within the phrase "thinking in its saying merely brings the unspoken word of being to language," should "be taken quite literally"? Heidegger first specifies that what is at issue is not precipitately treating "bringing to language" as a figure of speech. By thinking through this phrase, he suggests, we can come to treat language as "on the way," that "language . . . *is* only in this mysterious and yet for us always pervasive way," whereby language is no longer a system of conventional signs but a movement from originary openness into speech. Taking this phrase "literally," "the inconspicuous deed of thinking manifested itself. For to the extent that we expressly think the usage 'bring to language,' a usage destined to language, thinking only that and nothing further, to the extent that we retain this thought in the heedfulness of saying as what in the future continually has to be thought, we have brought something of the essential unfolding of being itself to language" (P 274–75/192). The literalism Heidegger envisages here, then, far from implying perfect correspondence of word to referent, let alone the banishment of verbal artifice, serves as a challenge to thinking to suspend any precipitate categorization or domestication of the phrase as figurative, in order to ask what the phrase "bring to language" might mean. With startling, even performative reflexivity, Heidegger concludes that only in thinking literally the phrase "bring to language" might "the essential unfolding of being" first itself be "brought . . . to language." The saying of the truth of being (*aletheia*), far from constituting an "unmediated revelation," takes place as we attend to our own usage of words so as to reframe the boundaries of the thinkable.

This is a thinking of the literal far removed from what, in "Anaximander's Saying," Heidegger scathingly brands the "formal correctness" of a "literal" translation (OBT 252/309). A translation is "faithful," Heidegger contends, not when it replaces the words of the original with their equivalent in the second language, but when its "words are words that speak out of the language of the matter" (OBT 243/297); the translation must "translate itself" into the thinking taking place in and through the words of the original. These two divergent instances of the word *literal* will elicit the perhaps banal observation that Heidegger's word usage changes depending on context. They also demonstrate his awareness of how an ossified linguistic habit can obstruct us from being able to think "the matter" to be thought. However, this has a far more precise consequence for the language in which thinking can take place. First of all, the *literal* translation, being characterized by "formal *correctness*," would thus block itself off from an anterior mode of truth, which is precisely what Heidegger searches for as the "matter" to be thought; when we *ought* to take a phrase literally, by contrast, it is precisely in order to suspend our disbelief and resist treating the phrase "bringing to language," insofar as it does not furnish a "correct" statement, as merely figurative. And secondly, as Karen Feldman wryly observes, it transpires to be Miller himself for whom "the figurative/literal or linguistic/phenomenal distinction is essential and insuperable."[14] In order to "think" Anaximander's saying, Heidegger wishes to suggest, we must translate ourselves into "the language of the matter," something which we achieve not simply by employing particular words, but by bringing the thinking that guides these words to manifest itself in them: this is the "bringing to language" which for Heidegger characterizes "thinking in its saying." His focus on "the matter to be thought" suggests that, if our thinking takes place in and through language, then, far from amounting to a "reification" of words,[15] the words become increasingly protean as we think in and through them; these words engender thinking but are subsequently transformed by the thinking that inhabits them. If this "matter" is in some way independent of the words we use, it is nevertheless only as we think in and through these words that this "matter" can first come to be thought.

In short, at issue in both the injunction to take a phrase literally and the denunciation of literal translation is the possibility of a renewed experience with language that would open up a space for thinking. Might it be in this experience with language that the "metaphoricity of Heidegger's text" resides? Again, this question is not restricted to matters of Heidegger's philosophical idiom. Ricoeur cites Heidegger's contention that the phrase "words like flowers," far from being "metaphorical," constitutes the awakening of the largest view in which "the word is brought forth from its inception" and "makes World appear in all things" (OL 100–1/207–8), only to riposte—"is this not what *live* metaphor does?"[16] The distinction between "dead" and "live" metaphor finds an analogue in Greisch's opposition of "simple" to "true (*veritable*)" metaphor. While Heidegger's critique applies exclusively to the former, it also serves as the basis for a "true" metaphor whose "iconic function" is "to cross a threshold, to accomplish a passage, to affront the Strange," and to "bring the Invisible to be seen."[17] Similarly, Casenave argues: "Heidegger's rejection of the label 'metaphor' is due to his falling prey to the same misunderstanding which is held by the tradition which he criticises. That is to say, he adopts the view of metaphor which sees metaphor as a deviation of word use, a deviation from the word's proper meaning."[18] Heidegger's discussion of *Über-tragung* constitutes a powerful critique of the "substitution theory of metaphor"; his thinking would nevertheless "complement" a theory of metaphor that focuses on its "creativity," its cognitive effects at the level of "discourse or performance."[19] Reading against Heidegger's own statements on metaphor and focusing on the shape of his thinking and his own writing practices, Casenave suggests, would strengthen an account of how "metaphor, by its deviance, suspends or disengages the reference of literal language" and thus "reorganizes our vision of reality."[20] Heidegger would in this case become a precursor to cognitivist accounts of metaphor, or "blending," which are currently prevalent in cognitive science, linguistics, and literary criticism.[21]

Yet the salvaged, nonmetaphysical concept of metaphor that Heidegger would thus offer differs from cognitivism insofar as it appeals to an ontologically anterior mode of language, and calls into question the model of linguistic meaning as reference. If "Heidegger's writing appears metaphorical from within the defined limits of the standard way of talking about things," this is because the writing is "attempting to move with the fundamental way-making of language and thereby remain at a level more fundamental than the metaphorical-literal distinction."[22] But if this metaphor is ontologically anterior to the "metaphorical-literal" distinction, this begs the question as to why we should retain the term *metaphor* at all. After all, Heidegger rejects it, partly for pragmatic reasons—its etymological associations of carrying-over, the historical baggage it has picked up in hermeneutics, poetics, Bible scholarship as well as philosophy—and partly to avoid lumping together diverse features of linguistic performance under one category. Heidegger's complaint that metaphor is metaphysical is not simply a judgment on the "interpretation of beings" it assumes, but also its history and the uses to which it is put. And moreover, the category and concept of metaphor risk blinding us to the sheer diversity of linguistic artifice as it is employed by both poets and philosophers; to equate Heidegger's own artifice first with metaphor and subsequently with metaphysics would besimply to confirm this blindness.

A Predicament for Reading

The terms *metaphor* and *metaphoricity,* be they explicitly of a nonmetaphysical or a cognitively creative kind, sit uneasily with the aporetic reflexivity of Heidegger's own "text." But this extends to any attempt to provide the diversity of verbal artifice with a single name. Karen Feldman identifies in Heidegger a "rejection of figuration, without a compensatory offer of a concrete alternative,"[23] and the attempts to salvage the term and category of metaphor within Heidegger's text do appear to have a compensatory dimension. But they also risk contravening the very problem Heidegger attempts to grasp. If naming is to trace, and thereby "bring to language," something that otherwise remains unnameable, then the attempt to identify a rhetorical category for this bringing-to-language would end up imposing a homogeneity upon a writing that thinks precisely through its verbal and stylistic diversity—and in the same gesture cutting against the grain of this diversity. This is exacerbated if we remember the self-description Heidegger gives in which, in the years after *Being and Time,* he was brought to "abandon [his] own path of thinking to namelessness [*im Namenlosen zu lassen*]" (OL 29/114), where such "namelessness" becomes the very condition for naming. Perhaps the most intriguing question in the Heidegger metaphor debate is why there is such a need to give a label to the linguistic operations through which Heidegger thinks and argues. And, conversely, how this thinking and arguing *resists* being categorized, and in particular resists being categorized as *metaphorical.*

This becomes clear in the rather practical difficulty we face as to how to characterize the "metaphors" Heidegger employs without falling into terminological imprecision. When Derrida argues that Heidegger's "own text . . . appears more 'metaphoric' or *quasi*-metaphoric than ever, at the very moment when he defends himself from it,"[24] one is struck by his evasiveness. Heidegger's text "appears," not "is," "more 'metaphoric'"—the scare quotes around "metaphoric" then emphasized by the equivocating "*quasi-*" (italicized for further effect) that subsequently qualifies it. Derrida's evasiveness here is no so much slippery as salutary, reflecting a "metaphoricity" at once tangible and yet tangibly hard to determine. Indeed, it might seem that Heidegger's "text" is characterized as metaphoric due more to its deviation from the supposed norms of philosophical discourse than to any employment of the specific rhetorical figure that is called "metaphor." As he recognizes later, with regard to Heidegger's famous house of being: "We are . . . no longer dealing with a metaphor in the usual sense, nor with a simple inversion permutating the places in a usual tropical structure."[25] The "metaphoricity" of this text is not simply a deviation from "usual" philosophical language, but also from "usual" metaphorical language.

Here, the term *metaphoricity* is being deployed almost to endow the unusualness of Heidegger's idiom with the philosophical dignity of technical rhetorical terminology. But in this, the technical vocabulary of metaphor loses technical precision, becoming a catchall to describe a general sense of anomalousness. Stellardi meets this problem head-on when he divides Heidegger's metaphors into two basic types, each firmly embedded within an ontic analysis of language. Firstly, he suggests that the writing is meta-phorical because it employs "the frequent intervention of extraordinary contexts . . . in order to make certain otherwise incongruous occurrences interpretable";[26] secondly, he suggests that Heidegger employs "open" met-aphor, that is, a figure that "opens up a possibility of meaning and leaves it in suspense."[27] Let us examine these two kinds of metaphor in turn.

Stellardi identifies in the phrase "language belongs to the closest neigh-bourhood of man's being" (PLT 187/11) two ordinary words, "belongs" and "neighbourhood," which are placed "in metaphorical position" next to two "philosophical" terms, language and being.[28] That there should be so hard-and-fast a distinction between "ordinary" and "philosophical" language might seem questionable, and in "Anaximander's Saying" Heidegger warns that the precipitate categorization of modes of discourse and thinking can lead us to interpret whatever does not conform to such categorization as aberrant. Here he looks at Theophrastus's claim that Anaximander applies a juridical vocabulary (*adike*) to beings in nature (*phusis*). Theophrastus's complaint is that "moral and legal concepts infiltrate the picture of na-ture," and reproaches Anaximander for "speaking more poetically than is necessary" (OBT 249/304). The similarity between Theophrastus and Stellardi is striking, and informative; where Anaximander has introduced a term from one vocabulary into a discussion of something to which this vocabulary does not apply, Heidegger's employment of the term *neighbor-hood* introduces an "ordinary" term into philosophical discourse. What Theophrastus terms "speaking poetically," Stellardi calls "metaphor."

Anaximander's saying, Theophrastus complains, has transgressed the boundary between the conceptual vocabularies of two mutually incom-mensurate realms, the juridico-legal and the natural-scientific. However, Heidegger counters, the boundary Anaximander has transgressed was set up by Theophrastus himself: the saying itself admits of no such boundary, and thus "no possibility of boundary transgression, no possibility of the illegitimate transfer of representations from one area to another" (OBT 249–50/305). It is only, Heidegger suggests, on the basis of this bound-ary and its purported transgression that Theophrastus can start to read the fragment; that is, he cannot read it other than as aberrant, and so is blocked off in advance from "the matter to be thought." His criticism articulates not Anaximander's own poetic way of thinking, but rather his own inability to make sense of this thinking.

Heidegger wishes to suggest that this "absence of boundaries between disciplines" is in fact a virtue of the saying. Heidegger continues: "it can well be that purely thought—free of over-simple categorization—the ac-tual structure of the matter comes to language" (OBT 250/305). In this, he would also challenge the implicit teleology through which Theophrastus reads Anaximander. Anaximander's unwitting conflation of conceptual vocabularies is ascribed by Theophrastus to the fact that a correct understanding of natural phenomena had not yet been developed: "Anaximander's saying speaks of justice and injustice, punishment and penalty, sin and recompense in relation to things" because "at this point an appropriate formula for a law of motion is still lacking" (OBT 248–49/304). As a result, he is consigned to "a primitive outlook [*Erleben*] . . . which interprets the world uncritically and anthropomorphically, and therefore takes refuge in poetic expression" (OBT 250/306). Theophrastus's reading shows itself to be anachronous in its imposing a later boundary categorization upon Anaximander's thinking; more significantly for Heidegger, it also demonstrates, apparently as a by-product but in fact central to its project, a conception of the poetic as, to borrow Heidegger's phrase from "The Origin of the Work of Art," an "aimless imagining of whimsicalities [and] flight of mere representations and fancies into the unreal" (OBT 45/60). Poetry is subsequently deployed to explain, and explain away, the moments where language does not conform to the requirements of philosophical conceptuality; yet it is precisely in his denigration of poetry that Theophrastus finds "the matter to be thought," that is, the presencing of being, withdraw from his grasp. In other words, the transformation of beings in *phusis* into "natural phenomena" coincides with the exclusion of poetry from truth, and with it the loss of a thinking capable of tracing the presencing movement by which beings come to presence. If Anaximander's thinking is "poetic," it is so in the very different sense of a "projective saying" (OBT 45/60) that shapes the modalities through which beings come to show themselves. In this it belongs to "the primordial form of poeticising in which, before everything else, language first becomes language" (OBT 247/303).

Anaximander's fragment thus points to a shared vocation of poetry and thinking: to open up a space for an encounter with beings, and one further way that the metaphoricity of Heidegger's text has been thematized is through its openness, and in the following chapter I will question this shared vocation in greater detail. For the time being, let us pursue the question of metaphor itself. As noted, Stellardi considers Heidegger's metaphors to be "open metaphors," and Bruns takes what he calls Heidegger's "dictum," "leave everything open" (OL 82/187),[29] to point to a chaotic openness of reference "designed to unsettle the normal procedures by which meanings get framed or fixed," and which he elsewhere compares to the experimentation of James Joyce in *Finnegans Wake*.[30] Heidegger's writing is radically "open" insofar as it resists semantic "closure." As Stellardi puts it: "the analogical circle is never closed."[31]

However, Heidegger is thinking openness at a level irreducible to semantics: where Bruns sees semantic indeterminacy Heidegger sees the openness of beings. This can be seen if we turn to his discussion of the "ambiguous ambiguousness [*zweideutigen Zweideutigkeit*]" of Trakl's poetry (OL 192/75), an ambiguity reducible neither to simple polysemy (what he terms "vague equivocations") nor even radical indeterminacy. He argues: "The ambiguous [*mehrdeutige*] tone of Trakl's poetry arises out of a gathering, that is, out of a unison that, meant for it alone, always remains unsayable. The ambiguity [*Zweideutigkeit*] of this poetic saying is not lax imprecision, but rather the rigour of him who leaves what is as it is, who has entered into the 'righteous vision' and now submits to it" (OL 192/75). Immediately striking is that ambiguity Heidegger identifies lies in the poems' *tone:* the cadences, the inflections, and voicing of the poetry that make up what I termed its "discursive whole." It is not simply the endless proliferation of the signifer. This ambiguity, he suggests, stems from the poems' gathering movement, a movement the poems themselves experience as an "unsayable" unison out of which they arise (this is what Heidegger calls the "site" of the poetry), but which they individually cannot grasp. The poems intone ambiguously as they cannot comprehend their own entry into sound—and yet, intoning ambiguously, they trace the gestation of their own singular sounding. Just as with the uncanniness that permeates the artwork in "The Origin of the Work of Art," the poem's "ambiguous" tone occurs as the poem first internalizes into its language, and then renders manifest, the abyssal relation of the truth of being to beings.

This leads to a crucial point. If Heidegger is denigrating metaphor because it is restricted to the ontic relations of words, his own thinking on poetry is not simply "ontological," as Kockelmans suggests, but is trying to inhabit the moments at which the "ontic" exceeds and exhausts itself. This means that his own thinking must inhabit the "ontic" if it is to engage with its limits. As we saw in Chapter 1, Heidegger in the *Contributions* conceives of the irruption of be-ing (*Seyn*) into the world in which we encounter beings in terms of the uncanny, foreign, and strange (C 326/463). That his writing should estrange itself (to use Bruns's apposite phrase) is simply a response to the exigencies central to tracing this movement. And in this respect, metaphor and metaphoricity describe less a tropological property of Heidegger's "text" than an exegetical predicament, a predicament faced by writer and reader alike: how, that is, from within a preexisting vocabulary, grammatical structure and meaningful framework, might one start to think beyond the interpretation of beings implicitly grounding and shape this vocabulary, grammar, and framework? This predicament is experienced perhaps most provocatively in the concluding lines to his 1960 lecture "Of Time and Being":

> If overcoming remains necessary, it concerns that thinking that explicitly enters Appropriation [*Ereignis*] in order to say It in terms of It about It.
>
> Our task is unceasingly to overcome the obstacles that tend to render such saying inadequate.
>
> The saying of Appropriation in the form of a lecture is an obstacle of this kind. The lecture has spoken merely in propositional statements. (TB 24/25)

Faute de mieux, Heidegger's writing inhabits the grammatical husk of the proposition, yet inhabits it uncannily, as though to render the propositional statement strange to itself. Insofar as the lecture as a means of disseminating thought publicly, and the proposition as a meas of formulating this thought, are "obstacles," Heidegger's thinking must necessarily become an aporetic exploration of these obstacles from the inside. Only thus can he first envisage articulating something like the "basic words" of which Kockelmans speaks.

■

Metaphor and metaphoricity, as terms employed to describe Heidegger's text, seek to familiarize a strangeness that itself continually calls into question such need for familiarity. Not only, however, is such unfamiliarity central to its attempts to search out and then to probe the limits of our thought; it also accords with a truth of being that demands that we preserve "the estranging and always unfamiliar" (C 29/41). His writing, then, necessarily advertises its own strangeness, all the while refusing to have such strangeness simply categorized, and domesticated, by recourse to the concept, trope, or philosophical constellation of metaphor. This leads to two conclusions. Firstly, that Heidegger's dismissal of metaphor as being metaphysical—like his similar dismissals of form, aesthetics, and so on—in fact opens on to a far larger meditation on the relation between thinking and how we read and write. Secondly, that if this constitutive ontic strangeness, the uncanny inhabitation of the propositional statement, leads us to deem Heidegger's "text" "metaphoric," then to deem it thus nevertheless serves to close us off from a deeper probing into what this inhabitation of the proposition might mean for philosophical idiom more broadly. To read Heidegger "rhetorically" is not to read him at all. Heidegger's thinking through language shows that verbal artifice can be reduced neither to an "other" to thinking that manifests itself as continual tropological play, nor as a relapse into "metaphysics" itself; rather, it becomes a way in which thinking can continually contest its own limits.

Seeing Hearing Thinking

I have argued that to ascribe to Heidegger's text the property of metaphoricity would be to domesticate the ways in which Heidegger thinks through and in language, thereby closing us off both to its diversity and to the unsettling effects so crucial to his wider project. Yet why should it be that metaphor, rather than any other category, plays this role of domestication? To answer this, I suggest that we take Heidegger's claim, in *The Principle of Reason,* that "there is the metaphorical only within metaphysics," at face value. At the beginning of this chapter, I argued that metaphysics, beyond its allusion to the history of the forgetting of being since Plato, is characterized in Heidegger's later work by the distinction between sensuous experience and a nonsensuous or super-sensuous realm. This conception of the metaphysical marks a change in focus from his earlier writings, for which metaphysics is grasped in terms of ontological difference and finite transcendence, as an "enquiry beyond or over beings that aims to recover them as such and as a whole for our grasp" (P 93/15). The move from "beyond beings" to "beyond the physical" must, I will argue, equally be understood alongside his retrieval (*Wiederholung*), from 1935 onwards, of the term *phusis.* The question of metaphor, as *meta-pherein,* is thus fundamentally bound up with his understanding of *phusis* both as a power within the human body, and within language.

The Intonation of Thinking

When Derrida observes, in "White Mythology," that "In *Der Satz vom Grund,* [Heidegger] stresses especially the 'sensuous/nonsensuous' opposition, an important trait but not the only, nor doubtless the first to appear, nor the most determinant for the value of metaphor,"[32] one senses that he does so with some puzzlement. It might not for Derrida be metaphor's "most determinant" trait, but the sensuous-nonsensuous opposition is nevertheless the "trait" that motivates and grounds Heidegger's entire thesis—the "trait," indeed, that leads Heidegger to deem a thesis on "the value of metaphor" necessary in the first place. The denunciation of metaphor in *The Principle of Reason* starts as a digression from a larger meditation on the relation between thinking and bodily experience, and particularly on whether we can hear an intonation of thinking in the supposedly atonal axiom, *nihil est sine ratione.* If, as I will argue, this is no digression but rather shows an organic unity in Heidegger's attempt to ask what an intonation of thinking might entail, then metaphor can only for Heidegger attain its significance when we attempt to think the exigencies of such an intonation.

The passage in *The Principle of Reason* where he turns to metaphor is the culmination of a thinking on the relation between bodily experience and intelligibility that extends back to the 1920s. In direct contradiction with a model of cognition that starts off with sense data and then tries to fill this sense data with meaning, Heidegger argues in *Being and Time:* "'Initially' we never hear noises and complexes of sound, but the creaking wagon, the motorcycle. We hear the column on the march, the north wind, the woodpecker tapping, the crackling fire" (BT 163/207). It is only on the basis of our orientation in the world that these phenomena become audible; to speak of "acoustic perception" is not to add a layer of precision, but to enact an abstraction from the originary givenness of meaningful sound, and impose upon this givenness a dualism alien to it. But this cannot reconstruct such givenness after the fact, and something that had started off as a basic fact of our experience is transformed into an insurmountable enigma. *The Principle of Reason* echoes this when it says: "Of course we hear a Bach fugue with our ears, but if we leave what is heard only at this, with what strikes the tympanum as sound waves, then we can never hear a Bach fugue" (PR 47/87). Central to Heidegger's thinking on both bodily perception and on linguistic meaning is the assertion that "Dasein hears because it understands" (BT 163/206); *understanding* is not the cognition of the present-at-hand, but the openness that guides Dasein's encounter other beings in the texture of intelligibility he calls "the world." Hence the attempt to understand language from out of the openness of human being-in-the-world will take place through a hermeneutic phenomenology of hearing.

In *Being and Time,* Heidegger speaks of a woodpecker tapping; in *The Principle of Reason* this has become a Bach fugue. And indeed, it is increasingly in his discussions of art that he encounters questions of bodily openness. His first references to metaphor, as noted above, are part of a wider critique of the "doctrine of symbolic images," both as an interpretive device for reading poetry and as a "metaphysical" ontology of the artwork which has its basis in the interpretation of the artwork as *allo agoreuei* or *sumballein* (OBT 3/9). Here again, the broader philosophical concern is that of how a material being can first become intelligible. It is to answer this question, Heidegger argues, that Hegel's philosophy of art, for him the culmination of "metaphysical" aesthetics, will hold that "this material thing"—the canvas and pigment of a painting, for instance—"is sublated [*aufgehoben*] into the painting and now is what it is only *through* the latter" (IH 17/19). It is by virtue of a structure of meaning that extends beyond the work's sensuous or phenomenal features that the canvas can cease to be brute matter and become spirit in a sensuous form. Not only is there "something over and above" the thingliness of the work: an intentional or mimetic content; there is something over and above the over-and-above itself, the deeper meaning behind the work. We move from *river* as a gesture of naming to referential term (a geographical phenomenon), and then from referent to abstract theme (the divine, for example).

In this, the question of metaphor, and of symbolic images more widely, points to an inner coherence between two central strands of Heidegger's thinking that I treated separately in Chapters 1 and 2: the thingliness of the artwork and the conception of language as a discursive whole that exceeds mere reference. In both cases, Heidegger is resisting a precipitate abstraction away from phenomenal experience—to a form above the materiality of the work, to a propositional content lying behind the wholeness of the naming gesture—in order to propose that this abstraction might in fact be the result of an impoverished understanding of such experience. That Heidegger should broach the question of metaphor and figurative language through a discussion of the intonation of a supposedly atonal axiom is teling: metaphor is seen to be one aspect of a wider wider-reaching thesis on *the meaningful phenomenality of words*. This is why a discussion of metaphor should arise out of this reappropriation of bodily hearing and seeing into a broadened notion of *thinking*. And this is why the sensuous-nonsensuous opposition becomes, for Heidegger, the "most determinant" trait for the value of metaphor.

And this is also why Heidegger, in attending to the intonation of Leibniz's axiom, feels obliged to enter into a discussion of metaphor and "metaphysics": "We come closer here to what can be brought into view as soon as we more clearly hear—and keep in our ear—the principle of reason in that intonation that we provisionally called the normative intonation: 'Nihil *est* sine *ratione*' . . . Our thinking should now bring into view what has really already been heard in the intonation. Thinking should bring into view something one can hear" (PR 46/86). The very notion of an intonation of thought already prizes it out of a purely nonsensuous realm; yet, curiously, such an intoned thinking "should bring into *view* what has really already been *heard*" (PR 46/86, my emphasis). It is this suggestion of a bodily thinking that leads him to counter, with barbed irony, "we are *quick on the draw* in explaining that thinking can be called a hearing and seeing only in a figurative sense [*übertragene Sinne*]" (PR 47/86, my emphasis). The figurative-literal distinction is here deployed as a means of explaining away a proposition that calls for thought as being aberrant; by deeming it figurative we absolve ourselves of the task of thinking, we shut off, rather than submit to, the unsettling effect of the language—and the thinking it articulates. And, critically, this explaining away and shutting off serve to return thinking to a purely nonsensuous realm. Metaphor is particularly germane for preserving the sensuous-nonsensuous dualism because, carrying over one linguistic token for another, it itself is grounded in and by this dualism.

The "metaphor" in question goes further than simply to conflate the sensuous and nonsensuous realms; it also conflates two sensuous procedures that any physiological determination of the body would ascribe to different organs. What is at issue is now not simply a framework for thinking the intonation of a propositional axiom; Heidegger is further calling into question the supposition that "our human-mortal hearing and viewing [has] its genuine element in mere sense reception" and thereby opening up the possibility, or at least thinkability, that "what can be heard can at the same time be brought into view" (PR 48/89). That is to say, if his "metaphor" questions the sensuous-nonsensuous distinction, and its attendant division of language into sensuous token and nonsensuous principle of reference, it also calls for a rethinking of our bodily experience. That the denunciation should arise during a critique of the "physiological" determination of the body whereby eyes and ears are reduced to seeing and hearing organs is in this respect by no means coincidental, but refers back to a greater concern about the orientation of the phenomenological body in the world. Heidegger thus performs an inversion: the eye becomes an organ only once it can see, the ear once it can hear, and both these require a prior open space in which seeing and hearing first become possible.

The Bodily and the Animal

As noted, this is a development of the attempt, already present in *Being and Time,* to grasp bodily experience in terms of the openness of human being-in-the-world. Yet, as has been lamented by many of Heidegger's more sympathetic readers, *Being and Time* itself has little, at least at first blush, to say about the body itself.[33] In the seminars he gave at the psychologist Medard Boss's house in Zollikon, Switzerland, between 1959 and 1969, Heidegger tries to address this lacuna in an exposition of the central features of the being-in-the-world of Dasein that he had outlined decades earlier. Here he insists that we can only grasp "our bodily spheres of existing" insofar as they "remain in the sway of being-human" (ZS 232/293), where being-human is defined as "the ecstatic sojourn in the clearing" (ZS

87/113). He continues: "We are not able to 'see' because we have eyes; rather, we can only have eyes because, according to our basic nature, we are beings who can see" (ZS 232/293). Yet here he gives extra emphasis to these "bodily spheres of existing," or "bodying-forth" (*Leiben*), whereby the human body, rather than being a physiologically determined "physical mass" (*Körper*) serves as the site of human openness.[34] It is as it "bodies forth" that hearing would be able to bring into view.

The distinction between *Leib* and *Körper* is first outlined in the 1936–39 Nietzsche lectures. In *The Will to Power as Art* he says, "we live insofar as we body forth [*Wir leben, indem wir leiben*]" (Ni 99/100, translation modified); and in *The Will to Power as Knowledge* he elaborates: "Life lives in that it bodies forth [*Das Leben lebt indem es leibt*]. We know by now perhaps a great deal—almost more than we can encompass—about what we call the body, without having seriously thought about what *bodying* is. . . . The bodying of life is nothing separate by itself, encapsulated in the 'physical mass' [*Körper*] in which the body can appear to us; the body [*Leib*] is transmission and passage at the same time" (N.III 79/509). The *Körper-Leib* distinction might seem specifically a question of how the body "can appear to us"; yet Heidegger also uses it to argue that "the human body is something essentially other than an animal organism [*Organismus*]" (P 247/155–56). Assertions such as this one and the claim that "Apes, for example, have organs that can grasp [*Greiforgane*], but they do not have hands" (WCT 16/18), have inspired an at times precipitate charge of a dogmatic human exceptionalism. Derrida, for example, sees Heidegger's thinking on animality as marked "with a humanism that," if "supposed to be nonmetaphysical . . . nonetheless inscribes . . . not *some* differences [between human hand and grasp-organ] but an absolute, oppositional limit."[35] Stuart Elden has observed the extent to which, Heidegger's discussions of animals focus almost exclusively on their "deficiency," whether it be the claim that "only man dies. The animal perishes [*verendet*]" (PLT 178/177), or the ascription to animals of a "poverty in world" (FCM 192–95/284–88).[36] In both cases animals are characterized by a double deficiency: not only is animal experience defined by a lack (of the capacity to die, of world), but this lack is analyzed in order to bring to light something specific to human Dasein.

When Heidegger describes the animal body as *Körper* and *Organismus*, however, his central point is that this arises from our lack of access to animal's peculiar mode of openness; if we understand it as lack or "poverty in world," it is because only as lack and poverty can we start to grasp this openness at all. It tells us little about animals themselves, but a great deal about man "insofar as the animal is viewed from the perspective of man to whom world-formation belongs" (FCM 271/394). In other words, that we should interpret animal captivity as a "poverty in world" demonstrates that we can only start to grasp the animal's "captivity" in terms of our own form of openness, world-formation. Thus Heidegger concludes that "through that apparently purely negative characterization of world in our examination of the animal's not-having of world, our own proper essence has constantly emerged in contrast" (FCM 272/394). And this arises out of a radical skepticism regarding the possibility of grasping the fullness of animal experience through empirical investigation, his discussion of the animal ending with the admission that "we have not yet clarified the essential organization of the organism sufficiently at all . . . the thesis that '*the animal is poor in world*' must remain a problem, and one which we cannot broach now" (FCM 273/396).

If animal openness thus reveals world-formation to be constitutive of human openness, it can do so by virtue of the successes and limitations of behavioral biology. That is to say, if we characterize the ape as having a *Greiforgan,* this is in no little part due to the mode in which it manifests itself to us, that is, as an organ serving a specific function, in this case "grasping." Such a functionalist interpretation is, however, ill-equipped to explain the fabric of human bodily comportment. Although grasping is also integral to the human hand, the hand is also characterized by a large gestural vocabulary far in excess of its grasping function: "The hand does not only grasp and catch, or push and pull. The hand reaches and extends, receives and welcomes—and not just things: the hand extends itself, and receives its own welcome in the hands of others. The hand holds. The hand carries. The hand signs [*Die Hand zeichnet*], presumably because man is a sign" (WCT 16/19, translation modified). The excess of the hand over its functional determination, it transpires, is not simply gesture, but *language.* Yet it is not simply that bodily openness is continually infused with the "signing" of language: inversely, "the hand's gestures run everywhere through language" (WCT 16/19). This link is made even clearer in his 1942–43 lectures on *Parmenides,* when he claims, "only a being which, like man, 'has' the word (*muthos, logos*), can and must 'have' 'the hand'" (Par 80/118). This adds a further dimension to the thinking of gesture we encountered in Chapter 2, as the hand's comportment becomes a metonym of bodying-forth as such, and consequently serves as the crux of a wider attempt to think alongside one another the *zoion* and the *logon* of Aristotle's determination of the human as the *zoion logon ekhon.*

The bodying-forth of humans happens only insofar as they have *logos,* yet only as they body forth can they first enter into language; such is the chiasmic relation that Heidegger traces. If the word first makes it possible for man to *have* the hand, it is by the same token the hand that "entrusts to the word the relation of being to man and, thereby, the relation of man to beings" (Par 84/124)—the articulation of beings that is the vocation of language.[37] This means that verbal comportment—not simply gesture, but speaking and writing—is understood by Heidegger as a mode of bodying-forth, something borne out by the two marginal notes he added to "The Origin of the Work of Art" and "The Way to Language" in the 1960s: *Sprache und Leiben* (*Lauten und Schrift*), and *Lauten und Leiben: Leib und Schrift*. If the first sees "sounding" and "script" as the points where body and language converge, the latter creates a chiasmus where *Leib* itself becomes the hinge relating *Lauten* to *Schrift*. The inscriptions and hand and voice thus become sites of an irreducible bodily dimension, anteceding and exceeding both the semantic determination of linguistic meaning and the physiological determination of the body. Yet we also find such inscription become the very opening of meaning: lying before and beyond the unity of verbal comportment and bodying forth is a powerfully *material* impulse into "sounded word" that would set into motion the movement or way-making (*Be-wëgung*) by which language first "speaks."

■

Heidegger's move from the question of a thinking that is "a hearing that brings into view" to a discussion of metaphor, then, is first of all motivated by the desire to anticipate and interrupt one means of rejecting the kind of thinking such a hearing would exact. But it moves beyond this, initially to ask what kind of speaking and writing can attend to human bodying-forth, and then to propose that, in fact, it is only as they body forth that speaking and writing are "brought to language." The critique of figurative language gives impetus to an attempt to think the body-language nexus anew; that is, it is the point of entry to grasping their shared opening as what in the Chapter 2 I termed a *bodily articulation*. This requires not simply that we see how both language and body are implicated in the same openness, but also that we can identify the irreducible bodily in language. And it is here that Heidegger turns, once more, to the sounding of poetry.

Rethinking Figure

Heidegger's denunciations of metaphor hold together the different yet interlinking strands of a tripartite critique of representation. Not only is he arguing against the conception of language as symbolic reference, and the mimetic model of the artwork as representing an intentional content, but he also opposes the model of mind as representing sense data by concepts. In each instance, this involves a reengagement with the aspects of language, art, and mind that are supposedly overlooked on the representationalist account; in each instance, this entails specifically revaluation of the status of the body, and a shift toward an ontological dimension that would describe beings' entry into presence—the "open" that antecedes and renders possible all ontic relations. The sounding and script of language are no longer considered as sensuous tokens, extraneous to actual meaning, but rather are returned to the bodying forth of language that constitutes the opening of linguistic meaning; the artwork's thingliness is no longer the material to be endowed with form and a content, but is understood as the medium out of which the work first comes to shape its own entry into appearance; the body is no longer a physiological organism receiving sense data, but is always already oriented in an intelligible world, open to the very horizon in which something like "sense data" can first appear. That metaphor should be implicated in representationalist models of linguistic and art meaning is not particularly surprising perhaps, its relation to the body-mind dualism more so; it is at the crux of the two that Heidegger's dismissal of metaphor attains is significance, both for his thought as a whole, and for poetics as a discipline.

Mimesis and the Body

As noted above, Heidegger's concern with the intelligibility of aural experience is, in *Being and Time,* elaborated by a discussion of a woodpecker tapping, whereas in *The Principle of Reason* this has been replaced by a Bach fugue. This indicates a close coherence between Heidegger's thinking on linguistic and bodily openness and his account of the thingliness of the artwork. This becomes explicit when, after discussing the Bach fugue (and the case of Beethoven, who, albeit deaf, "perhaps hears even more and something greater than before" (PR 47/87), Heidegger turns his attention to the distinction between seeing and visual perception: "If human vision remains confined to what is piped in as sensations through the eye to the retina, then, for instance, the Greeks would never have been able to see Apollo in a statue of a young man or, to put this in a better way, they would never have been able to see the statue in and through Apollo" (PR 47–48/88). "To see Apollo in a statue"—this is precisely the problem that led "metaphysics" to characterize art meaning by recourse to "symbolic images." Just as the "physiological" conception of the eye as receiving sensations cannot explain how this sheer data can become meaningful, the conception of the thingliness of the work as "brute matter" cannot explain how marble and plaster might first come to show a young man, let alone showing Apollo in the figure of this young man. In both instances, the sensuous-nonsensuous dualism is charged with reconstructing the originary openness out of which it first arises, and so the basic givenness of experience is transformed into an enigma.

Yet Heidegger at this juncture is not simply trying to demonstrate the insufficiency of this dualism for grasping either the irreducibility of vision to the activity of the retina, or the artwork to its basic thingliness, but argue that it is only on the basis of Apollo that the Greeks could see the statue at all. He introduces this inversion by saying "to put this in a better way"; but this "better way" in fact seeks to effect no less than an overcoming of the model of art meaning as mimesis. Rather, he suggests, the statue both engenders the "truth" that the god Apollo would reveal, and can only show itself as *Gestalt*—both as statue, and as statue *of Apollo*—on the basis of this truth. In this, he is recalling the account, given in "The Origin of the Work of Art," of the statue in the temple at Paestum by virtue of which "Tree, grass, eagle and bull, snake and cricket first enter their distinctive shapes and thus come to appearance as what they are" (OBT 21/31) where the statue attains its capacity to engender such firstness because, in its engagement with the limits of its earthly medium, it renders manifest the way in which this medium first enters appearance, and in so doing comes to trace the parameters by which beings in general enter into appearance, finally shaping the way in which such appearance takes place. The statue thus becomes one mode of "poetizing": a "projective saying" that renders possible a new mode of encounter with beings.

Such poetizing is not the exclusive preserve of linguistic art, but belongs to the respective gathering movements of each artistic medium; the work poetizes insofar as it "gathers" beings into a singular configuration in the open, and thereby shifts the parameters of this open. Thus Heidegger can claim, in his reading of Hölderlin's "Andenken" hymn: "the 'things themselves'" only become "the things themselves" by virtue of being "poetized," and therefore that it is only on the basis of an anterior poetizing that we can read the poem's (or artwork more generally) mode of depiction, or the that which it depicts, as "symbolic" (GA52 40). To treat the language of poetry as figurative, or metaphorical, in its engagement with the possibilities of its medium, would effectively reduce it to an after-the-fact play on the things themselves, and overlook the poem's own role in engendering the space in which "the things themselves" first becomes a viable category. No appeal to "the necessary rhetoricity of language" will suffice to account for the openness afforded by these words; indeed, such "necessary rhetoricity" is itself the function of a derivative conception of language, where deviation from ontic reference is understood as figurality and the rhetorical form has been separated off from the semantic content, instead of being the way in which such openness is brought about. Just as was the case with the physiological determination of the body, the discourse on metaphor, "figurative language," and "symbolic images" is blind to the originary openness that first makes it possible. Herein lies the inner coherence between the physiological approach to man as organism and the mimetic conception of art.

The *Principle of Reason* brings together these two strands of thought—the worlding capacity of the artwork and the bodying-forth of human being-in-the-world—in, and as, its critique of metaphor. However, it also remains at the level of bodily receptivity, "a listening that brings something to view" (PR 48/89). In the third of the lectures brought together as "The Nature of Language," by contrast, Heidegger focuses on the bodily production of words in vocalization, in whose sounding, a mode of verbal bodying forth, entry into meaning and entry into sound constitute one and the same movement. The voice thus becomes the locus for a conception of language that would exceed and antecede any sensuous-nonsensuous distinction: by approaching the voice from the perspective of bodying forth, Heidegger starts to offer an account of language as entry into sounding word.

This continues a train of thought first elaborated in the final, unfinished passages to the *Contributions to Philosophy:*

> It cannot be denied that, with what in language supports its conception as symbol for man, something is encountered that is somehow peculiar to language: the word in its *tone* and sound, the attunement of the word and the word's meaning, whereby, however, we once again think in the horizon of perspectives that arise in metaphysics, i.e., the perspectives of sensuous, nonsensuous, and supersensuous. . . . Likewise word's attunement and word's melody and saying's feeling-stress are objects of psychological explanation; and word's meaning is the matter for logical-poetic-rhetorical analyses. The dependence of this explanation and analysis of language on the kind of conception of man is now obvious. (C 353–54/502–3)

Heidegger here notes that the motifs such as the materiality of language, its affectivity, or its musicality, instead of showing a lack in a purely semantic account, in fact supplement it: by designating it as materiality we have in advance assumed the very sensuous-nonsensuous distinction that would split language into its ideal signification and material token. When we speak of the word's attunement or melody, we assume them to represent an emotional state of the speaker, and thus any explanation of this attunement and melody will take place not by looking at language itself but at the speaker's psychology. Even stress, the emphasis central to our being able to make sense of a phrase, determine its morphology, and so on, is taken away from *saying* and ascribed to the feelings of the *sayer*. At each point, these critiques of a dominant thinking of language in fact transpire to reinforce it, as they assume the basic interpretation of language as subjective expression, and the basic division of language from paralanguage.

In this discussion of word attunement, melody, and feeling-stress, Heidegger does not offer an alternative to the bad choice between a rationalistic semantics on the one hand, and a subjectivistic language on the other; he merely restricts himself to describing its limitations and lacunae, and its provenance in a flawed interpretation of human being. Similarly, in *The Principle of Reason* Heidegger for the most part restricts himself to complicating the figurative-literal opposition so as not to close off in advance a rethinking of bodily openness. "It is not unheard of," Heidegger says, "[that] human-mortal hearing and viewing doesn't have its genuine element in mere sense reception" (PR 48/89), the recourse to litotes indicative of an attempt less to establish a substantive account of a thinking experience that exceeds the sensuous/nonsensuous opposition than to keep open such a possibility. The scope of the discussion of metaphor in "The Nature of Language," by contrast, is at once narrower and more ambitious. Heidegger asks first whether, in the model of language as *semeia* ("sign," but also the etymological root of "semantics") which issues from Aristotle's *De interpretatione,* "the physical element of language, its vocal and written character, is being adequately experienced; whether it is sufficient to associate sound exclusively with the body *understood in physiological terms,* and to place it within the metaphysically conceived confines of the sensuous" (OL 98/204–5, my emphasis); again, he questions "whether the real nature of the sounds and tones of speech is thus ever experienced and kept before our eyes" (OL 98/205). However, Heidegger now goes one step further: if we attend to the way that language comes to sound, he suggests, this will at the same time afford a point of entry into a thinking of the body that exceeds the "physiological."

As in the *Contributions,* Heidegger first turns to that element of language that appears to have been left out in the account of the sign: where the *Contributions* speaks of word's "attunement" and "melody," and "saying's feeling-stress," we are now "referred to melody and rhythm in language and thus to the kinship between song and speech" (OL 98/205). Once again, Heidegger warns against "understanding melody and rhythm also from the perspective of physiology and physics"; yet here he probes deeper into the "property of language to sound and ring and vibrate, to hover and to tremble." Taking *Mundart,* dialect, as a basis for asking more about the mouth's role in the way of speaking, he suggests that in each mouth of each person, "the landscape, and that means the earth, speaks in them, differently each time. But the mouth is not merely a kind of organ of the body understood as an organism—body and mouth are part of the earth's flow and growth in which we mortals flourish, and from which we receive the soundness of our roots" (OL 98–99/205). The hovering and trembling of language, then, arise not simply from the vibrations of the vocal cords, but rather from the flow and growth of the earth. If in "The Origin of the Work of Art" the earth was situated in the medium of the work, it is now encountered within the opacity of the human body. It is through a focus on "body and mouth," and in particular the vocal element of a language that sounds, rings, vibrates, hovers and trembles, that Heidegger can point to the complicity between a linguistics that divides verbal utterance into sensuous sound and nonsensuous meaning, and a physiology that reduces the voice to physical organ. And, by grasping this ringing, vibrating, hovering, and trembling as a movement into sounding from out of the opacity of the body, he can start to overcome it. That is, the sounding of language is now conceived as a bodily site for language, arising out of an earth that inheres both in throat and in language itself, anterior to any sensuous-nonsensuous split. For the opening into sounding word, traced from the throat that withdraws from this word, allows for a movement from silence to sounding that is not a becoming-sensuous, but for which the sounding is the entry of beings into word itself.

The Flowering of Language

Making the link between the earth as thingly excess over intelligibility and the entry into sound of the word, Heidegger has started to get beyond the provisional nature of his earlier account of attunement, melody, tone, and sound. It is at this crucial juncture that he turns to three moments in Hölderlin's late poetry: in the hymn "Germanien," where we encounter language as "the flower of the mouth" (OL 99/205–6); the elegy "Der Gang aufs Land," where the word blossoms as do "the sky's blooms" (OL 99/206); and finally in the following lines from the elegy "Brot und Wein":

So ist der Mensch; wenn da ist das Gut, und es sorget mit Gaben
Selber ein Gott für ihn, kennet und sieht er es nicht

Tragen muß er, zuvor; nun aber nennt er sein Liebstes,
Nun, nun müssen dafür Worte, wie Blumen, entstehn. (OL 99/206)

(Such is man; when the wealth is there, and no less than a god in
Persons tends him with gifts, blind he remains, unaware.
First he must suffer; but now he names his most treasured possession,
Now for it words like flowers leaping alive he must find.)

In Chapter 2 we saw these lines bring Heidegger to "hear the sounding of language rising up earthwise [*dann hören wir das Lauten der Sprache erdhaft aufgehen*]."[38] He subsequently thematized this rising-up as coming both from the earth of the human body, and from the saying that withdraws from human speech: the "harmony" of the sounding of language is that which allows world to appear. This also brings Heidegger to articulate a far more developed thinking of human bodily experience: no longer merely the rebuttal of the "physiological" account of the body, but an account of the relation between the meaningful and the physical that would not fall back into a sensuous-nonsensuous dichotomy. He continues: "The sounding of the voice is then no longer only of the order of physical organs. It is released now from the perspective of the physiological-physical explanation in terms of purely phonetic data. The sounding, earthly of language [*Das Lautende, Erdige der Sprache*] is held with the harmony [*Stimmen*] that attunes [*einstimmt*] the regions of the world's structure, playing them in chorus" (OL 101/208, translation modified). Opposed to a purely "physiological-physical" explanation, the sounding of language is always already engaged within a dual movement of opening and opacity: it is at once the earthly and, through an earthly sounding, attuned into the harmony of the world. It is, Heidegger suggests, through engaging this dual movement within the human body itself that we will be able to grasp voice and throat beyond any sensuous-nonsensuous opposition. But it also gestures toward a far more complex thinking of the animality of the human body than that discussed above.

This is already latent in Heidegger's long meditation on the animal's poverty in world, something that has been teased out with particular dexterity by Giorgio Agamben in his *The Open: Man and Animal.* Agamben remarks a close, and striking, overlap between Heidegger's descriptions of animal "poverty in world" and of human *Grundstimmung.* The animal's worldly experience is described using a series of cognates of the verb *nehmen:* it is "captivated" (*benommen*), "behaves" (*vernehmen*) rather than "comporting itself." This reflects the animal's environment, *offen* (open) but not *offenbar* (disconcealed), where beings are "open in an inaccessibility and an opacity."[39] It is thus that, unlike "world-forming" (*weltbildend*) man, the animal is unable to set itself into relation with the world. Heidegger argues that man becomes capable of "world-formation" in the *Grundstimmung* of "deep boredom," in which he is "*taken* [hingenommen] by things . . . and often even *captivated* [benommen] by them" (FCM 101/153)—the very same words used to characterize the animal's relation to its environment. In deep boredom, then, would lie both the animality of man and the condition for man's overcoming his animality.

In this respect, the difference between man and animal lies not in their being captivated, but rather in the possibilities such captivation opens up. What marks off human deep boredom is its being experienced as a "being-held-in-suspense" which, like death in *Being and Time,* constitutes "the suspension and withholding of all concrete and specific possibilities."[40] Just as in *Being and Time,* when Dasein attains its authenticity by taking up thrownness as its "ownmost possibility," man becomes world-forming in *Fundamental Concepts of Metaphysics* when he takes this radical nonpossibility precisely *as nonpossibility,* and transforms this nonpossibility into an originary, albeit radically finite, making-possible. This contrasts with the animal, which is "unable to . . . suspend and deactivate its relationship [to its environment]."[41] It is the capacity to disclose closedness as such that serves as the impulse into open human comportment. The "animal" in man would thus be the opacity out of which each openness can first arise, "the *lethe* that holds sway at the centre of *aletheia.*"[42]

Already in the 1929–30 lectures, Heidegger sees the animality of man in terms of opacity, but also the distinction between man and animal in terms of the disclosure of this opacity. It is precisely this claim that we find when, in the *Parmenides* lecture series, Heidegger suggests that if "no animal has a hand," it is because "the hand exists as hand only where there is disclosure and concealment" (Par 80/118–19). That is, what transforms the grasping organ into a hand is its relation not only to language, but also to the countermovements of disclosure and concealment that continually shape and reshape the limits of the open. Instead of conceiving of language as effecting disclosure, and of the bodily dimension of language as antisemantic materiality that conceals, the originary unity of body and language requires that both disclose and both conceal, that both retain within themselves something of the animal opacity out of which they issue—and requires, moreover, that they bring this opacity to show itself. In other words, if the openness of the human body only takes place through an accompanying closedness, and if this openness is effected by *logos,* then this openness must at the same time be structured by an opacity shared by body and *logos* alike. This is what is at stake when Heidegger identifies, in the "earthing" flowering of the mouth, a bodily opacity that structures and inflects language's "rising up" from the inner depths of the body into sounding speech. Opposed to the physiological account whereby bodily processes would have linguistic meaning added to them, Heidegger wishes to suggest that it is language itself that arises out of the body to find voice: the bodily opacity of this earthly sounding is nothing other than language itself.

In this respect, it is not enough to say that, "words like flowers" diverges from the physiological conception of the human body through a "deviance" from the norms of discourse that "reorganizes our vision of reality"—nor to say that this "awakening of the largest view" is simply "what *live* metaphor does." Derrida has remarked the problems in any attempt to render metaphor "live" without any "dead" residue.[43] But even before this, Ricoeur's concept of "live" metaphor, both of poetry's "tensional" truth and the dialectic underlying speculative thought, "between the experience of belonging as a whole and the power of distantiation," presents metaphor as an epistemological and hermeneutic problem. Both poetic and philosophical metaphor lie at the level of "reference," as though Ricoeur considers the nonsensuous grounds of metaphor self-evident.[44] Insofar as the phrase "words like flowers" has permitted Heidegger to think something that had hitherto remained latent, not least in his earlier attempts to treat this question, we might want to conceive of the phrase, as Greisch does, as a *véritable* metaphor that "brings the Invisible to be seen"; yet this too we should resist. As de Man has observed, the motif of "bringing the invisible to be seen" is a paradigm case of figurative language: the master trope that "smuggles the wiles of rhetoric back into the hygienic clarity of semiotics."[45] In this respect, all "true" metaphor, instead of proving itself anterior to "the necessary rhetoricity of language," would inexorably be drawn back into it.

Notable in Greisch's account is that the processes by which language means, and renders intelligible, are primarily *visual;* in this, the words' sounding has surreptitiously been transformed into a rendering-visible, and the sounding itself lost. If Heidegger was indeed searching for semiotics' "hygienic clarity," then he would fall into the trap de Man outlines; in fact, his critique of metaphor issues from his critique, which I examined in Chapter 2, of the model of language underpinning such "semiotics." The anteriority that Greisch is searching for is in fact an anteriority to the very dualism that permits his category of *véritable* metaphor. Indeed, Greisch's visual trope, assuming that language has taken experience away from ear and mouth, shows itself to be deaf to that thinking that "must bring into view something we can hear" which motivates his critique of metaphor as *Über-tragung,* where we do not find so much a transition from hearing to seeing, as a confusion of the boundaries between the two.

Might we then say that the phrase "words like flowers" heightens our attention to the words' growth, flourishing, and so on, within the poem itself, insofar as the poem performs the very growth and flourishing it describes? This was Feldman's suggestion; but striking is how each performance or enactment she describes is presented as a kind of mimicking of the predicament Heidegger is concerned with, so that he would bring his reader to experience the predicament rather than simply to submit it to dispassionate reason. This notion of performance inheres at a purely semantic plane: we come to encounter a referent differently, and have it brought before us with particular force due to Heidegger's employment of "the order of performance and enactment"; but the basic assumption of language as sensuous token with nonsensuous reference is left unquestioned. If there is a performative at work in Heidegger's thinking of language, and in the lines of poetry he cites, then I would suggest that it is rather a gesture of opening up a space for thinking where one did not exist before—but that this thinking is necessarily embodied, and its language only *means* insofar as it *sounds.* If the order of performance is to have significance for Heidegger's thinking on metaphor, as I believe it should, then it must be grasped in terms of language's entry into appearance: this, after all, is what the flowering of words describes and performs. Heidegger considers the sounding of language to be both a showing and a *self*-showing; that is, it advertises other beings in appearance only as it advertises itself as something that appears, so that verbal language is grasped as a sounding. "Words like flowers" can only *show* (describe, illustrate, perform) if it shows itself (demands our hearing).

Heidegger's readers have thus far always considered his critique of metaphor to be a semantic and hermeneutic problem. But so long as metaphor and figurative language remains merely a hermeneutic problem, it is tied to the very sensuous-nonsensuous distinction that Heidegger is calling into question, and the scope and import of Heidegger's thinking will be occluded. Indeed, the critique of figurative language may well be cast as a critique of poetics, but only in the sense of poetics as "the doctrine of 'images' in poetry, of 'metaphor'" (GA 52, 40). It is, that is to say, a critique not so much of poetics as such as of a poetics that stays at the level of image, a poetics that reads poetry in terms of a symbolic content that has already been abstracted from the bodily whole of its poetizing, and thus closing itself off from its "naming power"—a poetics that sees itself as having an ostensibly *hermeneutic* vocation. This doctrine would not only domesticate the poem's naming as *mere* metaphor, but would at the same time reduce its mode of meaning to a signification that is itself structured by the sensuous-nonsensuous distinction that has effected this abstraction in advance. What Heidegger's thinking exacts, then, is a mode of attending to the bodily in language where it does not simply inflect meaning but become an inalienable part of language's *aletheic* showing. For this we need a salvaged poetics.

Gestalt *and* Bild: *Two Paradigms of Figure?*

But how are we to hear, let alone think, such a sounding? Indeed, it had been to grasp this sounding in greater detail that Heidegger first turned to the lines of Hölderlin quoted above. In his discussions of language's "word-attunement," of bodying-forth, and of a thinking whose "listening" calls into view, he notes the insufficiencies of earlier accounts of language and the body, but his thinking remains provisional. His sketches of the sounding of language lead in two contradictory directions, to the earth's opacity and to the understanding of being. It would seem that only with the hint given to him by these phrases of poetry, in which language becomes "the flower of the mouth" and "words [are] like flowers," can he come to give a positive account of how language and body intersect and open together in the *erdhaft* "rising up" of their sounding. That is, Hölderlin's lines make possible an encounter with beings that would otherwise have remained closed, and it is by thinking through this encounter that Heidegger can situate the bodying-forth of language in the voice's coming to sound. Hölderlin's lines do not simply describe a "voice" (*Stimme*) that can attune (*einstimmen*) beings into a harmony (*Stimmen*); they do not simply enact or perform this voice: they embody it—and indeed must do, if they are to sound in such a way that we can hear the voice's sounding rising up within them. The *erdhaft* rising-up that the lines name, in other words, is the very rising-up from out of throat and saying from which the lines themselves issue. And the lines will bring us to hear this rising up only as the lines' own voice holds together a sounding through which bodying-forth and language enter concomitantly into presence, while also bringing to sound that which withdraws into the opacity of the body, the countermovement to its own bodying-forth.

Heidegger here appears to be offering an implicit account of "poetic language," which recalls the *Gestalt* of the artwork in "Origin" that advertises its own entry into appearance and thereby "fixes in place" the relations between presencing and absencing that condition this appearance (OBT 38/52). Indeed, taking advantage of that fortuitous accident in the English language, one might then suggest that these lines constitute one such figure, or *Gestalt,* that far outstrips their figurative (*übertragende*) language or the image (*Bild*) they paint. Like the *Gestalt* in "The Origin of the Work of Art," these lines would point to the very movement by which they can come to sound, and would do so by engaging with and bringing to sound, the earthly provenance of this sounding. Working through the various interlinking meanings of *Gestalt* as figure, shape, and configuration, we could say: the lines would both sound in a singular shape (*Gesalt*), and yet shape (*gestalten*) the way in which we subsequently hear them, and render possible a different configuration (*Gestalt*) though which beings in general come to appearance—in this instance, a configuration that would exceed the sensuous-nonsensuous dualism itself.

And, moreover, it is as a *Gestalt* that these lines can bring thinking to grasp something beyond its own limitations, to expose itself to something that exceeds and resists it, to think that which, from within the categories and dichotomies of philosophical discourse, would otherwise remain unthinkable. In "The Origin of the Work of Art" Heidegger argued that the artwork engages with the limits of its own medium so as to render manifest these limits, and thereby to alter them; they thus "transport us . . . out of the realm of the usual" (OBT 40/54, translation modified). What we see here is these lines of poetry altering the limits of the thinkable through precisely such a transport. These lines demand that thinking should hear the sounding of language in the throat, and in this its limit is intimately related to the intonation of thinking, and its demand is that thinking should hear the intonation that is central to it, and yet which is veiled from it. And this requires that thinking develop a mode of hearing that does not simply reduce the poem's saying, and sounding, to metaphor, but rather lets it resound.

It would then be as a *Gestalt* that Heidegger can claim the tropes "words like flowers" and "the mouth's flower" resist and exceed their purely tropological determination, so that trope is never mere trope; it would be as *Gestalt* that they can come to name the *erdhaft* rising up of language, and allow thinking to hear this rising up. In this, Heidegger's analysis of the excess of "words like flowers" over trope is far from a naive denial that the phrase does not constitute a simile. Rather, it would be to claim that the concept of simile does not exhaust what is taking place here; and furthermore, that to read it exclusively as a simile would blind us to its capacity to sound, at which point it may well start to resemble a "herbarium." Yet, if the poem renders manifest this limit of thinking precisely in its divergence from the norms of thought underlying the physiological determination of mouth and word, does it not advertise this divergence by taking the *form* of a simile? And if this is the case, does not the phrase's very claim to overcome the sensuous-nonsensuous dualism depend on its using a figure of style governed by this dualism in advance? We are thus returned to the two exegetical possibilities discussed above. Firstly, Heidegger would be outlining, perhaps even against his own better judgment, a salvaged conception of metaphor; secondly, Heidegger's institution of a thinking beyond and before the figural-literal distinction is entangled in the "necessary rhetoricity of language" after all.

At this juncture, however, I would like to return to what I noted in the first section of this chapter: when Heidegger employs certain metaphorical phrases, it is with the negative and aporetic aim of using the language currently at his disposal (notably the propositional statement) in order to think the limits of this form of language, and indeed to inaugurate a thinking beyond these limits. It strikes me that the simile in Hölderlin's lines is functioning in an analogous way: it advertises its divergence from the norms of language usage by using the repertoire of expressive gestures open to it within these norms. Nevertheless, it would not be exhausted by such norms, and indeed would exact a thinking of language in excess of these norms, an excess that for Heidegger is characterized by its refusal of the sensuous-nonsensuous split that determines the model of linguistic meaning as signification.

In other words, although "words like flowers" first advertises its or aberrance through the form of a simile, the sounding it effects will not simply happen at the level of simile; and more precisely, these lines can only name the *erdhaft* rising up of words in throat by being themselves subject to this rising up. We must understand these lines, whatever excess over trope and "awakening of the largest view" they effect, not as a semantic excess but as a sounding that elides any split of sensuous to nonsensuous. The words would exceed their form as trope, then, not simply by reaching beyond any tropological determination, but insofar as they perform their own entry into sounding word—insofar, that is, as they undermine the very epistemological framework that grounds the concept of "trope." If the account of the poem's sounding is at first framed as a critique of the rhetorical and hermeneutic category of metaphor, then its ultimate target is the precipitate dividing up of sensory experience necessary to separate off a hermeneutic sphere. When Heidegger tries to think beyond the words' status as simile, he must attend to the words' sounding, through which they address their hearer and reader as an articulation that is verbal only as its site is bodily. Heidegger's denunciation of metaphor leads to a defense of poetics against hermeneutics.

Here, simile becomes one element in a repertoire of available techniques in the medium of poetry, to be deployed to as to render manifest the "naming power" hidden in the texture of this medium, and setting it into motion. Just as the propositional statement is a medium for thinking, but one from within which Heidegger will aim to inaugurate and engage a mode of thinking anterior to propositions, he will see these lines of Hölderlin to employ a simile in order to open up a space for an encounter with beings anterior to simile and to the conception of language that governs it. But this leaves one final question: if the excess over simile constitutes a sounding, then in what way is such a sounding actually *sonorous*? Particularly important in this regard is Heidegger's employment of the nominalized verb *lauten,* which, as mentioned in Chapter 2, is not simply a phonic phenomenon, but rather the continual movement into language and phenomenality. In this respect, it would not be sufficient to say that the sound would mimic this rising up, so-called verbal mimesis. Indeed, as we saw in Chapter 2, such employment of the nonsignifying sounds of language (*Wortlaut*) constitutes, for Heidegger, a derivative mode of sounding, and one that is directly equivalent to the construction of the literal-figurative opposition. In both instances, the originary totality of language as sounding is broken up into a dualism (of sound and sense; of literal reference and indirect forms of reference) that is ill-equipped to grasp the openness that rendered it possible, and from which it was derived. This is not to deny that poems use sonorous patterning or similes, but rather that, even when these techniques are deployed in order for the poem to grasp its own sounding, the sounding will subsequently be irreducible to these techniques. This would be poetry's constitutive excess.[46]

Here too I suggest that we approach this in terms of what Heidegger had termed the work's *Gestalt,* tracing and fixing in place the *erdhaft* rising-up of language through the "movedness" (*Bewegtheit*) it fixes in place and holds in tension (see Chapter 1). The sounding, then, would describe the work's entry into appearance in its broadest sense, the way in which it engenders our hearing, a hearing that goes beyond the bounds of auditory reception to embody our encounter with language more broadly. The sounding arises out of a "medium" of poetry that is not simply the "materiality" of the voice and throat that speaks poetry, nor simply the "necessary rhetoricity of language," but for which materiality and rhetoricity are instances of myriad expressive possibilities, neither one of which can be thought in isolation from the other. It is by opening on to a sounding that exceeds it, then, that the tropes "words like flowers" and "the mouth's flower" would engage and inaugurate a dimension of the medium of poetry to which trope is blind, and yet on which it depends.

■

If Heidegger's denunciations of metaphor then point toward a wholly original account of how phrases and motifs in poems can render manifest an openness at once bodily and verbal, we should not forget that they take place as digressions within wider discussions about thinking, language, and bodily experience. This means that despite the rarity of its appearances, metaphor lies at the crux of Heidegger's thought; but it also means that his thinking on metaphor remains incomplete, that he did not pursue the consequences of his all too brief, and on the face of it simplificatory, denunciations. At no moment is this more frustratingly articulated than in his sudden address to his listeners, just as he embarks on his reading of the phrases "the mouth's flower" and "words like flowers": "It must be left to you, my audience, to think about these verses in the light of what my three lectures are attempting, so that you may someday see how the nature of language as Saying, as that which moves all things, here announces itself" (OL 99/206). How precisely "the nature of language as Saying . . . announces itself" in the poem, Heidegger does not deign to specify—indeed, leaving this task to his audience and future readers resembles a somewhat patrician gesture toward the literary critics that, supposedly, would be left to debate the minutiae upon which the "thinking of being" will so blithely pronounce. We can also regret that, although Heidegger's discussion of these phrases leads him to articulate the sounding of language as it arises out of the opacity of throat and voice, his reading of the lines themselves show no such attentiveness to the way in which this sounds in the lines themselves, and contents itself rather with glosses of the words *mouth* and *flower,* instead of situating this sounding in the poem's use of its medium. That Heidegger should refuse to explain *how* we might come to "hear" this saying come to speak in the lines he cites, and that his brief analysis should take the form of a hermeneutician's gloss, even though his argumentation would call such a reading practice into question, is deeply problematic. Might it be that behind Heidegger's sovereign indifference to literary critical analysis lies an inability to read in accordance with the exigencies of his thought?

This question will be central to the rest of this book. If Heidegger's discussions of metaphor demonstrate what is at stake in our attending to individual figures in poems, and even hints at the direction such attention might take, then we will nevertheless need to see whether Heidegger's own reading practice lives up to his insights, or is even consistent with these insights. This both involves turning inward to ask why it is that the internal dynamics of Heidegger's thought preclude him from saying *how* this happens, and turning away from Heidegger, and back to that discipline which can and does engage with this *how*, and which might take these insights as a powerful possibility for future thinking, and a point of entry for reframing its central categories and practices. And this discipline, to whose categories and modes of questioning Heidegger here tacitly admits blindness, is *poetics*. Not, perhaps, a poetics steeped in the "doctrine of 'images,'" but a poetics whose intoned thinking can listen to the sounding of such lines and trace the movement of this sounding. If Heidegger's own readings of poetry situate themselves at the limits of poetics, then a poetics that would engage with Heidegger must repay the favor and identify the limits of his own thinking, must attend to the poems he reads precisely where his readings break off, where the thinking of being shows itself to be limited. This will be the task of the next chapter.

4

Reading Heidegger Reading

Ever since Max Kommerell described an essay of Heidegger's on Hölder-lin's "Andenken" as "a productive train-wreck" (*ein productives Eisenbahn-Unglück*),[1] Heidegger's readings of poetry have been subject to a critical skepticism bordering at times on outrage. To an extent this is unsurprising and even, one feels—in the light of his contempt for "the history of litera-ture and aesthetics" (EHP 21/7)—solicited. Yet the surfeit of commentary on Heidegger as a "train-wreck" exegete risks occluding the other term in Kommerell's oxymoron, or the possibility that the two are interlinked: that as the reading is, as it were, derailed, it opens on to aspects of the po-etry that would have otherwise remained inaccessible to thinking. This is something noted by George Steiner. It is true, he admits, that "on the level of normal expository responsibility many of his readings are opportunistic fictions," but yet "his commentary on Stefan George's poem 'Das Wort' . . . seems to me incomparable in its penetration and finesse. If he augments the fitful, reiterative texture of the poems of Georg Trakl, Heidegger's read-ing of 'Ein Winterabend' . . . is, nevertheless, a marvel of sympathy."[2] It is in particular Heidegger's purported lack of "expository responsibility" that has caused consternation. Yet it is not clear that we should approach his readings as exegeses in the first place. This is not simply to observe that cor-rectness was not, for Heidegger, a criterion of much consequence; rather, his *Erläuterungen,* often translated (and interpreted) as "elucidations" or "commentaries," are far more "soundings-out" of the poems, setting off from the poem to see where it will take his thinking rather than elucidating what the poem says and how it says it.[3] Cries of exegetical infidelity might easily miss the point, and interest, of Heidegger's *Erläuterungen,* closing us off from what is taking place in his encounters with Hölderlin, George, Trakl, and others.

If Heidegger is not doing exegesis when he reads, then we need not only to look in greater detail at his reading practice, but also to consider how we are to read Heidegger reading. This is most evidently the case when we ask what the relation is between the "sounding" Heidegger produces and the poem he takes as his starting point. One is tempted, for example, to identify the discrepancies between his readings and the poems he discusses; yet this would be to treat them as exegeses and to judge them as such. Nor, however, can we simply disregard the role played by the poems in his readings, as though they were themselves incidental, or indicative of his "opportunism." Not only would this render the relation between poem and reading arbitrary, and absolve Heidegger of any possible criticism of how he reads; it would also overlook why it is that Heidegger turns to particular poems at particular moments, what such-and-such a particular poem offers to his thinking, how this poem allows Heidegger—or so he claims—to gauge, and engage, the limits of his thinking; finally, it would blind us to the ways in which poems come to shape and mark this thinking.

My suggestion is that we approach Heidegger's readings from within his account of the "work-character" of the artwork. The artwork is only "at work," will only constitute a "setting into work of truth [*Wahrheit*]," when it is being read, listened to, or beheld, by what Heidegger calls the work's "preservers" (*Bewahrenden*) (OBT 44/59). We should consider Heidegger's readings of poems as themselves attempts at "preservation," which would "stand within" the openness of beings opened up, in a singular manner, by an individual poem, so as to "submit to the displacement" this openness effects on thinking. The readings do not claim to speak for the poems, or to determine their meanings, or even to analyze what the poems say and how they say it; they aim, rather, to "undergo" them in order to attain a thinking that is not identical to the poem, but which sets off from this encounter with the poem for an encounter with beings more broadly.

This supposes that poetry is indeed able to facilitate such a thinking and listening, and one of the questions we must ask is whether, and how, this is the case. So we must ask: What is it about *Dichten* (poetry or poetizing) that allows it to bring *Denken* (thinking) to confront and overcome its own limits? And, following on from this: if poetry can affect thinking thus, how can thinking subsequently give an account of poetry, and the way it is affected by poetry, that does not end up assimilating poetry into thinking, and thereby dissolving the very limits it aims to think? If Heidegger insists upon the unsettling otherness of poetry, then surely "thinking" cannot decide on the parameters of this otherness. One of the crucial questions for this chapter will be to see not only whether Heidegger's readings in fact succeed in becoming "preservations," but also whether the account Heidegger gives of *Dichten* and *Denken* provides an accurate depiction of these readings.

To this end, I will read Heidegger's readings at the points of transition between poem and preservation, to see the ways in which the poems inflect, mark, and shape the readings Heidegger gives, and to see how Heidegger's thinking responds to the exigencies of the poems. First, however, I will probe in greater depth the role of preservation, both in the ontology of the artwork found in "The Origin of the Work of Art," and within Heidegger's work more broadly. Preservation, I argue, is part of a thinking of ecstasis that dates back to *Being and Time,* and is articulated in his later work through the project of "undergoing an experience with language" (OL 57/159). Poetry becomes crucial for Heidegger because it is both within language, like thinking, and yet its modes of saying are foreign to thinking. This means two things: firstly, that to grasp the relation between poetry and thinking requires an account of the co-belonging foreignness of the two; secondly, that all reading of poetry involves a kind of translation of this foreignness.

By probing the theoretical concerns that motivate and guide Heidegger's readings, I will aim to address the critical response that these readings have received, and in particular the complaint that Heidegger disregards the radical indeterminacy of "poetic language." The purpose here is not to defend Heidegger from his critics at all costs: I wish merely to observe that any criticism must first of all understand what Heidegger's project is, as otherwise we risk accusing him of doing badly something he does not consider himself to be doing at all. Yet I will also argue that those critics that take issue with Heidegger for doing "bad" exegesis offer themselves a model of exegesis that Heidegger's thinking radically calls into question, notably as their analysis of the indeterminacy of "poetic language" operates on an exclusively semantic, hermeneutic level, which Heidegger's own account of language as a bodily articulation would move beyond. Not only, then, does a precipitate dismissal of Heidegger's reading practice undermine their critiques of this reading practice, but the very framework upon which these critiques are based is undermined by Heidegger's own work. If we are to account for the "train wreck" Kommerell observes in Heidegger's readings, we should understand what these readings are attempting to achieve, and ask whether they do in fact achieve them.

In other words, do Heidegger's readings do justice to his most powerful insights regarding poetry—from the "contest of measure and limit" that characterizes the work's engagement with its medium, to the rhythmicity of the work, to the bodily articulation of language, to reading as a "preservation" that "stands within" the openness brought about by the poems? Heidegger's readings, as we saw his discussion of Hölderlin's "words like flowers" in Chapter 3, rarely mention rhyme, prosody, or any of the other ways that this bodily dimension would be captured within the poem; nor do they describe the workings of the medium which are so central to his account of the artwork in "The Origin of the Work of Art." Can his readings "submit" themselves to the poems they read while overlooking such intrinsic features of poetry? Or might it be that these readings do submit themselves, but not in the way Heidegger claims? The third section of this chapter, which reads three moments of transition between poem and preservation in Heidegger's work, will pursue these two questions. I argue that Heidegger's readings only become successful "preservations" when the poems' treatment of their prosodic and figural medium comes to inflect the texture of the readings themselves. But the poems inflect the readings' texture in such a way as to remain veiled from the readings themselves: if at such moments Heidegger would be engaging with the limits of his thinking, then he is not able to account for these limits, or control the way in which these limits articulate themselves. Reading Heidegger reading, then, we see limits become apparent, and so we must not simply read Heidegger but read beyond him, just as he reads beyond the poems to which he turns, to think those limits he himself cannot think.

Standing in the Open of the Poem

In "The Origin of the Work of Art," Heidegger argues that the thingliness of the work is to be derived from its "work-character." We saw in Chapter 1 that he initially situates this "work-character" in the work's engagement with its medium, through which the limits of the medium are rendered manifest and the strife between world and earth, opening and withdrawal, that conditions these limits, is thus "set to work." Chapter 1 focused on was this strife, and how it is fixed in place in the work's *Gestalt;* however, when Heidegger pursues his description of the work-character, he argues that even though this account of the strife within the "work-material" is a necessary condition for setting the work "to work," it is on its own incomplete. The definition of art as the "setting-into-work of truth" in fact has "two meanings" (*ist zweideutige*): "On the one hand, it says: art is the fixing in place of self-establishing truth in the *Gestalt.* This happens in creation, understood as the bringing forth of the unconcealment of beings. At the same time, however, setting-to-work also means: bringing the work-character of the work into motion and happening. This happens in preservation [*Bewahrung*]" (OBT 44/59). In other words, the truth (*Wahrheit*) of the work, while only first rendered possible through its engagement with its medium, further depends upon its reception and, specifically, whether its audience, which Heidegger terms the work's "preservers" (*Bewahrenden*), allows "what is created to become, for the first time, the work that it is" (OBT 40/54). So—what is at stake when Heidegger displaces the "truth" of the artwork from the created artifact to its encounter with its preservers? And how will this inflect Heidegger's own readings?

The Preservation of the Artwork

The notion that preservation is necessary if the work is "to become . . . the work that it is" motivates much of Heidegger's writing on Hölderlin, Trakl, and George. In Hellenic Greece, artworks were, in Bernstein's phrase, "historically legislative," that is, they shaped the modalities through which beings entered into unconcealment:[4] the temple at Paestum, Heidegger tells us, "first structures and simultaneously gathers around itself the unity of those paths and relations in which birth and death, disaster and blessing, victory and disgrace, endurance and decline acquire for the human being the shape of its destiny" (OBT 20–21/31); similarly, "the tragedy" (Heidegger has Sophocles's *Antigone* in mind) "transforms that speech [of the people] so that now every essential word fights the battle and puts up for decision what is holy and what unholy, what is great and what small, what is brave and what cowardly, what is noble and what fugitive, what is master and what slave" (OBT 22/32). In short, art constituted "an essential and necessary way in which that truth happens which is decisive for [their] historical existence" (OBT 51/66). In the epoch of "aesthetics," by contrast, where beauty has been reduced to "subjective experience," and the work's engagement with its medium to "formal features and intrinsic charms," this legislative dimension is lost. While this has been taken to mean that, for Heidegger, all great art is Greek art,[5] I would argue that there is a far more measured thinking taking place at this juncture. In a revealing aside, Heidegger suggests that "even the oblivion into which the work can fall is not nothing: it is still a preserving" (OBT 41/55). That is, the truth of the artwork would lie precisely in contemporary humanity's inability to stand within the openness of beings it brings about: the unheeded artwork tells the truth of where we stand historically with art. Hölderlin's poetic corpus, written within the epoch of aesthetics but at the same time pointing to a nonaesthetic conception of art and poetry, does not simply await, but rather *demands* preservation. Rather than asking whether "great art"—that is, art that constitutes a "happening of truth"— can still be created, Heidegger wishes to ask whether it is possible for us to preserve extant, not-yet-great art into greatness. It is in this respect that Hölderlin's corpus "stands before the Germans as a test to be stood" (OBT 50/65; translation modified).

The word *origin* in "The Origin of the Work of Art" thus constitutes a double genitive. Not only does Heidegger ask where and how artworks originate; he also asks what kind of origin an artwork can be. And this, simply put, depends on how we behold the work. The question of reading practice therefore becomes crucial for Heidegger; but this brings with it the suspicion that it is, properly speaking, not Hölderlin's poetry which is "great," but Heidegger's "preservation" of it. When J. M. Anderson notes that "only as a consequence of thinking does the art-work culminate in its horizon,"[6] one might wonder whether the horizon of the artwork belongs to the work itself, or rather to the thinking that preserves it.

This motivates de Man's observation that "the source of the truth of the text then no longer resides in the text but in an awareness that lies beyond it; the commentary, the interpretation, really adds something to the poetic statement."[7] However, to suggest that the truth finds its source beyond the text would be to overlook Heidegger's insistence that the created work will shape the parameters of preservation. Indeed, de Man's employment of the (pointedly un-Heideggerian) term *text* here is revealing: he conceives of the relation between poem and reader as between literary artifact and exegete, and so is imposing on Heidegger's readings a terminology and model of exegesis that is alien to them (the text furnishes a "statement" to which we add a "commentary": this is a poetics of *content*). Preservation only reaches *beyond* the work as it constitutes a "*standing within* the open-ness of beings that happens in the work" (OBT 41/55; emphasis added). On the one hand, "what is created [will] become, for the first time, the work that it is" (OBT 40/54) only by virtue of our preservation; and yet, on the other, the "openness of beings" that preservation can stand within is dictated by the singularity of the work's engagement with its earthly medium. Barbara Bolt's summary is useful in this regard: "The work of the art opens onto possibility. In unconcealment (*aletheia*), the artwork opens truth in its own way."[8] The created work "opens" truth as a possibility, but does not actualize it. And yet, Bolt stipulates, it opens possibility *in its own way*, and thus delimits the kinds of preservation open to it. The artwork, as a "setting-to-work of truth," comprehends both the created work's engage-ment with its medium, and the horizon beyond the created work that the preservation takes up and renders actual; yet it cannot be attributed solely to either. Rather, the work "happens" in, and as, the points of contact, intersection, and divergence, between the created work and its preservation: it is at these moments that the work is most powerfully "at work."

The artwork, in other words, is conceived of as the matrix of the created work and its preservation—or, better, the matrix of the created work's engagement with medium and the inexhaustible plurality of preservations this engagement opens up. This subsequently guides what Heidegger is attempting to do when he reads—and thereby furnishes us with a means of evaluating his readings without turning them into "exegeses." For if the artwork lies in the points of intersection between created work and preservation, then Heidegger's claim to "preserve" the various poems he reads will depend precisely on how such points of intersection are negotiated. And it is precisely in negotiating such points of intersection that we start to see what preservation might mean as a proposition for *literary criticism*. In particular, if it is only as "standing within" the openness brought about by the created work that a preserving reading can take place, then how can our reading first come to "stand within" the poem?

To see this, one may recall the uncanny *Dass* of the created work, index of its thrust into the open. As the created work "is . . . itself transported into the openness of beings it itself opens up," it "carries us into this openness and, at the same time, out of the realm of the usual." It is insofar as we let ourselves be thus carried that we can become the work's preservers. Heidegger continues: "To submit to this displacement means: to transform all familiar relations to world and to earth, and henceforth to restrain all usual doing and prizing, knowing and looking, in order to dwell within the truth that is happening in the work" (OBT 40/54). The reading "preserves" the work, in other words, only as long as it submits itself to it, and thus dwells within the configuration of beings the work makes possible. And yet, this standing-within, rather than explicating the created work, *projects* from inside it in new directions, taking it as a catalyst to further thinking.[9] The poem, Bruns notes, serves for Heidegger's later readings of poetry as "an opening, a threshold, a line to follow or cross: in short, a *way* of taking it or of being taken by it."[10] The chiasmus is taking and being taken is crucial: only by submitting to the work, of "being taken by it," can thinking *take* its own path from within the openness the created work sets out. If Heidegger's own reading practice is not to contravene his thematization of preservation, in other words, such a standing-within should mark his own readings even as they take off from the created work.

How would this preservation relate to the practice of literary criticism, and the explication of literary texts? Heidegger is at pains to contrast preservation with "that merely cultivated connoisseurship of the formal features of the work" (OBT 42/57), which familiarizes the work by turning it, in one gesture, into both an object of science that can be categorized, taxonomized, and so on, and an object of pleasure, an object for consumption. He warns: "As soon as the thrust into the extra-ordinary is captured by familiarity and connoisseurship, the art business has already begun to take over the works" (OBT 42/56). In this, connoisseurship is not merely scholarship, but part of a tacit division of aesthetic labor: "The art dealer looks after the market. The art-historical researcher turns the works into the objects of a science" (OBT 19/29). Art becomes a commodity and an object of science in one and the same gesture. It is here that the artwork's transformative, *aletheic* capacity is domesticated, so that art lovers and specialists, who believe themselves to be conserving the works, are in fact simply perpetuating a kind of living death: "The 'Aegina' sculptures in the Munich collection and Sophocles's *Antigone* in the best critical edition are, as the works they are, torn out of their essential space" (OBT 19–20/29–30). The museum and the critical edition, as places in which to encounter artworks, ensure in advance that the work's "thrust" into the open has been blocked off.

And yet, Heidegger also speaks, presumably with Norbert von Hellingrath in mind, of "the careful handing down of works" which, while not constituting preservation itself, "can still offer a place to the work from out of which it can contribute to the shaping [*Gestalten*] of history" (OBT 42/56)—that is, can create the conditions in which preservation might take place, so that, to extend the metaphor, its living death becomes a dormancy waiting to awake. This suggests a more tempered relation between historical art and literary scholarship and the preservation that inhabits and articulates the work's truth. In Chapter 1 I suggested that Cézanne's *Portrait du jardinier Vallier* becomes a *Gestalt* in Heidegger's sense: a point of coherence in which are rendered manifest a complex of movements and countermovements between presence and absence, luminosity and opacity, and so on. This ontological dimension had hardly disregard painterly technique: Cézanne can capture such movements only because of the accumulation of technical advances from Delacroix to Courbet to Manet and Impressionism. This means, consequently, that only through an awareness of such technique can we attend to such movements, and thereby grasp the work's "firstness." What Heidegger seems to be suggesting in his mention of the "careful handing down of works" is that such technical and historical analysis provides basis upon which we can attend to the ways in which this painting constitutes a *Gestalt,* that, even though such analysis will not on its own stand within the work's truth, it may render possible a future experience, and standing-within, of the firstness the work affords. Heidegger's challenge to literary and aesthetic scholarship is to ask how we are to *stand within* these works, to *submit* our thinking to its uncanny *Dass,* and thereby bring this work to be *at work.*

An Ecstasis of Thinking

The relation between created work and preservation is marked by a curious uncanniness. Preservation seeks to "stand within the openness of beings" the work makes possible; yet it can only do this to the extent that the work insists upon its own solitariness and thereby advertises its singular thrust into openness, the *Dass* of its createdness. As a mode of thinking preservation is always engaged at the limit between created work and preservation—a limit the artwork inhabits, for so long as it remains at work. It is here also that we see the importance of preservation as a project for the thinking of being: by attending to the artwork, thinking confronts its own limits, and indeed has to inhabit an open that, strictly speaking, takes place beyond these limits. "Standing-within" takes place as ec-stasis: "the out-standing standing-within the essential separation [*Auseinander*] of the clearing of beings" (OBT 41/55; translation modified).

In this respect, the account of preservation continues and develops some of the central motifs from the account of "finite transcendence" in *Being and Time.* When he says, in the "Afterword" to "The Origin of the Work of Art," that its purpose is to "see the enigma that art is," not to "solve" it (OBT 50/66), we can recall another "enigma" central to Heidegger's work: the description of Dasein's brute thrownness in, where Dasein's "mood brings [it] before the 'that-it-is' [*Dass*] of its 'there,' which, as such, stares it in the face with the inexorability of an enigma" (BT 175/136). Throughout the exposition of preservation, in fact, Heidegger is developing themes from *Being and Time.* Preservation is "a knowing that is a willing," whose willing, far from being a "subjective" action "is the sober resoluteness of that existential self-transcendence which exposes itself to the openness of beings" (OBT 41/55)—an explicit allusion to *Being and Time*'s account of resoluteness as the mode of thinking that can grasp Dasein's thrownness, and the "nothing" that underlies it. In resoluteness, Dasein projects its thrownness as its "ownmost possibility," so that the "nothing" becomes an originary "making-possible" (BT 434–36/383–85); similarly, the projection of the preservers involves founding their thinking on the opacity of the earth. And indeed, the model of the artwork as "the creative preservation of truth in the work" is itself conceived along the lines of the "thrown-projection" which had characterized the "being-in" of Dasein's ontological determination as "being-in-the-world" (OBT 44/59). As the artwork takes over from Dasein as the site in which beings can be disclosed in their being, thrown-projection shifts from characterizing Dasein to characterizing openness as such. The created work is thrown toward its preservers, who must subsequently "project" their thinking from out of the unconcealedness thus "thrown open" (OBT 44/59).

In *Being and Time,* the thinking of *ecstasis* exacts, as it were, an *ecstasis* of thinking. As Dasein is brought before "the 'that-it-is' of its 'there,'" it must think this predicament without attempting to render it commensurate to calculation. A similar pattern is present in Heidegger's account of the preserver's confrontation with the work's enigmatic *Dass.* Preservation must grasp this *Dass* while allowing it to remain unfamiliar, uncanny, foreign, as only on the basis of this constitutive foreignness can the preservation first stand within the openness it furnishes and project from out of it. Heidegger's central critique of scholarship and connoisseurship is that they familiarize the work, and hence block off in advance the uncanny address the work would articulate to its potential preservers. And it is through a similar thinking of *ecstasis,* and in particular, the *ecstasis* of language, that leads Heidegger, in the 1957–58 lectures on "The Nature of Language," to turn to poetry.

Heidegger opens these lectures by saying: "The lectures that follow . . . are intended to bring us face to face with a possibility of undergoing an experience with language" (OL 57/159),[11] where "to undergo an experience with something" is thought in terms of our submitting to a displacement: "this something befalls us, strikes us, comes over us, overwhelms us and transforms us" (OL 57/159). Yet to undergo an experience with language is peculiar in that we can only experience language from within it. Rodolphe Gasché distills this problem when he notes that, "unlike other unfathomable objects, language is not unknowable because it exceeds the range of our faculties." Rather, it is the contrary: there is a constitutive "impossibility of stepping out of language to 'look at it from somewhere else.'"[12] The resistance of the "linguistic nature" of language to accommodate itself to our thinking, in this respect, is compounded by our inability to stand *outside* language, rather than our inability to inhabit it. Rather, Heidegger says, if we are to "speak of language" we must "let language, *from within* language, speak to us, in language, of itself, saying its essence" (OL 85/191, translation modified). And if we are to do this, to hear language "bring itself to language," we must find a way of rendering it foreign, so as to experience its withdrawal. It is at such moments that the linguistic nature of language will open itself to human hearing.

To experience this withdrawal of language into itself, Heidegger starts from the observation that we experience the withdrawal of language "when we cannot find the right word" (OL 59/161), recalling the broken equipment of *Being and Time,* which discloses the structure of relations that otherwise remain inconspicuous. However, in a gesture that directly echoes that of the overcoming of this analysis of equipmentality in "The Origin of the Work of Art," discussed in Chapter 1, Heidegger suggests that this is insufficient to grasp the withdrawal *as such.* For in such instances, the withdrawal of language does not enter into speech; and yet we wish to bring our own experience with language *into language.* There is, however, one instance where "everything depends on whether language gives or withholds the appropriate word": poetry. Dependent on language's movement into verbal articulation, and continually attempting to trace this movement as the enigma of his or her own artistic medium, "the poet . . . is compelled . . . to bring to language the experience he undergoes with language" (OL 59/162).

The poet becomes an exemplary figure for a thinking that wishes to grasp the withdrawal of the very language it inhabits. However, the significance of poetry for these lectures reaches beyond the poet's status as exemplar. If Heidegger initially turns to "the case of the poet" because the poet would attempt to articulate the experience of language's withdrawal, and therefore bring this withdrawal to speak, he subsequently justifies his turn to poetry by arguing that poetry, as a mode of saying, can bring thinking to stand outside itself. This has two, interrelated features. Firstly, thinking must, if it is to undergo this experience, give itself over to receptivity. As Gasché notes, this means that, while remaining a "thinking experience," "thinking . . . is not to be determined from itself";[13] but rather, "what thinking is and what it is to achieve" becomes "dependent, as it were, on thinking's neighbour, its other: poetry."[14] And secondly, thinking must, from within language, find a means of experiencing language as other, as foreign. The constitutive foreignness of poetry to thinking affords thinking a foreignness *of* language from *within* language. In both instances, it is as thinking attends to the displacements impacted upon it by poetry within language, that it can undergo an experience with language. Poetry brings thinking to encounter its own limits, to experience its own *ecstasis* within the language it inhabits. To "undergo an experience with language" necessitates the preservation of poetry.

What, then, is this peculiar relation between *Dichten* (i.e., a gerundive *poiesis* rather than an abstract concept or body of poetic writing) and *Denken* as modes of inhabiting language; and, moreover, how can these two first find themselves in relation? For this he returns to the series of cognates around the verb *reissen* which plays a central role in his tracing both the artwork's "fixing into place" the strife of earth and world in its *Gestalt,* and the movement through which the linguistic essence of language articulates itself in speech. Thinking and poetizing, Heidegger argues, are

> in virtue of their essence held apart by a delicate yet luminous difference, each held in its own darkness: two parallels, in Greek *para allelo,* by one another, against one another, surpassing one another each in its fashion. Poetizing and thinking are not separated if separation is to mean cut off into the non-relational. The parallels intersect in the in-finite. There they intersect [*schneiden sie sich*] with a section [*Schnitt*] that they themselves do not make. By this section, they are first cut, that is, engraved [*eingezeichnet*] into the incision [*Aufriß*] of their neighbourly essence. This design [*Zeichnung*] is the rift [*Riß*]. It wrests [*reißt . . . auf*] poetizing and thinking to their reciprocal nearness [*Nähe*]. (OL 90/196, translation modified)

The *Aufriß* is a "cut" that does not *cut off,* but rather, as it were, *cuts out:* it traces the outlines of *Denken* and *Dichten,* "delineates" them as Fynsk puts it,[15] but does so only on the basis of a prior tracing or delineation, that of the neighborhood in which the two first become discernable as what they are. *Aufriß* is elsewhere deployed to describe the "unifying element" of linguistic essence, and the sketching of the "intimacy" of earth and world in the artwork; here it brings the *Dichten* and *Denken* into "nearness" (*Nähe*). There is a danger of transforming *Aufriß* into a generalized concept, at the expense of each of its singular instances; nevertheless we can remark that on each occasion Heidegger is trying to think alongside one another the differential structure of beings' autodisclosure and that which conditions and secures such autodisclosure by opening up a space of articulation—as jointure, unifying element, or nearness—in which difference comes to manifest itself *as* difference. What is at issue is how to conceive of a differential movement that never becomes nonrelational.

It is for this that Heidegger will then trace this articulation of the neighborly separation of poetizing and thinking back to that originary setting-into-relation, *Ereignis:* "The nearness, which nears, is itself the *Ereignis,* out of which poetizing and thinking are referred towards the proper (*das Eigene*) of their essence" (OL 90/196, translation modified). This "proper" nearness that binds poetizing and thinking together, that opens up a shared space they will inhabit, is at the same time that which articulates the limits between the two. And it is this, finally, which permits thinking, in turning to poetizing to confront and gauge its own limits, to think that which conditions and renders possible such limits, but which remains, strictly speaking, beyond the limits of thinking as such.

Translating Our Thinking

Thinking can enter its own ecstasis only as the language it inhabits is rendered strange, only as it starts to trace the withdrawal of language from within this language; this motivates and pervades its encounter with poetizing. The two coinhabit the "proper of their essence" uncannily because, while both take place in language, the ways in which they employ language are foreign to one another. The task for thinking is to attend to this foreignness without thereby assimilating it into its own language: to read poetry is thus to engage with the exigencies of translation.

This exigency is not, in fact, restricted to his readings of poems, but extends to his encounters with Heraclitus, Parmenides, and Anaximander. Speaking of Anaximander's fragment, Heidegger argues that for translation to take place requires that "our thinking is translated" into the language and thinking of what is to be translated (OBT 247–48/303). He continues, "to make this thoughtful translation to what comes to language in the saying is to leap over a gulf," a gulf "wider and deeper" than the two and a half millennia separating the fragment from our "hearing" it because, belonging intimately to the fragment's "*unsaid*," "we stand right on its edge" (OBT 248/303). Once again, the abyssal nature of translation is inextricable from the proximity and mutual belonging of translation and original.

Heidegger's translation of Anaximander translates both from Greek to German, and from one historical epoch to another, but remains within the domain of thinking. He identifies an equivalent kind of translation within poetry, when Hölderlin translates Pindar and Sophocles. However, whereas Hölderlin did produce translations of particular works by these two poets, Heidegger argues in his lecture series on "Der Ister" that a project of translation finds its most compelling articulation in the late "river hymns," as it is here that we find Hölderlin's most concerted attempts to work out the challenges these two poets had posed him. In order to reach his "own" (*Eigene*), Heidegger argues, Hölderlin must expose his poetizing to a poetry that stands at the beginning of the history into which Hölderlin would enter; through these hymns he probes the earlier works so as to claim them for himself as an uncanny origin. Only as he confronts an "original" that is (linguistically and historically) foreign to him, and seeks to preserve this foreignness in his own language and thinking, can he articulate his "own." Uncanniness becomes the fundamental condition of the "proper." It is thus that Heidegger will intone: "Tell me what you think of translation, and I will tell you who you are" (IH 63/76).

The kind of translation involved in preservation is far removed from "the best critical edition" that would domesticate the work (OBT 19/29); rather, the translator seeks to translate *themselves* and their own, historically conditioned, language into the thrust and foreignness of the original.[16] Heidegger specifies: "Translating [*Übersetzen*] is not so much a '*translating*' [*Über-setzen*] and passing over into a foreign language with the help of one's own. Rather, translation is more an awakening, clarification, and unfolding of one's own language with the help of an encounter with the foreign language . . . an encounter with a foreign language for the sake of appropriating one's own language (IH 65–66/79).

The translation renders possible an "unfolding of one's own language" that is only opened up through an exposure to the foreign. Hölderlin would "appropriate" his own language insofar as his encounter with Sophocles opens up a repertoire of expressive possibilities within his German poetic idiom that had hitherto been unavailable. It is as Sophocles's work is internalized into a series of inflections within a wholly original poetry that it becomes "actual" for a new historical epoch.

How are these inflections to be seen in the poetry itself? Heidegger's own analysis of Hölderlin remains to a large part at a thematic level, and yet he is aware that one of the features from the Greek that helps Hölderlin to appropriate his own language lies in Greek versification. Such appropriation would extend beyond the assimilation of "artistic rules," the techniques of Greek versification, to touch upon "the essence of poetizing in an originary and essential sense" (IH 123/153–54). Yet it would not forego verse technique altogether: poetic preservation should be understood as a historical reactualization of the possibilities opened up by such technique, without reducing it to an exercise. It has been argued convincingly that Swinburne's translations of Baudelaire, for instance, subsequently seep into the texture of Swinburne's own poetry as a kind of "translation by treachery, foreign infiltration, poison fed into the veins of the native language, whereby the native language is an unwitting instrument of its own contamination."[17] Yet where Clive Scott speaks of "infiltration" and "contamination," Heidegger envisages an uncanniness and passing through the "foreign" lying at the crux of a poet's appropriation of their own language, and transforming this language into a site in which an encounter with beings can take place and be articulated. And this does not need to be a translation from one language to another (Ancient Greek to German; French to English). We might think of T. S. Eliot's adoption of prosodic motifs from the early seventeenth-century "metaphysical poets" as a means of constructing a free verse that remains metrically taut and highly sensitized to the shocks and disjunctures of early twentieth-century experience. In this, the prosody of Donne, Cowley, and others is not simply being replicated, but recast and transformed—as is, conversely, the twentieth-century vernacular as it confronts such rhythms. Here, the "artistic rules" are not simply *con*-served, but *pre*-served, and thereby directed toward a transformation of our experience with language, and indeed with the rhythmicity of our encounter with beings.

In the shifting accentual patterning of "The Waste Land's" iambic lines, the tonal equivocations that will pervade Swinburne's ballads, or in the counter-rhythms of prosodic units cutting against metrical lines that characterize Hölderlin's inhabitation of Pindaric forms, these poets do not "poetize something identical" to the poets they preserve. Yet, taking up and preserving this poetry, and, as it were, reactualizing it, the two poetries encountering one another at these junctures "say the Same" (IH 123/153). This "Same," while indicating a shared experience in the fabric of their poetry, would not refer exhaustively to all aspects of the poetry. When Eliot, for instance, adopts the "metaphysical poets" for his own modernist project, he only appropriates those prosodic inflections, and broader motifs (notably that "a thought to Donne was an experience; it modified his sensibility"[18]), which are germane to his own poetic project. A preserving translation does not in this respect claim to be exhaustive, nor that its "Same" is a total adequation, but rather takes this shared experience as an illumination, a starting point. It is in this respect that its own language comes to be marked by the co-belonging difference that characterizes the relation between original and translation, created work and preservation. In this, the element which allows the later poem to inhabit its precursor is based on constitutive difference; once again, we find a shape of thinking that elsewhere Heidegger has approached through the verb *reissen* and its cognates.

If this co-belonging difference is first of all characteristic of a "poetic dialogue" between languages and historical epochs, it would also demonstrate that all "coming to be at home is . . . a passage through and encounter with the foreign" (IH 54/67). Poetic preservation transforms the way we should think the "proper" and the "same." And if the uncanny homeliness to which Hölderlin's hymns attest points to something characteristic of human historicity in general, then we need to think, Heidegger argues, this historicity as such. Not only is it the case that "the poetic meditation on becoming homely must also for its part be of a historical nature and, as poetic, demand a historical dialogue with foreign poets" (IH 49/61). This historical dialogue inaugurated within poetry must subsequently be preserved by thinking.

And yet, this poses a problem. For, as Warminski has noted, Heidegger's interest in the dialogue is directed toward the "law [of] coming to one's own" that his own preservation will outline as the "law of history." But then it transpires that this dialogue is but one instance of this law.[19] Harries has lamented that Heidegger's readings, by narrowing their focus thus, are "too one-sided to do justice to the different ways in which we are claimed and moved."[20] This points to a wider worry. Heidegger warns against an exegesis that "would have reduced poetry to the servant's role as documentary proof for our thinking" (OL 63/166), because our extracting a paraphrasable content from the poem would obstruct the attempt "to undergo an experience with language." But just because poetry has not furnished documentary proof does not mean that it does not still assume a "servant's role": indeed, *Dichten* still permits thinking to "undergo" its "experience with language." Each turn to poetry is motivated by an attempt by thinking to confront its own limits, and so poetry becomes that which facilitates this "necessity of thought." Indeed, there is no little irony in the fact that poetry, by virtue of its resistance to an equipmental or instrumental determination of thingliness or linguistic meaning, is *instrumentalized* by the very thinking that wishes to think beyond equipmentality and instrumental thought: it becomes, that is, the instrument of choice for thinking's ecstasis.

But there is another aspect to this. If poetry is grasped as that which can be used by thinking as an instrument to allow thinking to confront its own limits, then poetry is domesticated after all—it becomes thinking's instrument. But if it becomes thinking's instrument, it cannot open thinking up to the radical uncertainty necessary for it to experience its own ecstasis. I will return to this point below: if poetry genuinely does bring thinking outside of itself, then *thinking will not be able to characterize the way in which this happens.* In this respect we might expect to discover that the ways in which poetizing takes thinking outside of itself are not the same as those Heidegger claims. We may well indeed find ourselves in a paradoxical situation in which, if Heidegger's readings are to respond to the exigencies of preservation, they must contradict his own presentation of their relation to the poems they read; that they do not "submit to the displacement" in the way Heidegger claims. Indeed, were Heidegger to be able to grasp this displacement in advance, his thinking could hardly submit to it.

■

At this juncture of the "Ister Hymn" lectures there are several different strata at which preservation is taking place. Hölderlin preserves the work of Sophocles through his dialogue, both in his translations and in the late hymns. Heidegger offers a translation of Sophocles, to preserve not only Sophocles's ode but also Hölderlin's translation and hymns. It is Hölderlin's preserving translation that affords Heidegger a point of entry into the thinking of the human taking place in Sophocles's ode which he aims to preserve; and conversely, this ode that facilitates Heidegger's preservation of the "home" and the "foreign" in Hölderlin's late hymns. Only as he preserves the poetic dialogue between Sophocles and Hölderlin themselves can he preserve the two poets and vice versa. He performs a reading of a reading, a translation of a translation, standing within and listening to the dialogue as it takes place, and thereby continually setting this dialogue to work. What I would like to suggest is that this approach might furnish us with a means of reading Heidegger's own readings. That is, by reading Heidegger's preservations of poems through those moments where his reading is in dialogue with the poem, at those points of intersection between the two, we can see how his readings negotiate the constitutive foreignness of the poem to Heidegger's own thinking, as this thinking seeks to stand within the poem, respond to it, and to project out from within it. Yet to do this we must ask in greater detail how these readings proceed, and, if they are not exegeses, how they thematize the foreignness of the poems they encounter. These are the questions I will pose in the coming section.

Heidegger's Reading Practice

By approaching Heidegger's readings of poets and poems as preservations rather than exegeses, we can cast new light on the oft-repeated charge that the readings are unfaithful to what is taking place in the poems he reads, and in particular, that Heidegger's readings impose on them a thematic and formal unity that they themselves resist. Fóti, for example, notes that the "intellectual constructs" of Hölderlin's late work demonstrate a "tenuous (and changing) character," whereas Heidegger "literalizes the poet's task of preparing a historical site for destinal transformation."[21] Fynsk voices a similar worry: "Hölderlin . . . consistently questioned in his later poetry the possibility of achieving a measured poetic saying like the one Heidegger ascribes to him and to Trakl."[22] These complaints echo Derrida's admonition that Heidegger has "always . . . skewed the asymmetry *in favor* of what he in effect interprets as the possibility of *favor* itself," and just as Derrida aligns such "favor" with "the accord that gathers or collects while harmonizing (*Versammlung, Fug*), be it the sameness of differents or of disagreements [*différends*], and before the synthesis of a system," what is at issue for these readings is Heidegger's apparent need to overcome the radical negativity of the poems he reads, and at the same time to overcome, or flatten, any potential discrepancy between these poems and the reading he gives.[23]

This suppression of thematic strands coincides, Fóti, argues, with Heidegger's "distressing tendency to neglect *lexis*";[24] and de Man similarly complains that Heidegger "ignores altogether all matters of poetic technique that had certainly been of great import to Hölderlin."[25] What is striking about these complaints is how Heidegger's refusal to read the *thematic* negativity of Hölderlin, Trakl, and others, leads him to ignore the *formal* aspects of these poems. For Fóti and de Man, it is at the formal level that these poems would then resist the readings Heidegger wishes to give of them. Yet this implies not only that Heidegger's readings are exegeses, but also that exegesis, even when concerning itself with "lexis" and "technique," is itself a kind of hermeneutic reconstruction. What I wish to argue in the following pages is that the shape of Heidegger's thinking takes a different direction, and responds to different demands; to deem his readings unfaithful is to expect of them something to which they do not pretend, but also to distort the way he reads.

Exegesis and Preservation

Indeed, Heidegger's thinking actually challenges a central motivating assumption behind many of these criticisms, namely that the defining characteristic of poetry is its resistance to semantic closure, a closure that reading, and especially philosophical reading, continually attempts to impose. Allen characterizes Heidegger's encounter with poetry thus: "For Heidegger the task of the language of philosophy was to articulate the meaning of being, but his encounter with poetic language has shown that this meaning can only be brought to language as a rupture, with which we can have no relation insofar as it severs all relation."[26] "Poetic language" institutes a world of nonrelationality, it resists, refuses, and withdraws from meaning as a stable, closed system; its measure and equilibrium is "always unstable and deferred."[27] Similarly, when Fóti complains that Heidegger, in his readings of Trakl, ignores the "poetic resources" through which Trakl "safeguards the enigma of manifestation," she suggests that such "resources" include "the juxtaposition of antagonistic figures and imagery without mediation and resolution, constant shifts of perspective which frustrate any effort to locate and define the figures, and a heightening of ambiguity through the use of tenuous subjunctive constructions and of conjunctions which convey uncertainty or plural possibilities."[28] But if these resources—irresolution, uncertainty, plurality, dislocation, indefinition—attain their effect as they "frustrate any effort" to situate the poem's figures and resolve its tensions, this implies that reading is nothing other than the "effort" to defuse this poetic play and institute a determinate and univocal meaning. This conception of reading is somewhat dubious, and indeed bears striking resemblance to the calculative thinking that tries to see inside the rock by breaking it open, only to see yet more surface (OBT 24–25/35–36). It may well be that when poetry is faced with such a mode of reading, it will resist and withdraw from it. Yet this seems more a function of the kind of reading at issue than of poetry itself. When Heidegger suggests that to attend to the artwork requires a thinking that will *see* the enigma without attempting to *solve* it (OBT 50/66), it would seem that he is articulating a mode of reading for which the poem's resistance to determinate meaning would not be experienced as frustration. Fóti's model of reading is one that reflects on its attempts to solve and calculate, but it is only within the framework of calculative thinking that these "poetic resources" attain their effect.

Just because Trakl's "poetic resources" resist a calculative reading, that is, does not entail that we should grasp them exclusively in terms of resistance to calculation, so that their defining feature should become their capacity to impart epistemic frustration or blockage. Rather, we should ask how they might engender, and inhabit, an openness of beings—what Fóti calls "the enigma of manifestation." As we have seen in the last two chapters, Heidegger's great insight is that such openness is not simply semantic but issues from a linguistic articulation in which the body is always already engaged. Indeed, it is striking that whereas Heidegger situates the "ambiguity" of Trakl's poetry in its "tone" (OL 192/75), the resources to which Fóti refers are emptied of this bodily dimension—cadence, prosody, rhyme—entirely. By remaining within the framework of calculative thinking, the poem becomes an exclusively hermeneutic, or antihermeneutic, phenomenon.

It remains to be seen, of course, whether Heidegger's own readings do justice to this bodily dimension; I will discuss this below. Before this, however, I would like to look in greater detail at Heidegger's purported ascription of closure to the poems he reads. I have argued that the criticism that Heidegger disregards the indeterminacy of the poems he reads is based on a questionable conception of reading; this critique also assumes that, if Heidegger is searching for a formal or thematic unity while reading a poem, he is thereby making the exegetical claim that such unity belongs to the poem itself. But if we approach the readings as preservations, aiming to "stand within" what the poems open up and project from out of this open, rather than as exegeses of them. Heidegger would respond to the poems as they challenge, and call for, thinking.

This would fundamentally shift our understanding of the relation between poem and reading. For instance, Avital Ronell takes the resistance of Hölderlin's "Andenken" from Heidegger's purported appropriation to say: "There will be no gathering home, even if the poet has projected a homeward turning"; Heidegger's inability to read this shows how the poem—and, by extension, poetry as such—has "trumped" Heidegger—and, by extension, "theory."[29] Ronell too approaches poetry through its epistemic negativity, resisting resolution of whatever kind ("gathering home" here attains a symbolic breadth). But she also neglects to ask whether this "projection" of a "homeward turning" that in the poem is left incomplete might in fact be what demands *preservation*. It is in this respect that Heidegger will feel that his "elucidations . . . spring from a necessity of thought" (EHP 21/7). Maybe this is how we should understand de Man's wry quip, "*Hölderlin says exactly the opposite of what Heidegger makes him say.*"[30] Heidegger would be attending to a thinking that takes place in the poem's tensions and lacunae as much as in any "measured saying" it might contain. Far from being a unified, unchanging whole, it is in its very inconclusiveness that the poem calls for the project, and projection (*Entwurf*), of "thinking preservation."

Textual Strategies

If this might appear as a simple and dogmatic defense of Heidegger's reading practices, my purpose here is in fact double. Firstly, I wish to note that many critics have taken issue with Heidegger on false premises, dismissing his readings without attending to what these readings are trying to do, and as a result missing their target. One is more likely to find a satisfying outlet for venting the many frustrations that Heidegger's readings provoke if one reads him on his own terms; if not, such criticisms can, as Warminski warns, easily "wind up being only so many refusals to read."[31] And secondly, these criticisms, overlooking the thinking behind reading as preservation, and the model of language as bodily articulation, are equally deaf to the real interest of Heidegger's work. A far more productive question would be to understand the demands that Heidegger makes of reading, and then to ask to what extent he himself lives up to these demands. This will be the approach that the rest of this chapter will take. Just because, in other words, we cannot evaluate Heidegger's readings on the criteria that would deem them successful, let alone "correct," exegeses, hardly means that we should not evaluate them at all. In short, to constitute a preservation Heidegger requires that the "sounding-out" (*Erläuterung*) does indeed submit itself to the poem and "stand within" its estranging force.

It is in this context that one should approach the reading practices that characterize his lectures on Hölderlin, George, and Trakl: his attention to individual figures; his onus on "hearing" the poem's intonation; his open disregard for poetic form. Before subjecting individual readings to scrutiny, I would like to discuss Heidegger's reading practice at a more general level. In a powerful critique, Kathleen Wright identifies four "textual strategies" that Heidegger employs in his first lecture course on Hölderlin's late hymns, which serve, she contends, as a means of endowing the hymns with a proto-Nazi gloss.[32] These "strategies" are (1) "to fragment the textual unity of 'Germania' by reading into it fragments drawn from Hölderlin's letters and poems"; (2) "to alter the tone or mood of the poem"; (3) "to disregard the tropology of the poem both by denying that Hölderlin maintains a distinction between the figurative/fictional and the literal/factual and by reversing the meaning of images," and (4) "to regender Germania by substituting a masculine for a feminine voice."[33] Although Wright's concern is with the 1934–35 lectures on "Germanien" and "Der Rhein" (the feminine and masculine voices of which Wright speaks), and Heidegger's readings have changed markedly by the time we reach the lectures that constitute *On the Way to Language,* this does not diminish their pertinence, as the features Wright identifies endure throughout his work. If it does transpire that Heidegger reads not only *opportunistically* (turning to a motif knowing that it will facilitate his argumentation) but also *strategically,* that is, employing certain techniques to ensure that his reading takes the direction he intends it to, then the claim that he is "undergoing" the poems, and engaged in an ecstatic standing-within, would appear somewhat disingenuous.

We have already seen the importance of figures, and the figurative-literal distinction, for Heidegger's readings of Hölderlin; and I take the fourth claim, about Heidegger's imposition of masculinity on Hölderlin's poetry, to be an extension of the third, insofar as it is organized around the question of trope in that "masculine" and "feminine" voices are taken to be indexes of a series of metonymic relations between figures and gender types, in which, for Wright, even the gender of nouns attains a political valence. As a result, I will focus on the first two "strategies": Heidegger's fragmentation of the poem and his attempts to alter the poem's tone or mood.

These two features in fact coincide in the prelude Heidegger gives to his lecture on "Hölderlin's Earth and Heaven": "If what Paul Valéry says of the poem is true: 'the poem—this prolonged lingering between sound and sense,' then the listening to the poem, and even the thinking which prepares such listening, lingers even longer than the poem itself" (EHP 176/153). This is, at first blush, a reiteration of the thesis on preservation:

thinking must prepare for the listening of the poem if it is to stand within the openness the poem renders possible, and furthermore, as the actualization of the poem, it will continue to "linger" as long as it continues to inhabit this openness, that is, as long as the work remains "at work." The poem, moreover, is now no longer simply a "textual unit": it has been reconceived as the matrix of this unit and its "listening" preservation. The very conception of the "work-character" of the artwork as lying in the ways in which it engages and demands preservers breaks the unity of the created work. Yet here, Heidegger is moving beyond the account of "creative preservation" found in "The Origin of the Work of Art": the poem-listening nexus has attained a "mood," it "lingers" (*zögern*), just as does the subject experiencing aesthetic pleasure in Kant's theory of judgments of taste.[34] Heidegger, then, wishes to ask what "lingering" might mean if, rather than taking it as merely the suspension (Valéry's word is *hésitation*)[35] between these two poles, we think of it as something that attunes and determines them, that is, if sound and sense are seen only to enter into opposition so long as they linger.

This nod toward Valéry's famous aphorism has been taken to mean that Heidegger's readings are "more devoted to sense than to sound";[36] however, I would argue that lingering becomes something like an intonation that cannot be ascribed to, situated in, or even fully explained by sound or sense, and yet pervades the two. "Lingering" would thus accord with those other "intonations" that, we have seen, constitute an enduring feature of Heidegger's engagement with poetry. Along with "modulation" and "tempo," it is one of the central features of "'poetical' discourse" in *Being and Time* (BT 205/162); in the 1934–35 lecture course (the one Wright contests), Heidegger is concerned with the "fundamental attunement" (*Grundstimmung*) that serves both as organizing principle for the poem as a whole, and as the means through which we can come to stand in its truth (GA39 25–28); it is, finally, as "tone" that, he suggests in "Language in the Poem," the ambiguity of Trakl's poetry comes to speak (OL 192/75).[37] In each case, intonation becomes a means of thinking the meaningful phenomenality of poetry while refusing the separation of bodily and linguistic openness into the sensuous and nonsensuous realms. Indeed, we find something similar in an earlier lecture Heidegger gives on Hölderlin's "Andenken," where he discusses the poem's "tonality" of "Greeting." Ronell summarizes: "Everything in the poem—the landscape, the tropes, figures, images—is in the end inflected by the Greeting."[38] Rather than being constructed out of verse and rhetoric, the poem's intonation, tone, or tonality, frames the way in which the cadences of verse form or rhetorical inflection first attain their value.

But would this not mean that Heidegger is able to make arbitrarily pronouncements on an unverifiable "tone" or "mood," which subsequently permits him—*strategically*—to read selectively, according to the tone and mood established in advance? What is striking is how the poem's tone *interacts* with its versification and rhetoric, rather than being posited unequivocally at an ontologically anterior stage. As I have argued throughout, it is only through attending to the ontic that the openness which conditions the ontic first becomes discernable; this attention, and attentiveness, moreover, serve to reframe the limits of this openness. Something similar, I would argue, is taking place between intonation and meter in Heidegger's discussion of two lines from Hölderlin's elegy "Brot und Wein" (strictly speaking a "strategy" of "fragmentation," as it takes place in his lecture series on "Der Ister"). Heidegger is probing one of the central themes of the lecture series: Hölderlin's poetizing of the relation between homeliness and the foreign and uncanny (*das Unheimliche*), and his use of the term *spirit* as the human inhabitation of the holy and the homely. At this juncture, he turns to the following two lines:

nemlich zu Hauss ist der Geist
Nicht am Anfang, nicht an der Quell

(namely at home is spirit
Not at the commencement, not at the source)

Crucial to Heidegger's gloss of these lines is the discrepancy between "commencement" and "source." If "commencement" and "source" mean the same thing (both mean "origin"), then we find that "spirit" is "at home" when it is "not at the source"; the "source," or origin, of spirit, cannot be determined in terms of homeliness, or else we find that "at home spirit is not at home" (IH 129/161). Heidegger then offers a different gloss of these lines, whereby spirit is "at home," and grounds the "being-at-home" of humans, yet "is not immediately homely in its 'at home.'" To read the first "not" as a "not yet," Heidegger argues, requires that we attend to how the lines are "unveiled poetically by the very order of the words and the intonation demanded by it" (IH 129/161). The first *Nicht* refers back to *zu Hauss*, and *am Anfang* qualifies this *Nicht*: at first, spirit is not at home, it is not at the source; the discrepancy between *Anfang* and *Quell* is grammatical as well as semantic. Yet this does not simply mean that, by returning to the source, spirit will be "at home." Rather, Heidegger elaborates, "In the beginning ['spirit'] is 'not at home' 'at the source.' This is why it must first become homely 'at the source,' and to do so, 'spirit' must first specifically go 'to the source'" (IH 130/162). Turning to the source will only render "spirit" "at home" as it constitutes a passage through the foreign.

This is why Hölderlin is, as a matter of necessity, drawn into dialogue with those poets already "at the source"—Sophocles and Pindar—and why this dialogue takes the form of a preserving translation which inhabits their poetry uncannily.

Key to Heidegger's reading, then, is how we hear the first "Nicht" of the second line. One aspect to this Heidegger does not mention (but which, we shall see, is a characteristic feature of Hölderlin's versification and on more than one occasion inflects Heidegger's readings), is the suspension between "nemlich zu Hauss ist der Geiste" and the "Nicht" that follows the enjambment. Indeed, Hölderlin's line ending not only retains the positive statement of spirit's being-at-home, but also creates a parallelism of "Nicht am Anfang, nicht an der Quell." It might thus appear that Heidegger, in arguing that the intonation of the line refers the first "Nicht" back to the previous line, and arguing that "am Anfang" is a temporal qualifier for "zu Hauss" rather than a parallel for "an der Quell," is quite simply dismissing the formal patterning the poem employs at this moment. Yet it also points to the contrapuntal fabric of these lines, that "Nicht" serves as something like a hinge between two different cadences at work concurrently. We might be tempted to approach them in terms of the discrepancy between meter and syntax, "the semiotic sphere and the semantic sphere";[39] Heidegger, by contrast, situates such counterpoint in the lines' intonation as it is engendered by the word order. Moreover, the tension between the phrasing and the metrical movement that suppresses it, through enjambment and the parallelism, would itself reflect the difficulty of thinking "homeliness" through its uncanny relation to its own origin, a difficulty that has been interiorized into the fabric of the poem's sounding.

Hermeneutic Violence

Heidegger's focus on this intonation contour leads him to read against the grain of the poem's meter, not to dissolve the meter but rather to set up a counterpoint of intonations irreducible to a simple tension between metrical and syntactic pauses. Rather than disregarding the intricacies of Hölderlin's verse art here, we could see Heidegger as reading "violently" against it, in order to draw out a feature that would otherwise remain veiled. This would echo his remark in *Kant and the Problem of Metaphysics,* that "in order to wring from what the words say, what it is they want to say, every interpretation must necessarily use violence" (KPM 141/202), and in his reading of Sophocles's *Antigone* in the *Introduction to Metaphysics,* when he explains: "If we restrict ourselves to explicating what is directly said in the poetry, the interpretation is at an end. And yet with this the interpretation stands for the first time at the inception. The authentic interpretation must show what does not stand there in the words and which is nevertheless said. For this the interpretation must necessarily use violence" (IM 173/124). This latter statement is not simply a reiteration of the first. In the reading of Kant, Heidegger is concerned with what the words "want to say" but what they cannot, that in the words which Kant would suppress; in the discussion of Sophocles we find an almost reverse relation: Heidegger searches out something *not* there in the words but which the ode nevertheless says. And this different relation to the "unsaid" brings with it a fundamentally different reading practice.

Kant, Heidegger argues, having recognized the abyssal nature of the question of being as it is opened up by the "Schematism," feels obliged to "shrink back" from his own insight (KPM 118/168). In order to show precisely how this question surfaces and is suppressed, Heidegger, in Anderson's formulation, "tries to *overcome* the language used by those to whom he responds," so as "to forcibly elicit from Kant's writings contributions to the dialogue which is human thinking of Being."[40] Far from breaking the unity of Kant's Critique, Heidegger is insisting on it—even to the extent of rejecting Kant's own attempt to supplement it with the "B-version."[41] By contrast, faced with Sophocles's depiction of the "overwhelming" sea and earth (IM 163/117), he passes by way of Hölderlin's translation of the ode. If in *Introduction to Metaphysics* this is left implicit, it becomes a central strand to his lecture series on "Der Ister" seven years later, in which Heidegger's translation of *deinon* as *unhemilich* is at the same time a translation of Hölderlin's own translation, *ungeheur* (IH 69–71/84–88). In the reading of Sophocles, but not of Kant, Heidegger's hermeneutic violence involves the "textual strategy" of fragmenting the unity of the text, and turning to supplementary material—and, more specifically, the supplement of translation, which, as we saw above, he thematizes as a co-belonging difference. Supplementing the poem, it would appear, is a way of grasping what poem and reading share, how they can say "the same," while remaining attentive to their reciprocal otherness.

Heidegger will quite happily read Kant immanently and even insist on the unity of his oeuvre even when Kant does not; yet faced with Sophocles's ode, he has immediate recourse to supplementary material. The first of these supplements is Hölderlin—another poet, but one writing in German during the epoch of "metaphysics"; the second is a "thinker" from the same epoch as Sophocles and sharing the same language: Parmenides. Each serves as a means of overcoming the foreignness of the ode, the one an intermediary, within thinking, from contemporary German into Ancient Greek, the other, within German, from thinking into poetizing; yet the very fact that Heidegger should appeal to such intermediaries at this juncture implies that his thinking, just as it aims to "stand within" the poem, is in fact denied direct entry. The incommensurability of the two modes of language in dialogue reasserts itself; Heidegger will only *listen* to the poem insofar as he listens to, and performs, the poem's refusal to give itself to his thinking, questioning and listening. The supplementary material is in this respect indicative of a far more generalized supplementarity, and this brings to the fore a central paradox of preservation: Heidegger must remain outside the poem, even as he attempts to stand within the openness it brings about. Maybe, instead of asking how Heidegger fragments the poems he reads, we should turn this question around: how do these poems mark, and even fragment, Heidegger's readings of them?

In particular, I would like to suggest, we find that the foreignness Heidegger encounters in Sophocles's ode is not simply one of historical epoch, language, and mode of saying. Searching for what is "said" in Sophocles's ode beyond the "words" Sophocles employs, Heidegger is drawn, as we saw in Chapter 1, to "the law of motion that arranges the words and verses, just as the *chorei* in verse 336 is placed at the point where the meter shifts" (IM 164/118).[42] Heidegger can only read Sophocles, and indeed, can only set up a violent reading, by looking at how the verse organizes Sophocles's own thinking, just as his reading of the lines from "Brot und Wein" would listen for an intonation that runs counter to the versification but which would also structure this versification. The hermeneutic violence in this respect is not exclusively hermeneutic, as its violence brings it beyond the semantic realm to engage with those aspects of meaning—metrical shifts, intonation contours, counterrhythms—which exceed the framework in which hermeneutics takes place.

∎

However, this poses a problem for Heidegger. When he offers a thematization of the relation between *Dichten* and *Denken,* aspects such as meter and prosody are conspicuously absent. Indeed, *Dichten* is removed not only from *Poesie,* but also from *Dichtung:* it is a mode of *poiesis* in language rather than a linguistic artifact. And yet both instances demonstrate that as Heidegger reads these poems—the ode from *Antigone,* the lines from "Brot und Wein"—he is drawn to confront, but also to depend on, their prosodic texture. Might it then be that the encounter between Heidegger's readings and the texts he reads, the points of contact, intersection, and divergence that characterize this encounter, takes place not within the framework that Heidegger suggests, but also in those aspects he does *not* discuss—namely, at the level of prosody? It would then be as the readings submit themselves to prosody that they exceed a purely hermeneutic framework, and rather grasp the poems' language as it sounds in a bodily articulation. It would be here that Heidegger's readings can start to be considered as preservations in which the poems are palpably and compellingly "at work." This is the suggestion that I will pursue in the next section.

Reading Heidegger Reading

In his account of the *Aufriß* of poetizing and thinking, Heidegger characterizes poetizing exclusively in terms of its significance for thinking: it is that which would allow thinking to think its own limits, and even— tentatively—think beyond these limits. But what features of poetizing would lead to there being a "delicate but luminous difference" between the two in the first place? Indeed, throughout Heidegger's oeuvre we find a striking overlap between what poetizing and thinking are meant to do. In "The Origin of the Work of Art," poetry, *Dichtung* rather than *Poesie,* is a "projective saying" that brings beings to shine and sound. Yet *Dichtung* is not alone in projecting an open encounter with beings; this is precisely the vocation of thinking. But in this case, as Heidegger recognizes in "Anaximander's Saying," "thinking is . . . poetizing—though not in the sense of poesy or song. The thinking of being is the primordial form of poetizing in which, before everything else, language first becomes language, enters, that is to say, its essence. Thinking says what the truth of being dictates. Thinking is the ur-poetry [*Ur-dichtung*] which precedes all poesy [*Poesie*]" (OBT 247/303). What separates *Dichten* from *Poesie* also separates *Denken* from *Poesie.* And conversely, the poetizing of Hölderlin, Sophocles, and others is considered to be a specific kind of thinking, in which we will find articulated a highly nuanced interpretation of the autodisclosure of beings. But if poetizing "thinks," and thinking is "ur-poetry," then it is once more unclear what this "delicate and luminous difference" is.

And yet, when Heidegger says that thinking "is . . . poetizing—though not in the sense of poesy or song," this implies that "the sense of poesy or song" retains a valence for poetizing which it no longer does for thinking. If in both thinking and poetizing "language first becomes language," then only in poetizing does language first become language through an engagement with poetic form. But this means that the distinction between *Dichten* and *Denken* is fundamentally *generic.* That is, what differentiates Hölderlin's "thinking" from Heidegger's "thinking," and Heidegger's or Anaximander's "poetizing" from Hölderlin's and Sophocles's "poetizing," is the kind of medium that language is in each case, and the possibilities of articulation these two media afford. Sophocles can transform his "saying" through a metrical shift; Hölderlin can open up an encounter with the uncanny origin through a counterpoint of intonation contour, syntactical line and metrical line; Heidegger, who does not employ meter, cannot.

This generic distinction is in tension, and even conflict, with Heidegger's own characterization of *Dichten* as that which takes thinking outside itself. And indeed, this is a tension, within Heidegger's work, between the categories of poetics, which would grasp poetry through its technical features, and those of thinking, which would approach poetry through its role in the event of being. In the latter characterization, *Dichten* is not only defined *by* thinking, but *in terms of* thinking. Simon Jarvis has recently argued convincingly that if one asks what poetry is, one ceases to ask "a poetical question" but rather a "philosophical" one. Any semblance of reciprocity within the relation between the two is done away with; "antagonistic cooperation" between the two—a term that, on the face of it, would seem a rather apt description for Heidegger's *Aufriß*—"ceases."[43] Within this "thinking dialogue," *Dichten* resembles an invention of "thinking." Similarly, when the artwork is called an enigma, to be seen but not solved, it is an enigma *for thinking*.

Yet if this is the case, it brings a fundamental problem for Heidegger's account of this enigma, and of the otherness of *Dichten* more broadly: namely, how can thinking both define the relation between poetizing and thinking and yet say that poetizing lies beyond the limits of thinking, withdraws from thinking's attempts to grasp it? If thinking can articulate, and circumscribe, the limits of the relation between poetizing and itself, then this thinking cannot confront these limits, because these limits have, in advance, been assimilated within the limits proper to thinking itself. If *Dichten* is an invention of thinking, then it will not be able to perform the role it was invented for. And if, by contrast, *Dichten* genuinely does bring about an ecstasis for thinking, in other words, thinking will not be able determine what it "is" in advance. This also means that those moments at which Heidegger's readings will submit themselves to poetry as "other" will only take place provided those aspects of *Poesie*—that is, those features that are central to poetic technique and yet the account of *Dichten* overlooks—come to mark these readings. It is to such moments that I now turn.

Reading Thresholds

One way to see this is to look for points of transition, within Heidegger's reading, from the poem's vocabulary and its repertoire of expressive techniques on the one hand, to Heidegger's own philosophical idiom on the other. One moment at which the transition from a poem's vocabulary into Heidegger's own vocabulary is particularly fraught is in the reading of Trakl's "Ein Winterabend" in "Language." The difficulty for this reading lies in how the poem can be said to *name* the harmonizing of the world's "fourfold": earth, sky, mortals, and divinities. How, that is, can Heidegger effect the transition from Trakl's vocabulary, and indeed the lexis of an individual poem, into his own far broader idiom? Fynsk calls this reading "an *exemplary* essay in that it constructs a kind of allegory of poetic language from a reading of Georg Trakl's poem 'A Winter Evening' . . . and does so within the framework of the dialogue between thought and poetry Heidegger pursues throughout [*Unterwegs zur Sprache*]."[44] This, however, is only to make the question of transition all the more fraught: what role could "allegory" possibly have in Heidegger's reading, especially after he has argued that, like metaphor, allegory is one form of "symbolic image" (IH 16/18)?[45]

The reading progresses stanza by stanza. The first stanza of Trakl's poem "calls" things to world (PLT 197/22), the second inverts this movement by calling world to things, and the third, naming the "difference" (*Entscheidung*) between world and things, thereby "gathers the bidding of things and the bidding of world" (PLT 203/28). In the first stanza, we are told that the bidding of "things to world" is complete when the line "wandering ones, more than a few" names "mortals." But why should these "wandering ones" signify "mortals"? Heidegger argues that this is because these wanderers take "dark courses" (PLT 198/23); in which case, the transition from the poem's lexis into Heidegger's idiom is dependent on the metonymic relation between darkness and death, a metonymy characteristic of Trakl's oeuvre as a whole—but nevertheless of metonymy as a figure of style which inflects both poem and reading. In the second stanza, which "bids world to things," Heidegger's "sounding" once again seems grounded in metonymic play. Lines three and four of this stanza read:

Golden blüht der Baum der Gnaden
Aus der Erde kühlem Saft.

(Golden blooms the tree of graces
Drawing up the earth's cool dew.)

Heidegger glosses:

The tree roots soundly [*wurzelt gediegen*] in the earth. Thus it is sound and flourishes into a blooming [*So gedeiht er in das Blühen*] that opens itself to heaven's blessing. It spans both the ecstasy of flowering and the soberness of the nourishing sap. The earth's abated growth and the sky's open bounty belong together. The poem names the tree of graces. Its sound blossoming harbours the fruit that falls to us unearned—holy, saving, loving toward mortals. In the golden-blossoming tree there prevail earth and sky, divinities and mortals. (PLT 198–99/23)

Trakl's "tree of graces" becomes the site of the "fourfold" by virtue of a series of conjunctions and verbal shifts that propel within Heidegger's argumentation. The tree "roots soundly" in the particular earth out of which its roots draw up dew, and, just as "sound" shifts from adverb (*gediegen*) to verb (*gedeiht*), so this earth is transposed, in Heidegger's reading, from this particular earth in which this particular tree has its roots into *earth as such:* that which "is sound." Rooting "soundly" in this "sound" *earth,* the tree itself becomes sound; and, in a further shift, this sound tree flourishes into "sound blossoming." The shifts and slippages developing within the words *earth* and *sound* allow Heidegger to situate in the soundness of both root and blossom the co-belonging of earth and sky. Making use of the polysemy of the German word *Himmel,* the tree's reaching into the sky transmutes into an opening up to "heaven's blessing," and this prepares us for the description of the tree's fruit as the "holy, saving" gift of divinities to mortals. Thus Heidegger can conclude: "The fourfold is the world. The word 'world' is no longer used in the metaphysical sense" (PLT 199/23).

Heidegger's transition from these two lines to his thinking of world, then, makes dextrous use of connotation, polysemy, and metonymic slippage. However, if such word usage takes place in the development of Heidegger's thinking *from* Trakl's lines, that is, if Heidegger's thinking projection out of the lines proceeds in this way, then we are returned to the question posed earlier in this chapter: if the artwork is actualized by the preservation, is the work's truth or content ultimately situated in this preservation? A facetious way of putting this would be to ask: does "world" happen in the lines themselves, or only in the dense linguistic movement of Heidegger's reading of them? It is, for example, striking that Heidegger makes very little of the "graces" in Trakl's trope, which we might have expected to evoke the divinities that Heidegger situates in the tree's "blooming." And in the same spirit we might observe that if earth and sky are joined by the tree by virtue of its having roots and blossoms, then presumably all trees span both the earth's sap and the sky. Is this link only first revealed by this poem; in which case, what about *this poem* engenders such revelation?

Earlier in the chapter I suggested that the truth of the work for Heidegger lay not in the preservation itself, but in the matrix between created work and its preservation. If the reading is to constitute a preservation, then, it ought to be marked by the poem it reads, and its truth will lie not in Heidegger's glosses of individual phrases ("wandering ones" as "mortals," the tree's "sound" roots pointing to a "sound" earth) but in the encounter between phrase and gloss—in the dense linguistic workings of reading and poem alike. So perhaps the feature that catalyzes Heidegger's reading will be Trakl's presenting the tree as the point at which "golden bloom" and "earth's cool dew" meet, which subsequently renders thinkable the tree's spanning earth and heaven. Heidegger focuses on "golden" as "light-giving" at this juncture (involving, one might add, the supplementary material Pindar's ode *Isthmians V,* and the phrase *periosion panton* to facilitate this reading), where light is to be understood as form of presencing, and light-*giving* as that originary appropriation in which beings are first *given* to be encountered: this particular lexical feature then would open up a train of thought wherein what at first appeared to be description subsequently serves as catalyst for the thinking of being, where the interaction of root and blossom, as a jointure of earth and sky, indicates entry into appearance as such, and in which "world" is bid to things. This is even more the case in the German, where *blüht* is the only verb in this line, meaning that the tree drawing up the dew from the earth becomes itself a kind of blooming, so that the poem's deployment of "lexis" is crucial to its rendering thinkable the tree's "blooming" as a site for the co-belonging of the "fourfold." The tree Trakl describes would then constitute what in "The Origin of the Work of Art" Heidegger had termed a *Gestalt:* a point of coherence in which beings enter into appearance in a singular manner. This is not to see the tree as a "symbol" for the fourfold: its movement is one of inaugurating, of opening up thinking, rather than of standing as a sensuous token for an ideal (in this case conceptual) content.

However, we might object Heidegger himself does not deign to give this kind of reading, does not deign to situate his glosses in the lexical density of the poem itself; we simply reconstruct the kind of reading he might have given, but he did not. As Fóti laments, it is not as if we cannot ascribe Trakl's attempts to grasp "the enigma of manifestation" to an identifiable palette of "poetic resources" (even if I would define these resources rather differently than she does). I would like to shift this question somewhat: might we find places in Heidegger's reading where these very features which are left out of his reading *nevertheless* surface, inflecting the reading and demonstrating its dependence on aspects of the poem which he apparently ignores? Indeed, if we are to take his conception of "preservation" as a standard for these readings, then the poem will only call things to world and world to things if these calls are responded to by its reader-preserver; the "dif-ference" of world and things will disclose itself in this singular manner only if the reading is marked by such singularity. This is why I suggested that, in reading Heidegger reading, we should read not only his response, but also the ways in which this response is engendered by the poem—the way in which the tree's "blooming" out of the "earth," for instance, is subsequently thematized in terms of presencing and withdrawal. Reading back from Heidegger's exposition to the lines themselves, one can ask how particular moments mark the transition from poem to preservation. If the poem genuinely does demand thinking, as Heidegger claims, then it will subsequently inflect, and inscribe, the thinking that responds to, and stands within, its demand.

This question attains greatest force when Heidegger turns to read the third stanza. Having called things to world and world to things, the poem now names the very process through which this calling becomes possible. Of particular interest for Heidegger is the stanza's second line, "Pain turned the threshold to stone [*Schmerz versteinerte die Schwelle*]." While "the threshold bears the between," Heidegger observes, "pain rends [*reißt*]" (PLT 201/27). The threshold, both joining and setting apart, becomes *Riß*, once again moving out of Trakl's and into Heidegger's vocabulary: it "calls the difference" (that is, the joining that separates) of world and things (PLT 201/27). Part of this calling of the "dif-ference," Heidegger suggests, lies in the fact that *versteinerte* is the only preterit in the poem. *Versteinerte*, that is, introduces temporal concretion (so to speak) and disjunction into what appeared at first the description of a nonspecific present; what Heidegger does not mention is a second temporal disjunction also taking place with this use of the preterit: namely the extra unstressed syllable that comes with its preterit form. The depiction becomes more tangible as the preterit gives it definition, and is upset (one is tempted to say, "rent," *gerissen*) by the prosodic effect on our experience of time in reading the poem; while Heidegger points to a shift in grammatical temporality, this is registered by the poem in a shift of prosodic temporality. Indeed, the "te" verb ending of *versteinerte* lies on a stressed syllable, emphasizing this change in tense, but also undermining the taut regularity of the poem thus far, as the weak schwa vowel cannot sustain the development of the line's phrasing and meter. This line is characterized by the alliteration of three stressed / ʃ / phonemes, each part of a compound consonant: /Schmer/, /steil/, and /Schwel/, demanding a slower voicing and making the relative weakness of the /te/ even more glaring. The rending of pain is thus directed against the line itself, as *versteinerte* is rent prosodically, just as it would solidify and stabilize the threshold that permits such "dif-ference" to articulate itself.

To see how this line can name a difference that both "rends" and acts as "threshold," where its limits serve at the same time as an articulation, a setting-into-relation, requires listening to a density in the poem far beyond that to which Heidegger's reading gives voice—one in which conflicting prosodic features result in a density that recalls the echo of "thickening" in the word *Dichtung,* famously played upon in Ezra Pound's assertion: DICHTEN = CONDENSARE.[46] The prosodic and figural movement of the poem, its syntax, its employment of verse technique, while notable for their absence from Heidegger's reading, in fact guide and shape it, as it were surreptitiously. The dialogue with the poem might not mention them, but they in fact condition the form, and direction, this dialogue takes. In this, it also furnishes a way of reading the encounter beyond simply asking whether Heidegger's transition from poem to fourfold is exegetically accurate: we come to restage—*preserve,* even—the encounter between reading and poem, but in such a way that the reading itself does not hold monopoly over how to define the terms on which the encounter takes place.

A Measure on Earth

Although the lexical and prosodic features of the poem shape and mark the transition between Trakl's words and Heidegger's gloss, they do not irrupt into the texture of Heidegger's own writing. By contrast, the discussion of Hölderlin's fragment "In lieblicher Bläue" in the 1951 lecture "poetically man dwells . . ." sees him enter into what I want to call a prosodic dialogue with the lines he reads. To see this, one can note in passing the editorial history of this poem, which, as Heidegger puts it rather euphemistically, "comes to us by a curious route" (PLT 211/187). The only extant version of the poem is found in Wilhelm Waiblinger's novel, *Phaëton;*[47] although this was a prose transcription, the original was said to be written in "Pindaric verse," and Hellingrath's Berliner Ausgabe VI (1923) renders it thus. In his lecture, Heidegger refers us both to this edition and to Beissner and Beck's second Stuttgarter Ausgabe (1951, the same year as Heidegger's lecture), which had returned the poem to its extant prose version. Heidegger opts to cite the verse version, so the thinking of measure will pass through an encounter not with the phrase: "Giebt es auf Erden ein Maaß? Es giebt keines," but:

> Giebt es auf Erden ein Maaß? Es giebt
> Keines.

Does it matter for Heidegger's reading that he chooses to quote it in verse? In short, yes. Quite simply, the enjambment of "es giebt / Keines," and the caesura between second and third syllables of the line following it, not only form part of Heidegger's understanding of this poem, but become crucial to the way in which the reading submits itself to Hölderlin's lines.

Heidegger will argue that the reason there can be no measure on earth is that "measure" serves as the jointure of earth and heaven. This means not simply that "earth" alone is not enough to provide a "measure," but also that it is only on the basis of this measure that man can "dwell on earth as earth." Throughout his argument, Heidegger continues the vacillation suggested by the enjambment of "es giebt / Keines," where the "Keines," being suspended momentarily, is evaded briefly, but whose ultimate appearance seems for this precise reason all the more inexorable. To place a negation after a line break is a characteristic gesture in Hölderlinian verse art, serving to open up a counterpoint not only between syntax and meter, but also between competing cadential lines. What is striking in Heidegger's gloss is how these lines are inscribed into the reading with a shock akin to that played by the suspended disclosure of "Keines" in Hölderlin's fragment. His exposition seeks to follow the ineluctable logic of Hölderlin's poetic train of thought, and within this framework, the enjambment-and-caesura dramatizes the possibilities of a measure "on the earth" before withholding such a possibility, its withholding rendered all the more final as its ictus lies at the culmination of a series of metrical and syntactical syncopations.

This finality marks Heidegger's reading (it is here that he finishes his citation of fifteen lines) as the point at which the poem's prosodic movement and that of its apparently inexorable logic are set in conflict. Just as this logic is interrupted, and its inexorability questioned, by the enjambment before "Keines," Heidegger's attempt to draw out the inner necessity of Hölderlin's lines undergoes interruptions and self-questioning, so that the necessity itself only becomes visible or comprehensible retrospectively:

This sky is the measure. This is why the poet must ask:
Is there a measure on earth?
And he must reply: "There is none." Why? Because what we signify when we say "on the earth" exists only insofar as man dwells on the earth and in his dwelling lets the earth be as earth. (PLT 224/201)

Hölderlin, looking at the sky, *must* ask about the measure on earth, and *must* answer "there is / none"; to this necessity Heidegger's response, which he tacitly places in the mouths of his audience as well, is a somewhat incredulous "why?" The apparent inexorability and smoothness of the poem's logic, emphasized by the accumulation, in Heidegger's exposition, of "the poet must . . . he must," conflicts with the incongruity of the conclusion. This is not simply the irruption of Hölderlinian negativity into the Heideggerian "path" to a "new arising" or "measured saying"—indeed, Heidegger's subsequent explanation of the unfolding of these lines, providing a new gloss to the phrase "on the earth," does nothing to soften the strangeness of that unfolding. Rather, it is only through such strangeness that the question of "on the earth," and in particular "dwelling" "on the earth" can come to be thought.

This is in fact a crucial aspect of the prosody of Heidegger's reading here. Just as the relation between philosophy and poetry is often seen in terms of negativity—the poem that "trumps" theory, the "resources" that "frustrate" our reading, a "poetic language" for which meaning takes place as rupture and nonrelationality—the rhythmic or prosodic aspects of language can be seen as in some way antimeaningful, irrupting into and undermining the attempts by thinking to establish an ideal content or signified.[48] Yet what we see here is a far more complex relation between the two. Firstly, the negativity of Hölderlin's *Keines* (and of the *Nicht* of "Brot und Wein") is not simply a poetic negativity against a "measured saying" that Heidegger attempts to extract from it regardless; rather, it is a mode through which Heidegger's reading comes to experience the poem and to articulate this experience in its argumentation. Secondly, as a consequence, we see that prosody itself is not an antithinking, or resistance to thinking, but rather, as the rhythm peculiar to verbal language, a mode in which thinking that itself progresses by attention to verbal language—not just Hölderlin's thinking, but Heidegger's, and not just his thinking about poetry, but his thinking that takes off from the poetry—takes place. The suspension of *Nicht* by the enjambment, in other words, does not simply open up the possibility of a different reading (*es gibt ein Maaß* after all), and thereby play a negative hermeneutic role. Rather, this suspension becomes crucial to how we are to attend to and think the withholding of this measure—a withholding that, as metrical, is necessarily bound by a measure of its own. What Heidegger would expel from this thinking is not the rhythmicity that engenders and exceeds presence, and which pervades our encounter with poetry, but prosody as a category of *poetics* that seeks to grasp this rhythmicity as a feature of the contours of verbal language, which is subsequently employed as an expressive technique within the poem. But it is precisely the *prosodic* texture of Hölderlin's verse—where the enjambment introduces a contradiction, and, followed immediately by a caesura, radically upsets the very forward motion it generates—that allows Heidegger to establish the nonmetrical *metron* which, he will argue, is how we should think the "measure" of poetry (PLT 219/196); prosody, in other words, plays an integral role in the very argumentation that would deem it inessential.

One might protest at this juncture that Heidegger's choice of the verse version is one further example of his opportunism, motivated by an intuition that the rupture that is afforded by the enjambment will facilitate the reading he wishes to give. But if this is the case, then it means that Heidegger is admitting—*pace* his categorical dismissals of "the schemes of metrics and poetics"—that line endings shape thinking, and the "ontological" meaning of Hölderlin's *Dichten.* Whether for tendentious reasons or an ingenuous response to the poem's prosodic movement, Heidegger is effectively according to enjambment a revelatory power, so that the verse structure engineers the kind of thinking that can *preserve* this poem; moreover, this verse feature subsequently inflects the reading that aims to preserve it, as the very suspension it was performing becomes a central feature of the argumentation Heidegger employs. The question as to whether Heidegger is being opportunistic and tendentious, and to what extent, is in this respect a side issue—such opportunism is itself predicated on the supposition that verse can impact thinking, a belief that elsewhere Heidegger so strenuously denies.

The shock that characterizes Hölderlin's poem, both in the suspension of the enjambment and in the unfolding of the train of thought in the preceding lines is a prosodic shock, and when it is internalized into Heidegger's own attempts to "preserve" this train of thought, it retains this prosodic character. The thinking of the earth that the poem sets into work cannot be extricated from its prosodic movement, and this prosodic movement inflects Heidegger's subsequent thinking of "dwelling" on "the earth." If Hölderlin's lines think prosodically, and give themselves to be thought prosodically, then no preserving reading can stand within the openness brought about by the poem without submitting itself to the prosodic movements and countermovements through which the lines unfold, and interiorizing these prosodic movements into its thinking.

How, then, can we identify these prosodic movements in Heidegger's thinking? Allemann and Krell both look to his written style: Allemann sees in Heidegger's syntax traces of the "hard rhythmic jointures" characteristic of Hölderlin's late hymns,[49] whereas Krell worries that these rhythmic jointures are "*insufficiently* hard."[50] Yet Hölderlin's "hard rhythmic jointures" are indeed present in Heidegger's discussion of "Es gibt / Keines"—not only as they inflect the *rhythms* of Heidegger's prose, but also, and first and foremost, as they inhere in the rhythms of his *argumentation.* Given that Heidegger's thinking on language continually resists the separation of the sensuous and nonsensuous, then were these "rhythmic jointures" to be restricted to its "sensuous" side, they would contravene his own insight. When Heidegger encounters the prosodic movement of "In lieblicher Bläue," he responds not through his own prosody, but in the rhythms of his argumentation, and the way this argumentation seeks to render something thinkable—

something like the "fugal" movement into intelligibility that in Chapter 1 saw to characterize his thinking of rhythm. Similarly, the dependence of Heidegger's train of thought on "In lieblicher Bläue" as *Poesie* explains why he should favor one version over the other; yet the argumentation appears deliberate, so that whatever tension there is between poem and preservation is held in check. But there are other points where this tension comes more powerfully to a head; when it does, it surfaces not simply rhythmically, in the way in which beings enter presence, but where such rhythm is registered *prosodically.*

A Rhythmic Reading

Heidegger gives his account of rhythm as "structure" while discussing another of George's late "songs"—"In stillste ruh"—one in which, "with particular clarity" (OL 148/229), we can see such "song" take place:

In stillste ruh
Besonnenen tags
Bricht jäh ein blick
Der unerahnten schrecks
Die sichre seele stört

So wie auf höhn
Der feste stamm
Stolz reglos ragt
Und dann noch spät ein sturm
Ihn bis zum boden beugt:

So wie das meer
Mit gellem laut
Mit wildem prall
Noch einmal in die lang
Verlassne muschel stößt

In stillest rest
Of a musing day
Suddenly breaks a sight which
With undreamed terror
Troubles the secure soul

As when on the heights
The solid stem
Towers motionless in pride
And then late a storm
Bends it to the ground:

As when the sea
With shrill scream
With wild crash
Once again into the long
Abandoned shell thrusts (OL 148/229–30; translation modified)

These are Heidegger's initial remarks after he has quoted the poem in its entirety:

> The rhythm of this song is as marvelous as it is clear. It is enough to suggest it with a short remark. Rhythm, *ruthmos,* does not mean flux and flowing, but rather structure [*Fügung*]. Rhythm is what is at rest, what structures [*fügt*] the movement of dance and song, and thus lets it rest within itself. Rhythm bestows rest. In the song we just heard, the structure shows itself if we pay heed to the one fugue which sings to us, in three forms [*dreigestaltig*], in three stanzas: secure soul and sudden sight, stem and storm, sea and shell [*Sichre Seele, jäher Blick, Stamm und Sturm, Meer and Muschel*]. (OL 149/230–31; translation modified)

Chapter 1 saw Heidegger refigure the question of rhythm around how beings come to "stay awhile" in intelligible experience, suggesting a distinction between this rhythmicity and the prosody of verbal language. Heidegger negotiates these two poles by way of a distinction between the phenomenal movement of words and the "rest" or "stillness" structuring and joining this movement. George's poem also probes the relation between stillness and movement, but presents it in a manner that appears to be diametrically opposed to Heidegger's: the destruction of stillness evokes the vulnerability of man faced with nature, and at first blush we might say that the poem charts this descent, rather than successfully embodied a resting-in-itself, as Heidegger has claimed. Yet Heidegger's central observation about the poem's compositional structure identifies a current within the poem that would counter this first interpretation. The colon at the end of the second stanza draws the second "As when" back to the first stanza. As a result, the poet, bent "to the ground as the storm bends the tree" in the second stanza, becomes "open" for the third stanza, where "the sea thrusts its unfathomable voice into the poet's hearing [*Gehör*] which is called 'the long abandoned shell'" (OL 149/231; translation modified). The colon, Heidegger argues, has engendered an openness to the world (somewhat akin to Dasein's "resolve" in *Being and Time*) in which the sea's unfathomable voice will first become audible, and man's hearing will first be brought to name, as "the long abandoned shell." Moreover, in *Gehör* Heidegger is punning on the "belonging" (*gehören*) that, we saw in Chapter 2, first secures our ability to hear (*hören*) language. If the poem's "rest" is ultimately restored, it is by virtue of its capacity to *name* our encounter with excess, and transform our receptivity toward this excess—and, crucially, to grasp this encounter as *linguistic*.

In this respect we should resist the precipitate conclusion that Heidegger, wishing to impose a unity upon the poem, would return to it the "stillest rest" that in the final lines is for George irrevocably broken, and where Heidegger rides roughshod over poetry's radical negativity and indetermination. Heidegger's reading does not deny the vulnerability George depicts so much as reframe its significance, namely in terms of renunciation. Throughout this short lecture Heidegger is concerned with the final couplet of George's poem "Das Wort":

So lernt ich traurig den verzicht:
Kein ding sei wo das wort gebricht.

[So I renounced and sadly see:
Where word breaks off no thing may be.]

Crucial to understanding the word's "breaking-off" is the "renunciation" that precedes the poet-speaker's discovery. Only when one has "renounced" can one attend to the withdrawal of language, whereby it will condition, or "be-thing" (*be-dingen*), the ways in which beings enter into presence. But, Heidegger argues, renunciation must itself be understood as a mode of saying, rather than "just a rejection of saying, . . . a mere lapse into silence" (OL 147/228). That is, if renunciation is to afford an insight into the withdrawal of language, it must remain bound up in this withdrawing movement. When Heidegger turns to "In stillste ruh," then, he will offer an analogy between the breaking of rest it performs and the "breaking off" of the word that George attends to in "Das Wort"; the "shrill scream" that reverberates throughout our hearing both exceeds language—its voice is "unfathomable"—and yet is an integral mode through which language engages our hearing. In both cases, Heidegger sees George to trace withdrawal and breakage as part of the movement that language is. The stillness of "In stillste ruh" is ultimately not the experience of peace that is shaken from outside, but rather a more fundamental stillness that frames the relation between silence and sounding. As in his reading of Trakl's "Ein Winterabend," this latter stillness only surfaces in language as it is broken; here too Heidegger is offering an allegorization of poetry's tracing of the movement from silence into sounding, and in particular of the way that the "peal of stillness" is only ever heard as a "broken silence."

But what of the poem's "marvelous, . . . clear rhythm?" As we have seen, Heidegger situates it the unfolding of a series of figures: "secure soul and sudden sight, stem and storm, sea and shell." If this might appear to be one further means of ignoring the concepts and reading practices of literary criticism, then prosody is not so easily suppressed; Heidegger mimics, and even condenses, a prosodic and alliterative pattern that reverberates throughout the song.[51] He enumerates the series of figures thus: *Sichre Seele, jäher Blick, Stamm und Sturm, Meer and Muschel:* the pattern of two stressed syllables separated by one unstress creates a kind of syncopation through which the poem both sets up a forward motion and presses back in on itself. Indeed, in order to retain this pattern, Heidegger turns *jäh,* adverbially describing *bricht,* into *jäher,* adjectivally describing *Blick;* this grammatical shift has a prosodic corollary, as the change in case from *jäh* to *jäher* also serves to undo the metrical contraction in George's line. Heidegger's adherence to the poem's prosodic movement would distort its grammatical movement; substituting *jäher* for *jäh* might reproduce the regularity of the poem's prosody but in the same gesture it imposes upon the poem a grammatical stasis. In addition to reading "rest" back into the poem through this openness to the world, his enumeration of the poem's figural movement brings its prosody and grammar to "rest."

This naming, Heidegger concludes, affords us a glimpse into the "be-thinging" (*die Bedingnis*) of language itself (OL 151/232); in the poem, the poet is "brought face to face with the word's mystery, the be-thinging of the thing in the word" (OL 151/233). Once more, Heidegger attempts to effect a transition from the poem's lexis into the vocabulary of his own thinking. However, if the equivalent transition in his reading of "Ein Winterabend" was allegorical, or quasiallegorical, attentive above all to the poem's metonymic power, so that its versification and prosody were suppressed even as they facilitated his reading, here it is on a prosodic level that the encounter takes place: both as the point of intersection between poem and preservation, and—crucially—as their point of *divergence.* We have seen in his discussion of the poem's figural rhythm that Heidegger retains the prosodic pattern characteristic of the poem, but in doing so outlines something like a reverse conception of the relation between movement and rest to that depicted by George. On Heidegger's reading, the poem's texture aims to reestablish the rhythmic intelligibility that was broken with the "stillest rest." In this, I noted, Heidegger's description of the poem's rhythm, which he aligned with its figural development, seemed to internalize the poem's meter; but, paradoxically, this internalization of the poem's prosodic patterning leads Heidegger to collapse, and even contravene, its broader thematization of temporal experience. If this amounts to an "incorrect" account of the poem's account of temporality, it also draws out a powerful and crucial tension within the poem, between its prosodic and rhythmic movements.

As I have shown, Heidegger aims not simply to follow George's account of the breaking of the "stillest rest," but to see in this breaking a more fundamental rest, which will structure the poem's prosodic motion while exceeding it. But when he comes to articulate such stillness, which is experienced through renunciation as a kind of "saying," his argumentation continues to be marked by the prosody of George's poem, and indeed his encounter with this prosody is transformed. Heidegger terms renunciation "the transformation of the saying into the almost concealed roaring song-like echo of an unsayable Saga [*die Wandlung des Sagens in den fast verborgen rauschenden liedhaften Widerklang einer unsäglichen Sage*]" (OL 150/231; my translation). In renunciation, then, George has traced the movement from the preverbal *Sagen* into the poem's speech; in its rhythmic jointure, it renders audible the *Sage* that joins the two together. Yet the prosodic transition central to such an allegory tells of a far more complex encounter between poem and preservation. Earlier, Heidegger's writing had echoed the ebb and flow of George's stress-unstress syncopations; now, by contrast, it exhibits a near-paratactic accumulation of adjectives, culminating in an almost "dactylic" progression of the cadence—*rauschenden liedhaften Widerklang einer unsäglichen Sage*—whose prosodic overflow seems like a release of the tension the poem had built up.[52] Indeed, Heidegger's writing here is remarkably *unlike* George's poem, as though it were reacting against the poem. In the poem, the feet remain for the most part disyllabic, and, even though not punctuated, the line endings also turn back inwards and refuse enjambment, thereby adding a further syncopation between syntactical and metrical lines. The fourth and fifth lines of each stanza have six rather than four syllables, and three rather than two stresses, yet the lengthening of the lines, far from creating momentum, serves as a further level of prosodic containment. If Heidegger is searching for a stillness beyond the broken stillness of the storm that bends the "solid stem" in George's poem, and a rhythmical "joining rest" whose *kinesis* of the poem overcomes the clipped dimeters through which it proceeds, then this anterior level of stillness and jointure is nevertheless registered *prosodically* in Heidegger's own reading; the preservation plays itself out as a counterpoint of these two divergent prosodic palettes.

Heidegger's account of the transformation effected through the poem's figural and rhythmic movement accelerates just as its response to George's poem becomes a release of the tension that the poem continually contains. But this release does not thereby defuse the tension. Rather, against its acceleration lies a countermovement: Heidegger speaks of an "echo" (*Widerklang*) that is at once *fast verborgen* and yet *rauschenden liedhaften*, and there is another "echo" as *Sagen* resurfaces in the oxymoronic *unsäglichen Sage*. This might be seen to unsettle the triumphant tone of Heidegger's "positive claim" for "renunciation" as that which "brings the relation to the word into movement [*bringt . . . in Be-wegung*] toward that which concerns each saying [*Sagen*] as saying" (OL 150/232, translation modified), to the extent that one might be tempted to claim that Heidegger's thinking is undermined, overrun by "the irruptions and caesurae of rhythm."[53] Above I argued against that thinking which would take rhythm to interrupt the construction of self-presence, suggesting that rhythm should not be grasped merely negatively, as antimeaning, but rather as a modality for the construction of meaning and presence; here we can see that the kind of "presence" constructed by such rhythm would be itself inflected with an absencing movement; similarly, meaning will be far removed from an ideal content, but will continually be implicated in the articulation of language in the body. In other words, it is precisely through such irruptions and caesura that Heidegger, at this point, thinks.

However, there is another question one might pose here. Heidegger's reading is attempting to effect a transition from the poem's "marvellously clear" rhythm to a silent rhythmicity anterior to the broken silence of the poem itself. But what irrupts into Heidegger's reading and overruns it is, precisely, *prosody* as a feature of verbal language, and which, when deployed as part of the "linguistic work" of *Poesie,* patterns the "broken silence" into a metrical scheme. In Heidegger's attempt to establish a poetic measure irreducible to prosody or meter, his argumentation was shown to be dependent on the prosodic feature of enjambment; here his attempt to articulate a rhythmic stillness takes place through an assimilation of the poem's prosodic patterning, which is then transformed into a reaction against this patterning—but which functions in the prosodic texture of his own text. The poems' prosodic textures catalyze his readings and demand preservation, and then subsequently irrupt into the preservation in unexpected ways, as Heidegger is forced to confront and to contest the limits of his own thinking.

∎

At such moments, Heidegger's attempts to overcome *Poesie* and establish a pure *Dichtung* are undermined by a dependence on those same generic features of *Poesie*—notably prosody and figure—that he appears to deem inessential. But what is particularly striking is that the very claim that these features are inessential contradicts many of the most powerful insights of

Heidegger's thinking. We have seen him refuse the form-essence opposition, arguing that form and rhythm, far from being decorative ornaments to artworks, are central to their singular presencing; metaphor, similarly, was shown to be not the combination of two entities to indicate a shared resemblance, but rather a means of engaging the limits of discourse in order to think beyond it; and, finally, the originary "way-making movement" of language was set on its way by verbal gestures which are bodily as much as they are semantic. He argues that a preservation of poetry will only "stand within" the poems it reads if it cannot gauge the parameters of such standing-within. For Heidegger to claim to set up a measure that does not engage meter, or to find a rhythm uninflected by prosody, or for him to define the relation between thinking and poetizing, is quite simply for him to contravene his central insights. Reading Heidegger reading, to this extent, involves not only reading the points of contact and divergence between Heidegger's reading and the poem he discusses, but also involves reading Heidegger *against* Heidegger.

But if Heidegger's readings deem meter and prosody to be inessential, as they did trope and figure, then it is perhaps unsurprising that these features should be so integral to Heidegger's most successful preservations: as well as the significance of meter and prosody, we have noted the centrality of metonymy to "Ein Winterabend," and of allegorization to both "Ein Winterabend" and "In stillste ruh." For preservation involves submitting thinking to a series of displacements over which it has no control; were it to have control, it would domesticate the poem anew, and render preservation impossible. Many critics have lamented Heidegger's assimilation of the poems he reads for his "thinking of being," and his refusal to allow different and plural voices within the poems to be heard. On the one hand, this refusal runs counter to Heidegger's model of preservation; but on the other, it also contradicts those moments in Heidegger's readings when we *do* find a plurality of voices, when the reading seems to stage the tension between the direction of Heidegger's *Denkweg* and the prosodic and figural movements of the poem itself. In this, the readings do bear out his account of preservation after all. But this notion of preservation calls into question his later description of poetry as *Dichten*: Firstly, because *Dichten* is formulated as an "other" to *Denken,* and as such is a construction of *Denken,* defined and delimited by *Denken.* Secondly, because the syncopations between Heidegger and the poems he reads, the points at which the encounter between poem and reading is most "at work," take place most strikingly at the levels of prosody and trope that the model of *Dichten* left out.

This leads to one final observation. If we are to read Heidegger *faithfully*—to read his readings as places where the "difference" of things to world and world to things is played out, where the *measure* that exceeds meter is rendered audible, as places that trace, through renunciation, the movement of language into the broken silence of the poem, that is, to read his readings as genuine preservations of poetry—then not only will we read him against the poems he reads, and read the poems back against his readings; we will at the same time read Heidegger against himself, read the processes of his readings against his insights into figure, trope, prosody, and rhythm. It is these insights which constitute Heidegger's most enduring contribution to poetics; and it is these insights which will guide the way we read Heidegger reading so that we can see how, often despite himself, he sets up compelling encounters with the poems in which the poems, as artworks, are thrillingly "set to work."

Conclusion

A Poetics of Limit?

At the end of the last chapter I observed that Heidegger's readings of poetry are not exegeses but preservations, and moreover, that these preservations become genuine encounters with the poems they read only when they are themselves unable to gauge the shape of this encounter. This led to a paradoxical situation in which Heidegger's readings are most compelling when they undermine his own portrayal of them. The first of these observations impacts on how we read Heidegger: if we take Heidegger's refusal of exegesis seriously, we cannot perform an exegesis of Heidegger's readings, but rather the preservation of a preservation. The second observation helps us to flesh this out further: to *read Heidegger reading* means to read *against* Heidegger, and *beyond* him; what Werner Marx has called *Weiterdenken,* the task of thinking further, is necessarily antagonistic.[1] That is, we read his *unthought* just as he seeks to read the unthought of the philosophical tradition, and project off from his thinking as he projects off from the poems of George, Hölderlin, Sophocles, Trakl and others.

I situated this preservation-of-preservation in the contours and fault lines we find when we stage an encounter between poem and reading, attending to both its points of contact and divergence, where the reading is characterized less by the claims it makes than by its lacunae, tensions, and aporiai. In particular I used Heidegger's most powerful insights on poetry—that the form of a poem, as the singular mode in which it presences, is central to its ontological vocation, or that individual figures engage with the linguistic norms at their disposal so as to think beyond the constraints of these norms—as a means of addressing the very *absence* of these insights from his readings. We found that when such insights do inflect the encounter between poem and reading, they do so subreptitiously: Heidegger's unthinking encounter with poetics becomes an integral part of his thinking on poetry. It is thus that we might—co-opting Heidegger's own vocabulary—stand within the possibilities his thinking opens up, not in order to construct a Heideggerian poetics, were such a thing possible, but in order to take his thinking as a starting point for posing those questions, and lines of questioning, that characterize poetics itself.

In this conclusion, I would like to sketch out some of these lines of questioning. First I will revisit some of the central arguments of the book, and indicate how they fit in with other debates in philosophical poetics. Then I will look at how Heidegger's thinking of limit plays itself out in some of the most powerful poetry since the crisis in verse of the 1880s—a moment at which a shift took place in the possibilities of poetry's measure whose reverberations are still felt today.

■

In Chapter 1, we saw that an artwork "sets up a world" when, through its engagement with the limits of its medium, it transforms these limits and thereby transforms the limits of the open region in which we encounter beings. Although my focus was on the supposedly formal aspects of an artwork—metrical constraints, linear and painterly perspective, diatonic harmony—one might identify the same phenomenon at a thematic level, such as when Flaubertian realism transformed what was deemed acceptable literary subject matter. For Jacques Rancière, Flaubert "democratizes" literature not merely by including characters from the rural middle classes, but by rejecting subject matter as a criterion for literature as such: "There is no longer beautiful or ugly subject matter. This does not simply mean, as it did for Wordsworth, that the emotions of simple folk are as appropriate for poetry as those of 'great souls.' It means, more radically, that there is no such thing as subject matter, that . . . the texture of the work lies in style, which is 'an absolute manner of seeing things.' "[2] Like Heidegger, Rancière endows this ostensibly formal shift with epochal significance: it reframes what he elsewhere calls the *partage du sensible,* which, like Heidegger's "open," is conceived as a kind of articulation (his translators offer "distribution" as keeping both the sense of division and of sharing/partaking) that delimits the space of possible experience. However, situating this shift within a history of democratic politics, Rancière's thinking gives an indication of how the historicity of the artwork, which for Heidegger is bound up with the *Volk*'s capacity to set itself up as a "historical humanity," might have pertinence beyond the nationalist overtones the word *Volk* had in 1930s Germany, and might illuminate very different forms of political engagement, which Heidegger himself might repudiate but which we can nevertheless see to be latent within his writings.

And yet, the shift Rancière describes, from subject matter to style and "literariness," does not call into question the form-content opposition as such, nor its attendant model of language. This model of language, and in particular the relation between linguistic meaning and bodily experience beyond the sensuous-nonsensuous distinction, was the focus of Chapters 2 and 3. Heidegger conceives of verbal language as a sounding anterior to the sound-sense split, and this was central to his attempt to grasp an originary *logos* which would first open up the space in which we can address beings verbally. Heidegger then asked how our verbal language usage might in fact transform this originary *logos,* and to this end offered a model of naming as a kind of performative bringing-into-presence. Yet for language to *name* beings entails a second movement, by which language sounds: naming is a self-showing as well as a showing. Language, Heidegger then argues, can only enter presence, and bring beings into presence, if it traces the absencing movement that bounds it, and this involves a revaluation of paralanguage, and in particular the voice. On Heidegger's account, voice is the site of language's "coming to sound" by virtue of its encounter with the bodily linguistic opacity out of which it arises. Voice acts, in other words, as the threshold of sounding and silence.

This, I mentioned, may well seem quite flagrant "phonocentrism", as vocal utterance secures the self-presence of the speaker. And yet, I argued, Heidegger's model of an excess of *phonē* over *logos* should give us pause. In *Speech and Phenomena* Derrida argued that voice facilitated Husserl's institution of self-presence because in vocal utterance we hear ourselves speak, meaning that, even though the utterance traverses the world sonorously and is heard by the speaker-listener as a sonorous, exterior entity, this speaker-listener "can let themselves be affected by the signifier that they produce without any recourse to exteriority, to the world, or to the non-proper in general." Voice thus passes through the nonproper and can be heard there but all the while remains proper to the subject.[3] But by the same token, Derrida counters, if voice did not traverse the world, did not become different to itself, then it could not effect this unique mode of autoaffection in the first place. Hence he will turn Husserl's argumentation upon itself: the basis of self-presence is the difference of *autos* to itself; the autoaffecting subject can only first constitute "the same" by passing through the "non-identical."[4] Derrida's account of voice's institution of difference is in this regard strikingly similar to *Being and Time*'s account of the voice of conscience, which comes "from be and from beyond me," and discloses the uncanniness central to Dasein's being-in-the-world, and thus renders possible a thinking of Dasein's finite transcendence. But in his later work, Heidegger sees the voice specifically as an engagement with an opacity within the human body. Not only would this opacity resist self-presence, but would generate presence only by exacting a radical openness to the absencing movement which bounds it. Heidegger might in this respect be seen to have performed a deconstruction of the voice *avant la lettre*.

As I discussed in Chapter 3, this is crucial to Heidegger's rejection of figurative language, and its carrying over of one linguistic token for another. At this juncture, Heidegger's thinking coincides with that of Gilles Deleuze. In his *Dialogues* with Claire Parnet, Deleuze explains how the "black holes" Guattari was working on merged with the motif of the white walls of a plane or screen that fascinated him at the time, as they realize that "black holes on a white wall are in fact a face, a broad face with white cheeks, and pierced with black holes."[5] Deleuze here is adamant that the result of such collaboration is not a "metaphorical" claim: "we don't say that is 'like' black holes in astronomy, that is 'like' a white canvas in painting."[6] Like Heidegger, Deleuze initially refuses the category of metaphor because it would domesticate an aberrant thinking into mere semblance; and, like Heidegger, this serves as part of a broader attempt to think the human body, and what Deleuze calls "faceity," against a physiological determination: the black holes that pierce the face's white screen become "intensities" of energy.

This, for Deleuze as for Heidegger, is a predicament for poetry as well as for philosophy, and he and Guattari approvingly cite Kafka's journal entry from 1921: "Metaphors are one of the things that make me despair for literature," contrasting metaphor with the "metamorphosis" one finds throughout Kafka's writing (most famously of Gregor Samsa into a giant bug, but also in the many instances of anthropomorphized animals and animalized humans). If "metamorphosis is the contrary of metaphor,"[7] this is because it dissolves the distance between words and the world, so that language is understood not as signification but through its "intensities." Not only is Deleuze's rejection of metaphor thus motivated by a critique of a representationalist epistemology and the model of language as signification, but it also gestures toward a language conceived of as movement, and for philosophical thinking to grasp this movement requires the articulation of "mobile concepts."[8] Yet when Deleuze discusses "tonalities without meaning" and an "a-signifying *intensive use* of language" he seems to reverse the sound-sense dualism rather than overcome it.[9] Here, what

Deleuze and Guattari propose seems similar to the tendency that Heidegger rejects when he proposes that we should trace in voice's capacity "to hover and tremble" the movement of sounding itself; instead of simply preferring tonality to meaning, Heidegger would grasp this tonality as the very opening of meaning.

This concern with the bodily articulation of language does not only find a corollary in recent currents in "continental" philosophy and literary theory. Something similar is being grasped in a figure Paul Celan employs in "Schieferäugige," from the 1967 collection *Atemwende*. The poem runs as follows:

SCHIEFERÄUGIGE, von
der schreitenden Gegenschrift am
Tag nach der Blendung erreicht.

Lesbare Blutklumpen-Botin,
herübergestorben, trotz allem,
von wissenden Stacheldrahtschwingen
über die unverrückbare
Tausendmauer getragen.

Du hier, du: verlebendigt
vom Hauch der im frei-
geschaufelten Lungengeäst
hängengebliebenen
Namen.

Zu
Entzifferende du.

Mit dir,
auf der Stimmbänderbrücke, im
Großen Dazwischen,
nachtüber.

Mit Herztönen beschossen,
von allen Weltkanzeln her.

SLATE-EYED ONE, reached
by the striding counterscript the
day after the blinding.

Readable bloodclot-messenger,
hither-died, despite all,
carried by knowing barbedwire-wings
over the undisplaceable
thousand-wall.

You here, you: quickened
by the breath of the
names
caught in the free-
shovelled lungbranches.

To-
be-deciphered you.

With you,
on the vocalcords' bridge, in the
great Inbetween,
nightover.

Shot at with hearttones,
from all the world-pulpits. (Celan, *Breathturn*, 234–35)

The stanza particularly germane for the current discussion is the fifth one
(ll. 16–19), which, picking up on earlier motifs—especially the "counterscript" (l. 2) and the "lungbranches" which breathe out names (ll. 11–13),
and its invocation of a "you" who is "to-be-deciphered" (ll. 14–15)—sets
up a parallel between the "vocal-cord-bridge" and a "great Inbetween" that
ceases to be merely the space between the vocal cords and becomes a space
for a broader encounter between speaker and addressee. The figure merges
the physicality and the relationality of the address that binds speaker and
addressee: the addressee comes to be situated within the speaker's throat,
and in the same gesture the throat itself ceases to be "proper" and starts
to inhabit, and co-habit, this "between." In this, Celan's lines evoke something remarkably close to what Heidegger identified in Hölderlin's phrase
"words, like flowers": a bodily articulation of language, in which the rising
up of language in the vocal chords opens up relationality as such.

Celan's relation to Heidegger has been well documented, both given
Heidegger's powerful influence on Celan's thinking and poetic practice,
and his interest in Celan's poetry, and as a result of their controversial
meeting in Todtnauberg on July 25, 1967.[10] Yet Celan also stands as a constant reminder of Heidegger's refusal to give any public recognition of
the atrocities committed by the Nazis between 1933 and 1945 and which
culminated in the Shoah, or to explain to any satisfactory level his own
entanglement with Nazism in the 1930s. For precisely this reason, some
critics have asked whether Celan might not offer a possibility for thinking beyond Heidegger. For instance, in "Schieferäugige" Celan does not
simply develop the Heideggerian problematic of a bodily relationality of
language, but adds to it the opening gesture "Mit dir," so that the bodily
articulation is framed by an intimate address, and thereby becomes an en-

counter with the other.[11] If for Emmanuel Lévinas, this engagement with the other amounted to no less than a wholesale rejection of the thinking of being, as the title of his essay ("Paul Celan: from Being to the Other") makes explicit, Krzysztof Ziarek sees the salience of Celan's poetry and criticism to lie in an ethical refiguration of Heideggerian themes. He proposes that we "see Celan's interest in Heidegger as a way of engaging the problematic of the listening of language, which, to use Heidegger's own term, remains 'unthought,'" notably by "exploring why the insights into ethics and politics that Heidegger gains by rethinking relationship to otherness do not compel his writings to respond to the horror of the Holocaust and the atrocities of the war."[12]

If Celan could then be seen to reframe the relation between human speech and the originary saying of language as an ethical relation, between I and thou, there is another aspect of Heidegger's thinking that has points of contact with an "ethics" of poetry. Chapter 4 looked at how notions of otherness pervade the model of the artwork as "creative preservation": the work is "at work" when the created poem, painting, or piece of music is preserved by its audience—when, that is, the audience does not simply appreciate the created work, nor interpret it, but rather "stands within" the open that the work brings about. Similarly, the mutual belonging of thinking and poetizing was grasped as a "luminous difference." A "preserving" reading not only resists exegesis, but, as ecstasis, or standing-outside-oneself, becomes an encounter with alterity. Even if this would for Heidegger remain a "thinking" relation (in which case we can question whether this alterity is in fact a mode of appropriation), then we also saw moments where Heidegger's readings do become inflected by the poems he reads, and in a manner beyond the readings' control, as they confront an otherness that they cannot themselves gauge.

How one might thematize this otherness, and read according to it, has been central to the "ethics of reading" proposed by Derek Attridge. For Attridge, one becomes "responsible for" the text by first of all being "responsive to" its otherness: "Responding responsibly to a work of art means attempting to justice to it as a singular other,"[13] that is, means attending to the singular shape in which this individual work addresses us. Echoing Heidegger's notion of "createdness," Attridge calls this singular shape the work's "inventiveness." Attridge prefers "invention" to "creation" both because of its connotations with originality, so that the "invented" and "inventive" artwork in question constitutes in some sense "a step into the unknown," and because the work only becomes "inventive" through "its reception by the culture at large,"[14] just as for Heidegger the created work thrusts into the open, but also requires preservation if it is to attain its *ale-*

theic power. But it is in Attridge's own "reading performances," where he reads not only the poem in question, but also the way in which this poem addresses, interpellates, and places demands on his reading as it progresses, that his "ethical" approach offers both a means of grasping Heidegger's encounters with poetry through the points of contact and divergence between poem and reading, and of tracing, in our own readings, the ways in which an encounter with a poem is "set to work."

But there is a further significance in the ways in which I-thou relations pervade both the poet's address and the reader's response. In "Schieferäugige" Celan introduces the address to an "other" as a first step to reconciling the poet's vocation of naming with personal intimacy. This I would suggest can be read as a *lyric* gesture as much as an ethical one, and where the "I-thou" address is emblematic of a broader attitude toward the world. Indeed, Celan himself depicts a "poem of a person who still perceives, still turns toward phenomena, addressing and questioning them"; if the poem is thus a conversation, it is a conversation whose breadth engages "phenomena" that cannot be bundled together simply into "the . . . other," but rather embody the sheer diversity and plurality of the world we inhabit.[15] The I-thou address becomes a figure for engaging this diversity, and demanding not simply a responsive reader, but a responsive cosmos: what is at issue is at once an openness to the world and a belief in efficacious speech. In a recent essay, Jonathan Culler has seen this to be the defining feature of lyric as a genre, for which poems "call to be calling, both to display their poetic calling and to mark the belief that language can sometimes make things happen, through acts of naming, highlighting, and reordering, as well as through the instigation of poetic forms that will repeat as readers or listeners take them up and articulate them anew."[16] Taking Culler's model of a lyric that "calls to be calling," hoping through its address to remake the world anew, we might see the hardwon intimacy of Celan's I-thou conversation to form the basis of what Heidegger calls poetry's "projective saying," whereby beings enter the open in a singular and transformative manner. In this respect, Celan's powerfully human address gives on to an address directed to the movement of language itself—a movement that, Heidegger had insisted, is itself "nothing human."

Central to this is the way Celan's poem engages and negotiates a series of overlapping and interlinked limits: between the *ich* and the two forms of *du* the poem addresses, both the *du* figured within the poem and the reader who, while assuming this figure, remains outside it; between the limits of registers, as the I-thou address shifts into a broader thinking that situates the "Inbetween" of language and the "Inbetween" of human interaction in the articulation of the vocal cords; between the physicality of the vocal cords and the opening of the "Inbetween" to which the vocal cords give voice; and between the countermovements of verse and syntax, where the parallelism of "auf der Stimmbänderbrücke" and "im Grossen Dazwischen" cuts against the line endings, something emphasized by the metrical regularity of "im / Grossen Dazwischen," and where the appeal to an addressee, "Mit dir," stands on a line of its own, such that its intensified prosodic weight means that while it inhabits the linkage of vocal cords and the great Inbetween that is opened up and given voice, it is also distanced from them.

And here we might see how the matrix of limits that pervade Heidegger's own thinking on poetry and poetics, and which *Sounding/Silence* has charted throughout, can inform our understanding not simply of these few lines of Celan, but of the repertoire of techniques that poetry more broadly has at its disposal, and its demand to be "sounded out" by its readers. For the poem's engagement with limits is twofold. On the one hand, it engages the limit between address and addressee, and Chapter 4 saw that the limit pervading our encounter with the poem both affords a mutual belonging and demands that, in order for such an encounter to take place, our thinking must step outside of itself and submit itself to the thrust of the poem it encounters. On the other hand, it confronts, and contests, the limits inhering in its own medium. As Chapters 2 and 3 showed, Heidegger probes the limit between the "sounding" of verbal language and the double silence out of which it arises, which inheres at once in the "linguistic essence" of language and in the opacity of the human body. Both poetry and philosophy attempt to think beyond their limits by probing their generic constraints: this motivated both the purported "metaphoricity of Heidegger's text" and his rejection of metaphor, while in "Origin" it led him to characterize the artwork's treatment of its medium as a "contest of measure and limit." That is, as a poem employs and deploys the full breadth of its "measure" in order to confront the limits of its medium, thereby shifting and transforming these limits, it comes to transform the sayable as such. In the next section, I will expand briefly some ways in which the contest of poetry's measure—and what my conclusion tentatively proposes as a poetics of limit—might be seen to take place.

◼

For Heidegger, the contest of measure and limit in the artwork's *Gestalt* leads to a transformation of the open and of the possible configurations of language. In this respect, perhaps the most powerful contestation of limits in modern poetry was the shift from linear to tabular form, what Stéphane Mallarmé described as a *crise de vers* in his seminal essay of that name. This also finds articulation in his poetic practice, most strikingly as *Un coup de dés jamais n'abolira le hasard* employs the page as a typographical space in which the eye attends to an enlarged prosody, and (as Heidegger once said) "bring[s] into view something one can hear." Through this single gesture, a series of meaningful inflexions attains a valence in poetry it had not previously had, transforming the scope of the written mark.

If Mallarmé's project in part stems from a frustration with the *alexandrin* of French meter, it is also motivated by a concern with *hasard* (chance) in language, and the question of how to bring the profusion and uncontainability of language's chance connotations and configurations into a single measure. Mallarmé does not do away with the measure of poetry, but rather refigures it: in place of a metrical frame that will tame this *hasard*, *hasard* becomes the guiding principle for the poem as a prosodic and visual performance. For Mallarmé, this shift in measure will then allow poetry to attain its vocation of "searching, faced with a fragment of great literary rhythms . . . and their scattering in shivers that are articulated into an instrumentation, for a means to achieve the transposition, into the Book, of the symphony or rather to take back what is ours."[17] Mallarmé, like Heidegger, is outlining an *ontologization* of poetry that will bring language back to "its essential rhythm."[18] The "Book" will become a threshold to the "rhythmic motifs of being," by internalizing these motifs into its own texture as "fragment" and "scattering"; for Maurice Blanchot, *Un coup de dés* provides a compelling sketch of a poet giving "measure" to this "immeasurable challenge."[19]

We find this gesture replayed in Ezra Pound's "imagist" statement, "In a Station of the Metro," another poem famed for its iconoclasm:

> The apparition of these faces in the crowd;
> Petals on a wet, black bough.[20]

If the poem is most celebrated for its condensed, laconic description, then this is itself engendered by a highly fraught standoff between metricality and nonmetricality. Later, in his Cantos, Pound would write: "To break the pentameter, that was the first heave,"[21] and here we can see "the pentameter" brought to breaking point. The first line in this two-line poem, tracing an intonation contour from the stressed fourth syllable (appari-tion) to the final stress (crowd), would mimic an iambic line; yet it coexists with an alternative rhythm where each semantic element in the line becomes a prosodic unit, of five, four, and three syllables, respectively. This was the scansion preferred by the first version of the poem, published in the magazine *Poetry* in 1913:

| The apparition | of these faces | in the crowd : |
| Petals | on a wet, black | bough |

Returning from tabular to linear form, Pound not only introduces a syncopation between two possible phrasings, but stages a contest between two
competing kinds of measure. This contest is in either case undercut in the
following line (the "image" the poem gives), where the three stressed syllables of "wet, black bough" impose a stasis that coincides with its focus on
the poetic image as a form of temporality, something further exacerbated
by the caesura between "wet" and "black," which in the 1913 version generates a tension between linear-syntactic and tabular-paratactic forms of
composition. And if the line alludes to James George Frazer's *The Golden
Bough,* then the word *black,* summoning up the grime and smoke of urban
life, insists once more on the poem's modernity just as does its caesura. Effecting a rupture within the poem's prosodic patterning, either in its quasi-
metrical linear version or in its tabular version, the poem confronts *both*
measures that had been set in contest with an implacable prose limit.

Like Heidegger, Pound understood the significance of poetry in epochal
terms,[22] and the shift from linear to tabular verse may also be considered
as a change of epoch. Celan's work, too, is often accorded epochal significance, both for its response to the Shoah and its riposte to Adorno's
observation that one cannot write lyric poetry after Auschwitz.[23] And yet,
when Heidegger reads George and Trakl, he at no point makes the claim
that they are bringing about a shift in the history of being, even if in their
engagement with the limits of their linguistic medium they interrogate the
limits the epoch of metaphysics itself. So what of poetry that is less icono-
clastic and which pursues and develops, rather than openly contests, the
measures the poetic tradition has passed down to it?

To see this, I would like to turn to one of the canonical works from the
middle period of Wallace Stevens, "The Idea of Order at Key West."[24] It
was written in 1934–35, the years of Heidegger's first lectures on poetry,
and its thematic similarity to the account of the artwork Heidegger outlines in these years is remarkable: the woman who stands at the sea's edge
and sings "sang beyond the genius of the sea," engendering in the speaker
and his companion an encounter with the "Inhuman" cry of the "veritable
ocean." This has led Phillip Stambovsky to treat the poem as an allegorization of what Heidegger called "*Werksein*": the sea is a "'self-secluding'
place that the singing sets in relief but never penetrates"; setting it in relief,
"the singer 'sets up' the world of her song"; and the speaker is portrayed as
"striving—making the *work* of art *his* work—to set up the world in which

he and his friend integratively grasp (in the sense of *vernehmen*) the singer's performance as art-work."[25]

And yet, Stevens seems more ambivalent as to whether this poem "sets up a world," and the poem verges throughout between the hope that "It may be that in all her phrases stirred / The grinding water and the gasping word" (ll. 12–13), with its exaltation embodied in its metrical regularity and the culmination of three rhyming line-endings (ll. 10–12, heard/word/stirred), and the more prosaic worry that "The ever-hooded, tragic-gestured sea / Was merely a place by which she walked to sing" (ll. 16–17). Either she is the "maker" of the world through her song, or the maker of the song alone, cut off from this world.[26] This tension reaches its climax in the fourth stanza:

> It was her voice that made
> The sky acutest at its vanishing.
> She measured to the hour its solitude.
> She was the single artificer of the world
> In which she sang. And when she sang, the sea,
> Whatever self it had, became the self
> That was her song, for she was the maker. Then we,
> As we beheld her striding there alone,
> Knew that there never was a world for her
> Except the one she sang and, singing, made. (ll. 34–42)

"Then" (l. 39) is not logical progression, but temporal succession—and indeed flatly contradicts what came before. After saying that "when she sang, the sea, / Whatever self it had, became the self / That was her song," he now introduces a crucial qualifier: it is a "world *for her*." Stevens is thus wavering between the worlding claims that Heidegger will make for the artwork, in which it is the work itself that "first brings forth the light of day, the breadth of the sky, the darkness of night" (OBT 21/31), and a subjective experience of beauty, where the transformation of the world is of the order of private epiphany. After the great claims hazarded in the previous lines, beauty becomes a kind of consolation. This becomes all the more poignant when Stevens's speaker turns to describe a different kind of measure, the lights of the fishing village, which in their own way give "order" to nature as they "portioned out the sea" (l. 49). The sheer disjuncture between the grandly elevating diction—"Fixing emblazoned zones and fiery poles, / Arranging, deepening, enchanting night" (ll. 50–51)—and the phenomenon it is employed to describe turns consolation into bathetic overreach; its keenly felt aesthetic impotence intimates an impotence of the aesthetic as such.

In the final, concluding stanza, Stevens suggests a common source for singer and fisherman:

O Blessed rage for order, pale Ramon,
The maker's rage to order words of the sea . . . (ll. 52–53)

The evocative address makes this an almost speculative statement, and the double genitive of "words of the sea"—either they are words that are "wrested" from the sea by the maker (as Dürer would have it), or they are words that the maker uses to name the sea—once more hints at a possible reversibility of song and world, the mutual making-appropriate that Heidegger called *Ereignis*. Stevens's "rage for order" echoes Mallarmé's attempt to trace the *hasard* of language in poetry; yet whereas Mallarmé set up a dialectic according to which *hasard* is not simply internalized into the poem but becomes its law, for Stevens "order" is aligned with the poem's metricality. As a result, the slippage into and out of strict iambic lines throughout the poem attains thematic significance. When it seems as though the woman's song will—however momentarily—transform "The meaningless plungings of water and the wind" into something "more" (ll. 28–30), it is striking that the syntactically obsolete "the" is added before "wind" in order to fashion a metrical scansion. The appeals to a subjective, solipsistic experience of beauty, by contrast, place meter and phrasing in tension. For instance, in "Knew that there never was a world for her," we not only hear an alternative scansion—"*Knew* that there *ne*ver was a *world* for her"—but also hear the central stress fall on the fourth syllable of the line, where around it the lines' phrasing and meter both cadence at the end of the line. That the word effecting such dissonance should state "never" serves to make it that much more powerful an interdiction on the worlding claims of art.

We could also see this dissonance as insisting on subjective voice ahead of the order of meter; just as Stevens focalizes away from the scene described to address "Ramon Fernandez," his voicing turns away from the collective aspirations of art to embrace a private diction.[27] Yet in Chapter 1 we saw Heidegger identify the sounding of Hölderlin's lines in the prosodic dissonance of its "apparent prose," where the dissonance furnishes not individual expression but the sounding of language as such. Similarly, if the individual voice diverges from the meter, it is also conditioned by it: only thus could this divergence attain its effect. This might suggest an analogy with the claim that subjective experience is dependent on an anterior "open" region; yet I would like to make a different point. In Stevens's poem, the measure is not simply the meter, but the repertoire of syncopations, inflexions, and cadences that are dynamized by the meter, by the turns to elevated diction and intimate address. And this leads to one further point. While the diction and prosody might be said to "mimic" what is said, to "echo" or contradict the sense, I would suggest that something else is taking place in Stevens's poem: adherence to and divergence from metricality are not figures for the poem's order but rather the agency through the question of order, and more broadly of the vocation of poetry, can be articulated and brought to sound. In other words, they constitute the measure through which the poem grasps its predicament, such that the poem becomes *a medium for thinking.*

■

But what of the relation between the poem as a medium for thinking and Heidegger's own account of the relation between thinking and poetizing? What is crucial in Stevens's poem is that whatever thinking takes place does so through an engagement with medium, a *use* that does not *use up.* This was also the case with Celan's "Schieferäugige," which attempted to grasp a bodily articulation of language through possibilities of verbal articulation specific to its own measure, notably its use of address, and the countermovements of syntax and prosody it sets in play. If Celan's poem traces the limits between sounding and silence it is not as a statement but as an engagement with syntax, prosody, address, and so on. In both cases, we find a striking overlap between Celan's and Stevens's concerns and those of Heidegger—for Celan, the bodily articulation of language, for Stevens the "maker" who strives for an art that will transform and not simply describe the world. But for Celan and Stevens, and not for Heidegger, categories such as prosody, trope, and address, can become the motors of their thinking. If Heidegger's thinking might therefore inform our readings of these poems at a thematic level, and illuminate what is at stake in the poems' arguments, then its greater significance will ultimately lie in grasping how these arguments take place through their exploration of medium: where the "between" of the vocal cords is established as the poem utilizes the possibilities of our own vocal cords, and the description of the maker's "rage" to "order words of the sea" has already intertwined words and sea through its grammatical reversibility—a reversibility that inheres within the words themselves.

And this leaves one final question. When faced with the obvious thematic overlap between Stefan George's poem "Das Wort" and his own account of language, Heidegger warned against reducing "poetry to the servant's role as documentary proof for our thinking." How would one prevent the poems of Celan and Stevens I have discussed from being relegated to such a servant's role? Above I noted that Stevens himself ultimately seeks consolation in private epiphany, and yet he evinces hope for a thinking in which beauty is no longer consolation but rather effects the very transformation of experience he feels unsure of offering. Similarly, the prosodic weight accorded to "Mit dir" served both to insist on the addressee's presence, and to separate the addressee off from the very "Inbetween" the poem hoped to open up. The poems end neither with a conclusion or resolution nor with simple irresolution; rather, they end with a *demand*—so that their singular reflection, on the body and voice as the site for an encounter with both language and other people, as the promise of art to transform the world, calls for a preservation to come. Both poems, that is, subsequently demand that our thinking not only attend to their own explorations of medium, but that it sets off from them into an exploration of its own.

And it is here that Heidegger's thinking attains one further significance. For Heidegger continually asserts that poetry is a form of language in which truth—that is, the openness of beings—takes place. In attempting to rethink form, rhythm, figurative language, or the way we read or "sound out" poetry, he is always concerned with this claim to truth. Heidegger's thinking offers insights into the relation between prosody and rhythm, the meaningful phenomenality of words, categories such as song, gesture, and melody—and the ways in which poetry, through its employment of sonorous patterning and trope—can effect a sounding. But in each instance, it will hold to the insight that poetry's salient feature is its treatment of its language as medium, and as a medium that can open up a singular space for an encounter with beings, and thereby shape the ways in which we experience and comprehend the world. If Heidegger's long engagement with poetry allows us to rethink some of the basic questions of poetics, then this is only because he poses the question of the truth of poetry, that is, the openness that it makes possible through its naming. If poetics is to think after Heidegger, to think from out of the possibilities Heidegger's thinking opens up, and to think beyond him, then it is with this question of truth that it must start.

Notes

Introduction

1. Here one can note a recurrent motif in Heidegger's thinking: the denigration of words of a Latinate etymology (here *Poesie* and *Literatur*) at the expense of Germanic words (here *Dichtung*).

2. The term *ontologize* comes from Adorno's critique of Heidegger in *Negative Dialectics* (trans. E. B. Ashton [London: Routledge, 1990], 100), although as will become clear, I am less hostile to this ontological move than Adorno.

3. For a powerful account of Heidegger's discussion of "ontological difference" in the *Contributions to Philosophy*, see Thomas Sheehan, "A Paradigm Shift in Heidegger Research," *Continental Philosophy Review* 22, no. 2 (2001): 7–8.

4. *Es gibt* literally means "it gives," which is the German equivalent to the English "there is."

5. See in particular Sheehan's "On Movement and Destruction of Ontology," in *Heidegger Reexamined: Art, Poetry and Technology*, ed. Hubert L. Dreyfus and Mark A. Wrathall (New York and London: Routledge, 2002), 320–28.

6. A longer version of the following pages can be found in my article "The Poetry-Verse Distinction Revisited, *Thinking Verse* I (2011): 137–60."

7. Hölderlin, *Essays and Letters on Theory*, trans. and ed. Thomas Pfau (Albany: State University of New York Press Press, 1988), 101.

8. Ibid., 102, translation modified.

9. Hölderlin's discussion of caesura's "counter-rhythmic interruption" that serves to balance the metrical line accords in this respect with Gerard Manley Hopkins's observation of how "the various means of breaking the sameness of rhythm and especially caesura do not break the unity of the verse but the con-

trary; they make it organic and what is organic is one." "Rhythm and other Structural Parts of Rhetoric," in *The Journals and Papers of Gerard Manley Hopkins*, ed. Humphry House (London and New York: Oxford University Press, 1959), 283.

10. See Philippe Lacoue-Labarthe, *Fiction du politique: Heidegger, art, politique* (Paris: C. Bourgeois, 1988), 41–45, and "La césure du speculative," in *L'imitation des modernes* (Paris: Galilée, 1985), 65ff.

11. Lacoue-Labarthe, *Fiction du politique*, 45.

12. Ibid., 44. Lacoue-Labarthe then relates caesura to the pure gift of being that Heidegger tries to grasp as *Ereignis* (46).

13. Allen, *Ellipsis: Of Poetry and the Experience of Language after Heidegger, Hölderlin and Blanchot* (Albany: State University of New York Press, 2007), 151–52.

14. Agamben, "The End of the Poem," in *The End of the Poem: Studies in Poetics*, trans. Daniel Heller-Roazen (Stanford, CA: Stanford University Press, 1999), 109.

15. Ibid., 115.

16. Ibid., 112.

17. Ibid., 114.

18. Ibid., 115.

19. Agamben *Language and Death: The Place of Negativity*, trans. Karen E. Pinkus with Michael Hardt (Minneapolis and London: University of Minnesota Press, 1991), 36.

20. Hugo Ott, *Martin Heidegger: A Political Life* translated by Allan Blunden (London: Fontana, 1988); Victor Farías, *Heidegger and Nazism*, ed. Joseph Margolis and Tom Rockmore (Philadelphia: Temple University Press, 1989).

21. "Only a God Can Save Us: The Spiegel Interview," in *The Heidegger Controversy*, ed. Richard Wolin (New York: Columbia University Press, 1991), 101.

22. Miguel de Beistegui, *Heidegger and the Political: Dystopias* (London: Routledge, 1998); Michael Zimmerman, *Heidegger's Confrontation with Modernity: Technology, Politics, and Art* (Bloomington: Indiana University Press, 1990); Julian Young, *Heidegger, Philosophy, Nazism* (Cambridge: Cambridge University Press, 1997). The opening line of Young's book is: "This work aims to provide what might be described as a 'de-Nazification' of Heidegger" (1).

23. Phillips, *Heidegger's Volk: Between National Socialism and Poetry* (Stanford, CA: Stanford University Press, 2005); Radloff, *Heidegger and the Question of National Socialism: Disclosure and Gestalt* (Toronto: University of Toronto Press, 2007). See also Richard Polt, "Metaphysical Liberalism in Heidegger's *Beiträge zur Philosophie*," in *Heidegger Reexamined*, ed. Hubert L. Dreyfus and Mark A. Wrathall (New York and London: Routledge, 2002), 209–34. This echoes comments given by Lacoue-Labarthe in *Heidegger, Art, Politics*, and Jacques Derrida in *Of Spirit: Heidegger and the Question*, trans. Geoffrey Bennington and Rachel Bowlby (Chicago: University of Chicago Press, 1989).

24. Such accounts include Annemarie Gethmann-Siefert, "Heidegger and Hölderlin: the over-usage of 'Poets in an impoverished time,'" in *Heidegger:*

Critical Assessments, ed. Christopher Macann (London: Routledge, 1992), 247–77. Kathleen Wright, "Heidegger and the Authorization of Hölderlin's Poetry," in *Heidegger: Politics, Art and Technology,* ed. Karsten Harries and Christoph Jamme (New York and London: Holmes and Meier, 1994), 164–74, and Richard Wolin, *The Politics of Being: The Political Thought of Martin Heidegger* (New York: Columbia University Press, 1990), esp. 109–10.

25. Exceptions to this necessarily schematic generalization include Phillips, *Heidegger's Volk,* Beistegui, *Heidegger and the Political,* and Kathleen Wright, "Heidegger and the Authorization of Hölderlin's Poetry." Andrzej Warminski also tries to link the political stakes of Heidegger's readings of Hölderlin to both his politics of the 1930s and the question of reading poetry more generally in "Monstrous History: Heidegger reading Hölderlin," *Yale French Studies* 77 (1990): 193–209.

26. To my knowledge, the German *in all dem* does not, as Fried and Polt's translation of it as "for all that" implies, set up a counterpoint between two statements. Whereas Fried and Polt would have it that it is despite Germany's lying in the pincers that it is "the most metaphysical" nation, it seems to me that Heidegger wishes to suggest that it is a consequence of Germany's position.

27. Michael Hamburger, trans., *Hölderlin: Poems and Fragments* (London: Anvil Press, 1994), 482–83. (*Wo aber Gefahr ist, wächst/Das Rettende auch.*)

28. Löwith, "The Political Implications of Heidegger's Existentialism," 176.

29. See, for instance, Lacoue-Labarthe, *Heidegger, Art, Politics,* 56.

30. Johannes Fritsche, in fact, traces "rightist" politics back to paragraph 74 of *Being and Time,* in which "the right-minded Daseine will save the 'they' by destroying the world of the 'they' and by replacing it with one that in ensouled by the properly present origin," *Historical Destiny and National Socialism* in *Being and Time* (Berkeley: University of California Press, 1999), 44. Fritsche reads the terms *erwidern* and *Widerruf* ("[to give a] reciprocative rejoinder" and "disavowal" respectively in Macquarrie and Robinson's translation), in chapter 74 of *Being and Time* as saying that the tradition must be re-read it in terms of the authentic origin, in order to bring about rupture with the present and create an alternative, *authentic* present, an idea propounded by many "rightist" ideologues of the era.

31. It is worth noting a tendency, in discussions about Heidegger and Nazism, for our knowledge of 1930s and 1940s German history to impute Heidegger with a far worse crime than his sympathy toward the Ernst Röhm wing of the Nazi Party in the early 1930s (Heidegger resigned the rectorate ten days before the "night of the long knives"): tacit support and complicity in the "final solution." Given the horror of what happened, and Heidegger's consistent refusal after the war to recognize this, such a tendency is perhaps understandable. But it misrecognizes, amongst other things, the nature of Heidegger's own engagement with the Nazi Party, which, in 1933 was very different from what it would become by 1945. It was reprehensible, but nothing in comparison to the utter abhorrence of what was to come.

32. Hofstadter translates *staatgründende Tat* as "the act that founds a political state" (PLT 60). Hubert Dreyfus, in his "Nihilism, Art, Technology, Politics," summarizes: "the U.S. Constitution, like a work of art, has necessarily become the focus of attempts to make it explicit and consistent and to make it apply to all situations, and, of course, it is fecund just insofar as it can never be interpreted once and for all. The founding of a state could also refer to the act of a charismatic leader such as Hitler," in Charles Guignon, ed., *The Cambridge Companion to Heidegger* (Cambridge: Cambridge University Press, 2006), 357. For an example of Heidegger's apparently nationalistic pathos on sacrifice, see "Schlageter," in *The Heidegger Controversy,* 40–42.

33. Gerald Bruns relates this to a movement from the account of the artwork as "orphic" to "hermetic." See *Heidegger's Estrangements: Language, Truth and Poetry in the Later Writings* (New Haven, CT: Yale University Press, 1989), xviii–xxvi. Hugo Ott intimates that this is due to Heidegger's own response to the failure of National Socialism, as he saw it, and the trauma of the defeat in World War II. See *Martin Heidegger: A Political Life,* 14–19.

1. For the First Time

1. Bruns, *Heidegger's Estrangements,* 37.

2. Adorno, "Parataxis: On Hölderlin's Late Poetry," in *Notes to Literature,* 2:109–49, 114; Meschonnic, *Le Langage Heidegger,* 368.

3. de Man, "Patterns of Temporality in Hölderlin's 'Wie Wenn Am Feiertage,'" in *Romanticism and Contemporary Criticism,* ed. E. S. Burt, Kevin Newark, and Andrej Warminski (Baltimore, MD: Johns Hopkins University Press, 1992), 50–73, 71.

4. Christopher Fynsk, *Heidegger: Thought and Historicity* (Ithaca, NY: Cornell University Press, 1986), 146.

5. Heidegger, to my knowledge, only uses the term "finite transcendence" in *Kant and the Problem of Metaphysics*; however, in his seminal *Heidegger: Through Phenomenology to Thought* (The Hague: M. Nijhoff, 1963), William Richardson argues convincingly that it constitutes one of the guiding threads of his thought (Richardson's reading indeed ascribes great significance to the *Kantbuch*).

6. Heidegger's evidence for the decadence and worthlessness of literary criticism is a study about "the camel in Arabic literature"; something whose absurdity is such that he feels obliged to add, for extra effect, "I'm not making this up [*nicht etwa erfunden*]" (GA39 16).

7. This is understood by J. M. Bernstein as "truth-only cognition," which, he argues, constitutes both the basis of aesthetic thought since Kant and the problem that all aesthetics seeks to resolve. See *The Fate of Art: Aesthetic Alienation from Kant to Adorno* (Oxford: Blackwell, 1992), 5.

8. Here it is standard to follow Meyer Schapiro in noting that Van Gogh's peasant shoes, so central to Heidegger's essay, belonged not to a peasant woman, but to the artist himself, the standard response being that, insofar as Heidegger's concern

is with the modalities of appearance, rather than the ontic identity of one entity (a pair of shoes), this does not trouble Heidegger's central thesis. With this rejoinder comes the proviso that Heidegger should have known better all the same, and that the fact Heidegger should have read into this painting a whole pathos of peasant experience is certainly indicative of a certain pathos in his work. Schapiro, "The Still Life as a Personal Object—A Note on Heidegger and van Gogh," in *Theory and Philosophy of Art: Style, Artist, and Society* (New York: George Braziller, 1994), 139ff., and Derrida's reply in *The Truth in Painting,* trans. G. Bennington and I. McLeod (Chicago: University of Chicago Press, 1987), 257ff.

9. This is the phrase first coined by Alexander Pope in his "Essay on Criticism," which has become canonical for the doctrine of "verbal mimesis," Émile Audra and Aubrey Williams, eds., *Alexander Pope: Pastoral Poetry and An Essay on Criticism* (London: Routledge, 1962), 281.

10. Greenberg, "Modernist Painting," in *Collected Essays and Criticism, 4:* Modernism *with a Vengeance, 1957–1969* (Chicago and London: Chicago University Press, 1993), 85–93, esp. 87, 92; Fried, "Art and Objecthood," in *Art and Objecthood: Essays and Reviews* (Chicago and London: Chicago University Press, 1998), 148–72, 153.

11. In this, Heidegger is endowing with ontological value what Greenberg sees as paradigmatic to modernist painting: "Whereas one tends to see what is in an Old Master before one sees the picture itself, one sees a Modernist picture as a picture first" ("Modernist Painting," 87).

12. This would contradict the characterization of Heidegger's thinking of language given by Richard Rorty: "When a word is used frequently and easily, when it is a familiar, ready-to-hand instrument for achieving our purpose, we can no longer hear it. Heidegger is saying that we need to be able to hear the 'most elemental' words which we use . . . rather than simply using these words as tools" ("Heidegger, Contingency, and Pragmatism," in *Essays on Heidegger and Others,* 34–35).

13. Aristotle, *Metaphysics* trans. Hugh Lawson-Tancred (Harmondsworth, UK: Penguin, 1998), 10.

14. Christopher Fynsk, "The Use of the Earth," http://abdn.ac.uk/modern thought/archive/publications/earth.php, accessed November, 29, 2010.

15. I borrow this phrase from Fynsk, *Heidegger: Thought and Historicity,* 150.

16. Victor Shklovsky, "Art as Device," in *Theory of Prose,* trans. Benjamin Sher (Elmwood Park, IL: Dalkey Archive Press, 1990). J. M. Bernstein (*The Fate of Art,* 88) and Andrew Bowie (*From Romanticism to Critical Theory,* 6–7) both discuss Heidegger's relation to ostraniene.

17. Shklovsky, *Theory of Prose,* 6.

18. Ibid., 6.

19. Ibid.. This would seem to shadow the epistemological structure of Kant's thesis that the aesthetic judgment "is indifferent to the existence of the object," and is not "based on concepts" (Immanuel Kant, *Critique of Judgment,* trans. Wer-

ner Pluhar (Indianapolis, IN: Hackett, 1986), 51)—even if Shklovsky's conception of form insists upon a sensual and affective element not so readily to be found in Kant.

20. Krzysztof Ziarek proposes "traversal" as a translation for *Erfahrung*; see Ziarek, *The Historicity of Experience: Modernity, the Avant-Garde, and the Event* (Evanston, IL: Northwestern University Press, 2001), 68. For a detailed account of the relation between Heidegger's thinking of experience and that of "life philosophy," see David Farrell Krell, *Daimon Life: Heidegger and Life-Philosophy* (Bloomington: Indiana University Press, 1992), 78–84.

21. Radloff, *Heidegger and the Question of National Socialism,* 323. Bruns adopts a similar position in speaking of its "uncontainability within any conceptual framework" (*Heidegger's Estrangements,* xxiii).

22. Marc Froment-Meurice, *That is to Say . . . : Heidegger's Poetics,* trans. Jan Plug (Stanford, CA: Stanford University Press, 1998), 154.

23. Ibid., 152. I will look more precisely at the relation of this thinking of the earth to the difference between signifier and signified in chapter 2.

24. Mark Sinclair, *Heidegger, Aristotle, and the Work of Art* (Basingstoke, UK: Palgrave Macmillan, 2006), 136, emphasis in original; Robert Bernasconi, *The Question of Language in Heidegger's History of Being* (Atlantic Highlands, NJ: Humanities Press, 1985), 35.

25. Paul de Man, "Phenomenality and Materiality in Kant," in *Aesthetic Ideology* (Minneapolis: University of Minnesota Press, 1996), 90. See also his "The Resistance to Theory," in *The Resistance to Theory* (Manchester: Manchester University Press, 1986), 11.

26. Michel Haar, *Song of the Earth,* trans. Reginald Lily (Bloomington: Indiana University Press, 1993), 100.

27. For a history of materialism that pays particular attention to the trope of how to render visible the phenomenological nonavailability of matter, see Daniel Tiffany, *Toy Medium: Materialism and Modern Lyric* (Chicago: University of Chicago Press, 2000), 178–79.

28. This term, too, I borrow from Sheehan ("On Movement and Destruction of Ontology"), who employs it to explain how the movement between presence and absence that structures an entity's appearance at the same time renders this entity intelligible for thinking.

29. Cézanne painted Vallier on several occasions late in his life. Julian Young takes the painting in question to be one of the 1906 versions, which is characterized by its light colors including patches of white to endow it with an unfinished quality (it was indeed one of the final paintings he completed before his death that year) and make it resemble the watercolor sketches he also made; see Julian Young, *Heidegger's Philosophy of Art* (Cambridge: Cambridge University Press, 2001), 153ff. However, the earlier paintings of Vallier, one of which dates from 1902 and another was being worked on over a long period up until his death, aim to capture the dark weariness of Vallier as my brief description does above. My reasons for opting to read Heidegger's poem in terms of this poem are double: firstly, because

its pathos seems far more in keeping with Heidegger's tastes, as they are expressed in his discussion of Van Gogh's "peasant shoes"; secondly, because these are the paintings where the "in-standing stillness" that, we shall see, Heidegger attributes to Vallier, really seems to be at issue.

30. Haar, *Song of the Earth*, 98 (*Chant de la terre*, 197); Fynsk, *Heidegger: Thought and Historicity*, 142.

31. In claiming that the *Riß* is thus rendered manifest, I am taking issue with Derrida's claim that it "has no proper and independent phenomenality"; see Derrida, "The Retrait of Metaphor," in *The Derrida Reader: Writing Performances*, edit. Julian Wolfreys (Edinburgh: Edinburgh University Press, 1998), 124. The following chapters will dedicate a great deal of space to this essay; here, I would merely like to note that it is both striking and revealing that Derrida should say: "I arbitrarily interrupt my reading here, I cut it with a slash at the moment when it would lead us to the *Ge-stell* of the *Gestalt* in the adjoinment of which (*Gefüge*), der *Riss sich fügt* [the trait joins itself]" (127). The moment, that is, that the question of the phenomenal *Gestalt* arises, Derrida interrupts his reading, as though to elude that aspect of Heidegger's discussion of *Riß* which does not accord with the direction in which Derrida wishes to take it.

32. Fynsk, *Heidegger: Thought and Historicity*, 155.

33. Radloff, *Heidegger and the Question of National Socialism*, 9–13. This is perhaps most evident in Heidegger's oeuvre in his claim, in *Being and Time*, that "initially we never hear noises and complexes of sound, but the creaking wagon, the motorcycle. We hear the column on the march, the north wind, the woodpecker tapping, the crackling fire" (BT 163/207). He reiterates this in "The Origin of the Work of Art": "Much closer to us than any sensation are the things themselves. . . . To hear a bare sound we must listen away from the things, direct our ears from them, listen abstractly" (OBT 8/16), although he subsequently rejects this interpretation of thingliness, because it "brings" the thing "too close" (OBT 8/16).

34. The role played by Jünger's thought in Heidegger's writings of the 1930s onwards has received particular scrutiny with respect to his relation to the Nazi party at this point. See, for example, Wolin, ed., *The Heidegger Controversy;* Pierre Bourdieu, *The Political Ontology of Martin Heidegger,* trans. Peter Collier (Cambridge: Polity, 1991); Zimmerman, *Heidegger's Confrontation with Modernity;* and Radloff, *Heidegger and the Question of National Socialism*. Discussions of Jünger, however, are complicated by his own equivocal relation to Nazi doctrine; see Jeffrey Herf, *Reactionary Modernism: Technology, Culture, and Politics in Weimar and the Third Reich* (Cambridge: Cambridge University Press, 1984), esp. 70–109.

35. Again, Heidegger insists on the historical dimension of this, taking this thinking of "limits" to say that we only learn "who" a historical humanity is "when humanity steps into the confrontation of beings by attempting to bring them into their being—that is, sets [*stellt*] beings into limits and form [*Gestalt*]" (IM 153–54/110).

36. Indeed, Heidegger first introduces the term *Aufstellung* when noticing that, when we hang a painting in an exhibition (*Ausstellung*), we set it up (*auf-*

stellen). However, such *Aufstellung* is immediately distinguished from *Erstellung* (constructing).

37. Hofstadter favors the first translation, Young the second. Heidegger in fact employs both meanings at different moments in his exposition. The verb *verstellen* has come in for critical scrutiny regarding Heidegger's relation to National Socialism. For, if truth is, as he says in "On the Essence of Truth," at the same time "errancy" (P 151/93), and if, in "The Origin of the Work of Art," truth shows itself only in dissembling, then this seems to absolve him of personal responsibility for his own "greatest blunder" (cited in Richard Wolin, "French Heidegger Wars," in *The Heidegger Controversy*, 295); this argument has been proposed by Thomas Sheehan, "Everyone Has to Tell the Truth," *Continuum* I, no. 1 (Autumn 1990): 30–44, and Werner Marx, whose diagnosis is particularly eloquent: "Heidegger's coordination of the powers of error and sham with those of the luminous presents an extreme danger" (*Heidegger and the Tradition*, 248). Indeed, one gets the impression that Young's translation is itself attempting to foreclose this line of argument. Yet *verstellen* also offers a possibly intriguing approach to the *Gestalt*. If, as Froment-Meurice notes, the earth cannot be "said" without being "disfigured" (*That is to Say . . .* , 153), and yet must enter into the world in order to set this world up, then it does so in a figure (*Gestalt*) that is itself disfigurement. Indeed, this prospect makes it, Bruns suggests, "difficult to resist a temptation here to improvise a Heideggerian theory of metaphor on the basis of this conception of *Gestalt* or *Doppelgestalt* as refusal and figurality in which something manifests itself—enters into the open—as something other than itself or other than usual" (*Heidegger's Estrangements*, 41). In the rest of the thesis, I shall translate this term as *disfigurement*, in order to retain its intimate relation to the work's *Gestalt*.

38. This is an early usage of a term which, in Heidegger's postwar writings, will come to describe the "enframing" according to which beings are interpreted in accordance with the requirements of calculative-technological thinking (see, for example, "The Question Concerning Technology"; BW 309–41). Despite several differences between the two articles, Heidegger's later thinking of the term (as is noted in the appendix to "The Origin of the Work of Art" (OBT 54/GA5 74), takes this account of the *Gestalt*, and of *morphe*, as the basis for his subsequent thinking. Indeed, one similarity is that term, in the 1949 lecture, is introduced through another discussion of the cognates of *stellen* (BW 326–28/28–31), and Heidegger again argues that the "essence" of *Ge-stell* is intimately related to the question of poetry, which he here approaches in terms of *poiesis* (BW 326/28).

39. Stambaugh transliterates ρυθμος as rhusmos.

40. Henri Meschonnic, "The Rhythm Party Manifesto" trans. David Nowell Smith, *Thinking Verse I* (2011): 165.

41. Jünger, *Rhythmus und Sprache im deutschen Gedicht* (Stuttgart: Ernst Klett Verlag, 1952), 15. He continues to argue that "each attempt to isolate [time] from language must cause confusion for metrics," something that would seem to articulate, perhaps more specifically than Heidegger ever did, Heidegger's own aversion to the "schemes" of metrics. A more recent account that renews with added verve

this train of thought can be found in the work of Simon Jarvis, and particular the 1998 essay "Prosody as Cognition," and its rallying cry: "to the general economy of nihilism which is our experience of time as though it were an object prosody opposes the reality of the duration of our experience" ("Prosody as Cognition," *Critical Quarterly* 40, no. 4 [1998]: 11). Yet Heidegger's account of "jointure" also poses a fundamental challenge to Jarvis's thinking, as it transposes the "reality of the duration of our experience" away from the fabric of subjective experience and on to the presencing movement of being itself.

42. Allemann, *Hölderlin und Heidegger* (Zürich and Freiburg im Breisgau: Atlantis Verlag, 1954), 177.

43. Staiger, *Basic Concepts of Poetics,* trans. Janette C. Hudson and Luanne T. Frank (University Park, PA: Pennsylvania University Press, 1991), 188–89. He also suggested that the three existentials of state-of-mind, discourse, and understanding should ground a division of genres into lyric, epic, and drama respectively.

44. See, for example, David Farrell Krell, *Lunar Voices: of Tragedy, Poetry, Fiction, and Thought* (Chicago: University of Chicago Press, 1995), 75–76; Véronique Fóti, *Heidegger and the Poets: poiēsis/sophia/technē* (Atlantic Highlands, NJ: Humanities Press International, 1992), 1–8; David Halliburton, *Poetic Thinking: An Approach to Heidegger* (Chicago and London: University of Chicago Press, 1981), 59–76.

45. Krell, *Lunar Voices,* 65.

46. Ibid., 60.

47. Ibid., 65.

48. I take the term *dynamization* from Yuri Tynianov's *Problems of Verse Language,* trans. Michael Sosa and Brent Harvey (Ann Arbor, MI: Ardis, 1981), 153.

2. The Naming Power of the Word

1. In this mixture of privilege and anomaly, Heidegger is by no means alone. Kant, for example, at once insists that fine art is paradigmatically nonconceptual, and yet it is poetry's discursivity that places it above the other arts. Indeed, Kant notes this paradoxical relation when he says that poetry "offers us, from among the unlimited variety of possible forms that harmonize with a given concept, though within that concept's limits, that form which links the exhibition of the concept with a wealth of thought to which no linguistic expression is completely adequate, and so poetry rises aesthetically to ideas" (*Critique of Judgement,* 196).

2. Bruns, *Heidegger's Estrangements,* 50.

3. See, for example, Rorty, "Wittgenstein, Heidegger, and the Reification of Language," in *Essays on Heidegger and Others: Philosophical Papers, vol. 2* (Cambridge: Cambridge University Press, 1991); David White, *Heidegger and the Language of Poetry* (Lincoln: University of Nebraska Press, 1978); Cristina Lafont, *Heidegger, Language, and World-Disclosure,* trans. Graham Harman (Cambridge: Cambridge University Press, 2000); as well as the essays in Kockelmans, ed., *On Heidegger and Language* (Evanston, IL: Northwestern University Press, 1972). It is nevertheless worth recalling Heidegger's own rejoinder to such accounts, in the

letter to William Richardson that constitutes the preface to Richardson's *Martin Heidegger: Through Phenomenology to Thought:* "The distinction you make between Heidegger I and II is justified only on the condition that this is kept constantly in mind: only by way of what [Heidegger] I has thought does one gain access to what is to-be-thought by [Heidegger] II. But the thought of [Heidegger] I becomes possible only if it is contained in [Heidegger] II" (xxii).

4. The distinction between sign and symbol as modes of linguistic reference is a nuance to which Heidegger gives no real attention, although he dismisses both at various points in his work. For a canonical account of this distinction, see Saussure, *Course in General Linguistics,* trans. Wade Baskin, ed. Charles Bally and Albert Sechehaye in collaboration with Albert Reidlinger (London: Fontana, 1974), 68.

5. Both the terms *Rede* and *Ganze* have posed difficulties for translators. Macquarrie and Robinson render *Rede* as "discourse" or "talk" depending on context; Hubert Dreyfus, by contrast, suggests the word "telling" as a means of grasping the specific connotations of the German word. He explains: "*Rede* literally means talk, but 'discourse' is too formal and too linguistic for what Heidegger includes under this term." *Being-in-the-World: A Commentary on Heidegger's Being and Time, Division I* (Cambridge, MA: MIT Press, 1990), xi. However, this strikes me as problematic, not least as it implies precisely the communicative act that Heidegger is trying to call into question. For this reason, I will retain the term *discourse,* and *discursive* for its adjective. By contrast, *Ganze* is often translated as "totality"; the danger here is that we provide Heidegger's idiom with a far more technical, and Latinate, vocabulary than he would favor (one can hardly imagine his describing this as a *Totalität!*).

6. Aler, "Heidegger's conception of language in *Being and Time,*" in *Martin Heidegger: Critical Assessments,* 4:29–30.

7. This is at the basis of Heidegger's famous claim that he will "liberate grammar from logic" (BT 209/165). Indeed, in *History of the Concept of Time,* he offers a far more grandiose project: a "scientific logic" which would takes place as "a *phenomenology of discourse, of logos*" (HCT 264/364)

8. R. L. Trask and Peter Stockwell, *Language and Linguistics: The Key Concepts* (London: Routledge, 2007), 204–5. They note that it "is sometimes used more narrowly, to include only voice quality, and sometimes more broadly, to include most or even all aspects of **non-verbal communication**" (ibid., bold type in original). Whether a language without loudness, pitch, tempo, and so on, is in fact possible, is a moot point. For an illuminating discussion of these and related problems, see N. Burton-Roberts, P. Carr, and G. Docherty, eds., *Phonological Knowledge: Conceptual and Empirical Issues* (Oxford: Oxford University Press, 2000), especially Burton-Roberts, "What and Where is Phonology? A Representational Perspective," 39–66.

9. In this, Heidegger's thinking anticipates some recent developments in discourse analysis, where a pragmatic approach to intonation has shown the extent to which intonation contours are central to the intelligibility of the syntactic and

lexical components of verbal language. See, for example, Ann Wennerstrom, *The Music of Everyday Speech: Prosody and Discourse Analysis* (Oxford: Oxford University Press, 2001).

10. In both the Macquarrie-Robinson and Stambaugh translations of *Being and Time*, *Bedeutsamkeit* is rendered "significance" and *Bedeutung* is rendered "signification." For reasons that will soon become clear, I am going to remain with the far more imprecise, and perhaps inelegant, translations "meaningfulness" and "meaning."

11. For an account of Heidegger's "tautological thinking," see Allen, *Ellipsis*, 44.

12. Aler, "Heidegger's conception of language in *Being and Time*," 28.

13. The definitions come from Charles Guignon's reading of this passage in *Heidegger and the Problem of Knowledge* (Indianapolis, IN: Hackett, 1983), 116.

14. Guignon, *Heidegger and the Problem of Knowledge*, 117.

15. Ibid., 118. He subsequently concludes that we should read Heidegger through this latter, "constitutive" view, as it accords better with his later work.

16. Cristina Lafont, *Heidegger, Language, and World-Disclosure*, 7. Lafont's is a highly significant work, not least as it seeks to place Heidegger not simply within the history of Husserlian phenomenology, but also as engaging with a series of questions that would link him to various figures in the "analytic" tradition of philosophy. In this instance, Lafont looks at how this axiom brings Heidegger together with other proponents of meaning holism, including not only the late Wittgenstein, but also Quine, Putnam, and Davidson.

17. Ibid., 70.

18. Lafont, *Heidegger, Language, and World-Disclosure*, 15.

19. In *History of the Concept of Time*, the "signs" in question are firstly our "taking" the "south wind" as a "sign of rain" (HCT 206/281), but then Heidegger turns to "produced signs," examples of which are "arrows, flags, the storm ball in the marine weather-bureau, signal arms, road signs, and the like" (HCT 207/282). Interestingly, Heidegger refuses to give a genealogy of these signs from out of a symbolic function based on resemblance, rather referring both signifying and symbolic functions to the discoveredness of being-in-the-world.

20. Curiously, Taylor Carman takes this to mean Heidegger is setting up a distinction between "signs that indicate and signs that signify, *Zeichen* and *Bedeutungen*" ("Was Heidegger a Linguistic Idealist?," 210). This shows us precisely how difficult it is for us to imagine linguistic meaning as *not* being some kind of sign. Indeed, Heidegger's own choice of the term *Bedeutung* was knowingly imprecise. In an apologetic aside during his lecture series on the *History of the Concept of Time*, Heidegger regrets the inadequacy of the term: "I frankly admit that this expression is not the best, but for years I have found nothing better" (HCT 202/275).

21. Dastur, *Heidegger: la question du* logos (Paris: J Vrin, 2007), 170–71.

22. Agamben, *Language and Death: The Place of Negativity*, 26. Halliburton, by contrast, relates the Saussurean distinction to the later distinction Heidegger makes between *saying* and *speech*: "saying implies the whole scope and possibility

of any worldly act, including speaking, naming, and other modes" (*Poetic Thinking,* 55).

23. Lafont, *Heidegger, Language, and World-Disclosure,* 67. Lafont takes this to demonstrate that Heidegger offers "a *reifying* interpretation of the ontological difference" (73), which would treat the ontological and ontic as a separation analogous to Kant's distinction between transcendental and empirical, *a priori* and *a posteriori.* She continues: "This reification of the difference engendered a systematic blindness vis-à-vis the new possibilities that it opened up, for to take those possibilities seriously would amount to reinterpreting the ontological difference in a way opposed to the requirements of transcendental philosophy, perhaps in the sense of Saussure's purely *methodological* distinction between signifier and signified."

24. This point is made by Sheehan in "*Hermeneia* and *Apophansis,*" when he observes, "words are signs not of mental images but of being-in-the-world." "*Hermeneia* and *Apophansis:* The Early Heidegger's Reading of *De Interpretatione,*" in *Heidegger et l'idée de la phenomenology,* Franco Volpi et al. (Dordrecht: Kluwer, 1988), 74. Yet he too treats words as "signs."

25. Ferdinand de Saussure, *Course in General Linguistics,* 67–70.

26. Given the various discussions about Heidegger's potential relation to Saussure, it is notable that at this juncture he opposes *Zeichen* (*signe*), rather than *Bezeichnendem* (*signifiant*), to *Bezeichnetem* (*signifié*). This would imply ignorance, or at least disregard, of Saussure's own division the sign into *signifiant* and *signifié,* so that linguistic reference takes place within the sign itself (see Saussure, *Course in General Linguistics,* 17–20).

27. As though to force the issue, Heidegger directs his audience to his lecture on "Plato's Doctrine of Truth."

28. See, for example, Jean Greisch, *La Parole heureuse: Martin Heidegger entre les choses et les mots* (Paris: Beauchesne, 1987), 393, Froment-Meurice, *That is to say . . . ,* 67ff.

29. Froment-Meurice, *That is to say . . . ,* 71. Froment-Meurice suggests that "showing," with its "supreme identification" of the sign with what it shows, constitutes no less than the "teleology" of "metaphysics" (70).

30. Jennifer Gosetti-Ferencei, *Heidegger, Hölderlin, and the Subject of Poetic Language* (New York: Fordham University Press, 2004), 43; Robert Moynihan, "Interview with Paul de Man," *Yale Review* 73, no. 4: 602.

31. This latter absence is particularly striking, given the importance of mediation and immediacy for Husserl and Hegel, two crucial figures in Heidegger's own development.

32. This characterization is given by Karsten Harries, "Heidegger and Hölderlin: The Limits of Language," 11.

33. Derrida, "The *Retrait* of Metaphor," 125. See also Karen Feldman, "Heidegger and the Hypostasis of the Performative," *Angelaki* 9, no. 3 (2004): 157–67.

34. Allen, *Ellipsis,* 158ff.

35. Hans Ulrich Gumbrecht, "Martin Heidegger and his Japanese Interlocutors: About a Limit of Western Metaphysics," in *Diacritics* 30, no. 4 (Winter 2000): 83–101. Discussing a later passage (OL 45/144–45), Gumbrecht says: "Only the most unconditional admirers of Heidegger will not find embarrassing this concluding (self-)congratulation on his master interpretation of Japanese culture, as only Heidegger addicts will never wish that he had (at least sometimes) dispensed of his etymological speculations" (96).

36. Halliburton summarizes this predicament nicely when he says: "Saying designates what must be in order for anything to be, including the totality of the world. But if that is the case, then saying must somehow reach beyond what we normally think of as linguistic (though of course without ceasing to encompass the linguistic)" (*Poetic Thinking*, 193).

37. Jean-Luc Nancy, "On a Divine *Wink*," in François Raffoul and David Pettigrew (eds.), *French Interpretations of Heidegger: An Exceptional Reception* (Albany: State University of New York Press, 2008), 169.

38. Ibid. Nancy makes this point explicit some pages later: "At issue here are structure and movement; movement—the wink—as the structure of différance, whose motif or motivation is in the process of moving Derrida toward what always motivated him: the absenting of presence at the heart of its present and its presentation, and, correlatively, the spearing open of the sign and the heart of its relation to itself, and then the hollowing out of a nonsignifying passage at the heart or *joint* of the sign" (173).

39. Ibid., 172. This energy would be opposed to the *energeia* that Humboldt identifies in linguistic meaning.

40. Ibid., 179. He continues: "The wink belongs to all non-phenomenological looking." The difficulty of using the term *organ* in Heidegger's thought has been intimated above, and will be examined in greater depth in the next chapter.

41. This passage brings together two strands which, in *History of the Concept of Time,* are treated separately. Discussing the manifestational dimension to language, Heidegger argues that "one oneself and the being-in-the-world at the time likewise become manifest, even if only in having the dispostion 'manifested' through intonation, modulation, or tempo of discourse" (HCT 263/363–64). In this way, he seeks to give an account both of discourse that does not assume an "internal" subject expressing themselves through "external" language, and at the same time of a mode of linguistic manifestation irreducible to semantic reference. It is ten pages later, at the end of his discussion of language, that he notes: "articulated discourse can help first by grasping possibilities of being for the first time which before were already always experienced implicitly. The discoveredness of Dasein, in particular the disposition of Dasein, can be made manifest by means of words in such a way that certain new possibilities of Dasein's being are set free. Thus discourse, especially *poetry,* can even bring about the release of new possibilities of the being of Dasein. In this way, discourse proves itself positively as a *mode of maturation,* a *mode of temporalization* of Dasein itself" (HCT 272/372).

This implies that at some point in the period between the 1925 lecture series and Heidegger's writing *Being and Time* he comes to see these two moments—non-semantic, nonreferential manifestation and the disposition of Dasein—as meeting in poetry. Yet it also leaves relatively untouched a tantalizing possibility—that of the relation between poetry as a "mode of temporalization" and ecstatic temporality. In Chapter 1 we saw the extent to which Heidegger continues, albeit perhaps obliquely, this concern in his discussion of rhythm; later in this chapter I will suggest that it equally infuses his thinking on rhythm and on the temporal relation between said and unsaid. However, it is never, at least not to my knowledge, taken up explicitly.

42. Dastur, *Heidegger : La question du* logos, 176. She aligns this "life" with "what linguists (Saussure, Hjelmslev, Jakobson) name the syntagmatic axe, which constitutes a transversal reference within the language itself" (ibid.).

43. Ibid., 164. My claim is that poetry is not deduced from one of these moments, but engages all four.

44. *Sein und Zeit,* 443 (note to p. 161). Heidegger's notes are also included in Joan Stambaugh's translation, 151.

45. We can also note that when Heidegger is discussing being-toward-death, through which anxiety comes to disclose the nothing, that he makes the one literary reference of *Being and Time,* to Tolstoy's short story "The Death of Ivan Ilyitch" (BT 495/254).

46. Crowell, "Making Logic Philosophical Again," in *Reading Heidegger from the Start,* ed. Theodor Kisiel and John van Buren (Albany: State University of New York Press, 1994), 59.

47. This limit also motivates, albeit in a very different manner, Heidegger's discussion, in *Basic Problems of Phenomenology,* of a passage from Rilke's *The Notebooks of Malte Laurids Brigge,* his first reading of a poetic text. Heidegger introduces the passage by stating: "Poetry, creative literature, is nothing but the elementary emergence into words, the becoming-uncovered, of existence as being-in-the-world" (BPP 171–72/244). The "world" of the novel, and the "being-in-the-world" of its narrator, "leap toward us from the things" described in an "elemental . . . way" (BPP 173/246). Once again we find language conceived of as movement, the invocation of emergence anticipating Heidegger's later discussions of the "rising up" of beings in *phusis.* Such emergence, moreover, while being situated in a *description,* would exceed any referential determination of language; the passage performs the entry into discoveredness of the world, rather than simply articulating a world that has been discovered in advance. If this seems consistent with Heidegger's understanding of language as a whole of its discursive moments, it also troubles the account of the discoveredness of the world and the role of language within it. For, Heidegger suggests, the "world" that the passage evokes "has been unconsidered and not at all theoretically discovered" (BPP 173/246–47); Rilke's poetic discourse, in other words, grasps beings before circumspective understanding, through the "hermeneutic 'as,'" has made them available for verbal articulation. It has interrupted the teleology by which meanings accrue into words. The read-

ing of *The Notebooks of Malte Laurids Brigge* does not, however, engage with those vocal elements of language—intonation, modulation, and tempo—that lie at the basis of his theoretical outline of "'poetical' discourse" in *Being and Time*.

48. David Farrell Krell's *Daimon Life* offers a powerful account of Derrida's engagement with this passage (257–60).

49. This would contradict the account given by Abraham Mansbach, according to which "the call is not a voice from outside, but an unmediated expression of the self to its own self" (*Beyond Subjectivism: Heidegger on Language and the Human Being* (Westport, CT, and London: Greenwood, 2002), 54). We have already noted that "mediation" is a problematic category through which to approach Heidegger's thinking on language; what I would like to note here is that the "expression" Heidegger envisages would manifest the constitutive difference or ecstasis that characterizes Dasein's being-in-the-world. In this, Heidegger would appear to anticipate the analyses given by Derrida of the Husserlian motif "hearing oneself speak," in which the very voice that is designed to serve as self-present ground for the transcendence of the subject in fact shows up the impossibility of such presence, and the differential structure of all autoaffection. Derrida, "Speech and Phenomena," in *Speech and Phenomena, and Other Essays on Husserl's Theory of Signs,* trans. David B. Allison (Evanston, IL: Northwestern University Press, 1973), esp. 78–86.

50. Aler, "Heidegger's Conception of Language in *Being and Time,*" 33. He continues: "The response to the call of conscience obviously is merely small talk. Such a response is an attitude within the world: man projects himself resolutely and silently toward the most proper possibilities of Being." Taylor Carman ("Was Heidegger a Linguistic Idealist?") similarly argues that discourse serves as "a form of expression and communication distinct from and more primordial to language" (210), precisely because it responds to a "call of conscience" that doesn't speak in words. When he tries to elaborate on this, he refers to "facial expressions and bodily postures" (ibid.).

51. Aler, "The Conception of Language in *Being and Time,*" 34.

52. Haar, *The Song of the Earth*, 111.

53. Froment-Meurice, *That is to say . . . ,* 56. Plug translates *terrestre* as "terrestrial."

54. Fynsk, *Language and Relation: . . . that there is language* (Stanford, CA: Stanford University Press, 1996), 27–30.

55. Fynsk, *Language and Relation,* 98. This "broken silence," it is worth reiterating, can occur in both speech *and* writing.

56. Derrida, *Speech and Phenomena,* 12.

57. Fynsk, *Language and Relation,* 131.

3. Heidegger's Figures

1. As a corrective to the ever-expanding Heidegger-on-metaphor debate, Joseph Kockelmans wryly observed: "Heidegger has really made only some very brief statements about the relationship between metaphor and metaphysics. This

fact seems to suggest that he did not think the issue of metaphor to be of very great philosophical significance. If he would have shared the views of Derrida and Ricoeur he would have devoted an entire lecture course to the problems involved." "Heidegger on Metaphor and Metaphysics," in *Martin Heidegger: Critical Assessments,* ed. Macann (London: Routledge 1992), 294.

2. In this, one might sympathize with Paul Ricoeur's complaint that metaphysics in Heidegger's thought is little more than "an after-the-fact construction . . . intended to vindicate his own labour of thinking and to justify the renunciation of any kind of thinking that is not a genuine overcoming of metaphysics." *The Rule of Metaphor Multi-disciplinary Studies of the Creation of Meaning in Language,* trans. Robert Czerny with Kathleen McLauglin and John Costello (Toronto: University of Toronto Press, 1977), 311.

3. Jean Greisch, "Les mots et les roses: La métaphore chez Martin Heidegger," *Revue des Sciences Philosophiques et Théologiques,* 57, no. 3 (1973): 445. Indeed, central to Greisch's article is the recognition that "the interrogation on metaphor in Heidegger must explicitly . . . analyse how metaphor actually functions within Heidegger's discourse" (435).

4. Jacques Derrida, "The *Retrait* of Metaphor," 115. This passage is indeed designed to show the convergence of his thought on Heidegger and metaphor with that of Greisch and Ricoeur.

5. J. Hillis Miller, "Slipping Vaulting Crossing: Heidegger," in *Topographies* (Stanford: Stanford University Press, 1996); Giuseppe Stellardi, *Heidegger and Derrida on Philosophy and Metaphor: Imperfect Thought* (Amherst, NY: Humanity Books, 2000).

6. Paul Ricoeur, *The Rule of Metaphor;* Jean Greisch, "Les mots et les roses," and *La Parole heureuse;* Gerald Casenave, "Heidegger and Metaphor," *Philosophy Today* 26, no. 2 (Summer 1982).

7. Kockelmans, "Heidegger on Metaphor and Metaphysics," 313.

8. Ibid., 312. Kockelmans argues that Heidegger's critique of metaphor is restricted to the discussion of "basic texts," that is, "texts that genuinely reflect the thinking of Being and texts that 'result' from original poetizing." This would mean that Heidegger's concern is not with poetry as such, but only with the basic texts (Hölderlin, George, Trakl and so on) that happen to be poems. The interlacing between ontic *Poesie* and ontological *Dichtung,* however, is far more porous than such a reading would allow for.

9. Moynihan, "Interview with Paul de Man," 602.

10. Miller, "Slipping Vaulting Crossing," 238.

11. Ibid., 226. Miller continues, "the careful reader should always be wary when a writer says he or she is expunging all tropes. It is just then that the most powerful effects of figuration, powerful in part because obscured and unacknowledged, are likely to be doing their work" (238), and here we come also to see a further stake in his reading of Heidegger—that behind his supposed Cratylism, and ideological "confusion of linguistic with phenomenal reality" lies an explanation of, and philosophical continuity with, his relation to National Socialism.

12. Giuseppe Stellardi, *Heidegger and Derrida on Philosophy and Metaphor,* 133.

13. Miller says of this latter, in riposte to de Man: "To say 'language speaks' looks like prosopopoeia to me" ("Slipping Vaulting Crossing", 152).

14. Karen Feldman, "Heidegger and the Hypostasis of the Performative," 163.

15. This worry is most eloquently expressed by Richard Rorty, "Wittgenstein, Heidegger, and the Reification of Language," 50–65.

16. Ricoeur, *The Rule of Metaphor,* 284. Ricoeur makes a distinction between the poetry whose metaphor "sketches a 'tensional' conception of truth for thought" that comprises variously the "tensions between subject and predicate, between literal interpretation and metaphorical interpretation, between identity and difference" (313), and Heidegger's own idiom, which is "a mode of thought that unceasingly rectifies itself" as it tries to make possible an encounter with what he attempts to think, and to this end will "base its work upon the dynamism of metaphorical utterance" (312).

17. Greisch, "Les mots et les roses," 455. Indeed, in *La Parole heureuse* he will argue that this amounts to no less than "another, 'non-metaphysical' conception of metaphor" (210). Greisch notes at the beginning of "Les mots et les roses," "the originality of Heidegger's thought is not the result of a new theory of metaphor" (434); nevertheless, he sees in Heidegger's thinking a concept of "metaphor" far removed from the standard, "metaphysical" conception which subordinates metaphor to a representational paradigm of language, concluding his 1973 article with the tremulous claim: "metaphor is dead: long live metaphor" (455).

18. Casenave, "Heidegger and Metaphor," 141.

19. Ibid., 142.

20. Harries, "Language and Silence," in *Martin Heidegger and the Question of Literature,* ed. William V. Spanos (Bloomington: Indiana University Press, 1979), 155–72.

21. For a lucid overview of this trend, see Monika Fludernik, "Narratology in the Twenty-First Century: The Cognitive Approach to Narrative." *PMLA* 125, no. 4 (October 2010): 924–30.

22. Ibid., 146.

23. Feldman, 164–65. *Enact* is very much the operative term for Feldman, who argues that "Heidegger's explicit rejection of metaphor and symbolic representation constitutes a step in his texts in the evocation of, or access to, the order of enactment and performance" (157).

24. Derrida, "The *Retrait* of Metaphor," 119.

25. Ibid., 120.

26. Stellardi, *Heidegger and Derrida on Philosophy and Metaphor,* 137.

27. Ibid., 139–40.

28. Ibid., 137–38.

29. Bruns, *Heidegger's Estrangements,* 126.

30. Ibid., 128. For his references to *Finnegans Wake* see 45, 54.

31. Stellardi, *Heidegger and Derrida on Philosophy and Metaphor,* 149. This does, of course, beg the question as to how they can be analogical if interrupting the first structure of their analogy through their openness.

32. Derrida, "White Mythology," in *Margins of Philosophy*, trans. Alan Bass (Brighton, UK: Harvester Press, 1982), 226n29. Derrida discusses this note (note 19 in the French original) in more detail in "The *Retrait* of Metaphor," 108.

33. Kevin Aho in *Heidegger's Neglect of the Body* (Albany: State University of New York Press, 2009) attempts to address this throughout Heidegger's work, both to temper the criticisms leveled at Heidegger by Sartre, Merleau-Ponty and others, but also to ask why such a lacuna first appeared in his work, and how he subsequently tried to address it.

34. The translators of the *Zollikon Seminars* render *Körper* as "corporeal object," so as to preserve the etymology, and to highlight the antagonistic relation, so central to Heidegger's terminology, between Germanic and Latinate terms. As so often, the Germanic *Leib* is the authentic term, which allows for a thinking that would escape the precincts of metaphysics, whereas *Körper*, derived from the Latin *corpus*, is weighed down with a history of the forgetting of being.

35. Derrida, "Heidegger's Hand (*Geschlecht* II)," in *Psyche: Inventions of the Other, vol. II*, ed. Peggy Kamuf and Elizabeth Rottenberg (Stanford, CA: Stanford University Press, 2008), 40–41. As with the question of the metaphoricity of Heidegger's text, Derrida focuses his attention on Heidegger's overcoming of metaphysics; the setting up of an "absolute, oppositional limit" simply draws Heidegger back into the metaphysico-dialectical tradition in opposition to which his account of human Dasein had been developed.

36. Stuart Elden, "Heidegger's Animals," *Continental Philosophy Review* 39, no. 3 (2006): 279–81. See also Miguel de Beistegui, *Thinking with Heidegger: Displacements* (Bloomington: Indiana University Press, 2003), 115ff, and *The New Heidegger* (London: Continuum, 2005), 15ff. It is worth noting, however, that Heidegger sees this as "a poverty which, roughly put, is nonetheless a kind of wealth" (FCM 255/371).

37. This leads Heidegger to embark on a striking disquisition about the proliferation of typewriters (*Schreibmaschinen*, writing machines) in contemporary society (this is 1942–43; one can only imagine what he would have made of the *iPhone*). "The typewriter," he argues, "tears writing from the essential realm of the hand, i.e, the realm of the word," to constitute "the irruption of the mechanism in the realm of the word" (85). The fact that the use of typewriters is so often justified by their facilitating easy written communication is, for Heidegger, merely a further example of how the technological-calculative conception of language is divorced from the possibility of the disclosure of being. He concludes: "The typewriter veils the essence of writing and of the script. It withdraws from man the essential rank of the hand, without man's experiencing this withdrawal appropriately and recognising that it has transformed the relation of being to his essence." Derrida feels obliged to note that this sudden focus on *writing* as the bodily inscription central to the opening of meaning does not absolve Heidegger of the charge of logocentrism and phonocentrism, which "dominate a certain very continuous discourse of Heidegger's—whatever the lateral or material motifs that shape it simultaneously" ("Heidegger's Hand," 48–49).

38. Here we should diverge from Hertz's translation of *erdhaft* as "like the earth," with the unfortuitous irony of its introducing a simile just at the moment that Heidegger disputes the place of simile in Hölderlin's poem.

39. Giorgio Agamben, *The Open: Man and Animal*, trans. Kevin Attell (Stanford, CA: Stanford University Press, 2004), 55.

40. Ibid., 67.

41. Ibid., 68.

42. Ibid., 69.

43. Derrida, "The *Retrait* of Metaphor," 111.

44. Ricoeur, *The Rule of Metaphor*, 313.

45. de Man, "Hypogram and Inscription," in *The Resistance to Theory*, 50.

46. A somewhat different account of the "metaphysics" of "verbal mimesis" is proposed by Simon Jarvis in his "The Melodics of Long Poems," *Textual Practice* 24, no. 4 (2010).

4. Reading Heidegger Reading

1. Letter to Gadamer, dated December 22, 1941, cited Andrzej Warminski, *Readings in Interpretation* (Minneapolis: Minnesota University Press, 1987), 204; originally in Kommerell, *Briefe und Aufzeichnungen, 1919–1944* ed. Inge Jen (Olten and Freiburg im Breisgau: Walter-Verlag, 1967), 403. The trope of modern transportation is rather prominent in descriptions of Heidegger's exegeses. Dahlstrom, for example, having noted "the appearance" that Heidegger's "dialogues" with the poets "frequently" have of "being rapacious monologues," goes on to compare Heidegger's *Denkweg* to "a modern autobahn bulldozed and asphalted over country roads." Dahlstrom, "Heidegger's Artworld," in *Heidegger: Politics, Art, and Technology*, 125. Given Heidegger's own pathos of untouched countryside and peasant life, and his claim that aeroplanes and autobahns might shorten distance, but cannot bring "nearness," such tropes (a train wreck, the "bulldozing" motorway) could be considered unfortunate.

2. Steiner, *Heidegger* (London: Fontana, 1978), 137.

3. This point is made by Bruns in *Heidegger's Estrangements*, 60.

4. J. M. Bernstein, *The Fate of Art*, 71.

5. In addition to Bernstein (131–35), this claim is made by Bernasconi (*The Question of Language in Heidegger's History of Being*, 35–37), and Young (*Heidegger's Philosophy of Art*, 65). All three give powerful arguments to suggest that for Heidegger only preaesthetic art can be great art, even if this poses problems regarding the prominent role played by Van Gogh's peasant shoes in "The Origin of the Work of Art," and of Hölderlin throughout Heidegger's writings of the period (notably the 1934–35 lecture course on the hymns "Germanien" and "The Rhine" and the lecture "Hölderlin and the Essence of Poetry"). Young calls the appearance of the peasant shoes an "anomaly" (65).

6. J. M. Anderson, "Since the time we are a dialogue and able to hear from one another," in *Man and World* 10, no.2 (1977): 126. Halliburton also speaks of the poem "as a kind of horizon, which, though projected by the poet, the poet never

quite reaches" (*Poetic Thinking*, 192). We find a more concrete example of this analysis in Harries, "Language and Silence," when he says that Heidegger's Trakl readings involve thinking through and bringing to fruition a nonmetaphysical happening of "world" for which Trakl's poetry "prepares" us but which it "lacks the strength to establish" ("Language and Silence," 167).

7. de Man, "Patterns of Temporality in Hölderlin's 'Wie wenn am Feiertag . . . ,'" 65.

8. Barbara Bolt, *Art Beyond Representation* (London: I. B. Tauris, 2004), 112.

9. I borrow the term from Hans Ulrich Gumbrecht in his lecture at the *Collège de France,* "Pourquoi Heidegger?," February 2010.

10. Bruns, *Heidegger's Estrangements,* 181.

11. If there are some important differences between the preservation of "The Origin of the Work of Art" and the later readings of poetry, many of these reflect fundamental changes taking place within Heidegger's thinking as a whole. Thus the transformation of preservation into an individual rather than a collective act coincides with a change in tone in Heidegger's postwar writings. This coincides with Heidegger's move from the orphic to the hermetic identified by both Bruns (*Heidegger's Estrangements,* esp. xix–xxi) and Young (*Heidegger's Philosophy of Art,* esp. 52–56), from the resoluteness of Dasein to *Gelassenheit* awaiting the "sending" of being, or from the shift in Heidegger's interpretation of the "forgetting of being" from a human forgetting to being's forgetting of humans (and consequently, rather than destruction of history of metaphysics allowing us to think the unthought of this tradition, we have been abandoned by being and can only await and prepare for its coming—an eschatology of being, as it were).

12. Gasché, "Perhaps: a modality?," in *Of Minimal Things,* 184.

13. Ibid., 180.

14. Ibid., 181.

15. Fynsk, *Language and Relation,* 66.

16. We can see here a deep kinship between Heidegger's thinking on translation and that of Walter Benjamin, for whom translation must be seen as a preservation of the foreign in one's own language ("The Task of the Translator," in *Illuminations,* ed. Hannah Arendt, trans. Harry Zohn; London: Cape, 1970, 69–82), and who also cites Hölderlin's translations of Sophocles and Pindar as paragons of such translation. While this may give onto a broader affinity between the two thinkers, it might also imply a shared influence. Benjamin thus cites Rudolf Pannwitz: "Our translations, even the best ones, proceed from a wrong premise. They want to turn Hindi, Greek, English into German instead of turning German into Hindi, Greek, English . . . The basic error of the translator is that he preserves the state in which his own language happens to be instead of allowing his language to be powerfully affected by the foreign tongue" (cited 80–81). Heidegger would argue that it is only through the thrust of this foreignness that one can come to appropriate and inhabit one's own language.

17. Clive Scott, "Translating Baudelaire," in *The Cambridge Companion to Baudelaire,* ed. Rosemary Lloyd (Cambridge: Cambridge University Press, 2006), 194–95.

18. T. S. Eliot, "Metaphysical Poetry," in *Selected Essays* (London: Faber, 1951), 287.

19. Warminski, "Monstrous History: Heidegger Reading Hölderlin" (203). One can note, for example, that because this law of history is the law of homecoming, the relation between Hölderlin and the foreign as *unheimisch* becomes crucial to Heidegger's thinking of the history of being: "It is this reading of *Unheimlichkeit* on the basis of *Unheimischkeit* and in turn on the basis of man's relation to being that allows Heidegger to interpret the choral ode in terms of the ontological difference" (200). Note here also that Heidegger nevertheless does subordinate this translation (and law of history) to the thinking of being. Warminski then argues that this law is undermined by Heidegger's attempt to place the relation between *home* and *foreign* into a binary opposition, and thus overlooks the tripartite system Hölderlin sets up (German, Greek, Egyptian).

20. Ibid., 169. Harries sees this thematic blindness as testament to the sheer difficulty involved in trying to think beyond metaphysics (170).

21. Fóti, *Heidegger and the Poets,* xviii.

22. Fynsk *Language and Relation,* 34.

23. Derrida, *Specters of Marx: The State of the Debt, the Work of Mourning, and the New International,* trans. Peggy Kamuf (London: Routledge, 2006), 32.

24. Fóti, *Heidegger and the Poets,* 23.

25. de Man, Heidegger's "Exegeses of Hölderlin," 250. On a similar note, as I discussed in Chapter 1, Adorno argues that Heidegger ignores "the agency of form," transposing the poem onto the level of "message" ("Parataxis," 114).

26. Allen, *Ellipsis,* 189.

27. Ibid., 150.

28. Fóti *Heidegger and the Poets,* 24.

29. Ronell, "On the Misery of Theory without Poetry," *PMLA* 120, no. 1 (2005): 29–30.

30. de Man, "Heidegger's Exegeses of Hölderlin," 254–55. He continues, "it is already a major achievement to have, in a dialogue of this sort, the two interlocutors manage to speak of the same thing."

31. Warminski, *Readings in Interpretation,* 46.

32. Kathleen Wright, "Heidegger and the Authorization of Hölderlin's Poetry," 170. The question of Nazism reverberates throughout the question of Heidegger's exegetical technique when it comes to Hölderlin. Warminski sums up what is at stake in the question of "whether 'Hölderlin' is indeed who Heidegger thinks he is" when he notes that, if "it is only in Heidegger's dialogue with Hölderlin that we can begin to think what Heidegger means by history, *our* history, and 'the Germans'," then in getting Hölderlin "right" lies Heidegger's absolution from nationalism ("Monstrous History: Heidegger reading Hölderlin," 195). This point is also touched upon by Annemarie Gethmann-Sifert when claiming that "it can be shown that in Heidegger's way out of political activities [*Gemächte*], and in his way back into the power of poetizing [*Dichtens*] and thinking, the reason for the political error of misjudgement repeats itself in such a way that the factual deci-

sion turns out to be based on principle" ("Heidegger and Hölderlin: The Over-Usage of 'Poets in an Impoverished Time'," in Macann, *Heidegger: Critical Assessments*, 247), and when Harries summarizes: "Heidegger, the great questioner, betrayed himself when he found Hitler, and once again when he found Hölderlin, or rather his version of Hölderlin" ("Introduction" to *Heidegger: Art, Politics, Technology*, xv).

33. Harries, "Language and Silence," 170–71.

34. I am indebted to Ross Wilson for this point. Kant says: "We *linger* in our contemplation of the beautiful, because this contemplation reinforces and reproduces itself" (Kant, *Critique of Judgement*, 68).

35. Paul Valéry, *Rhumbs* (Paris: Société des Médecins Bibliophiles, 1929), 121.

36. Krell, *Lunar Voices*, 56.

37. We have also seen the importance of intonation for thinking, as elaborated in his analyzes of Leibniz's principle of sufficient reason in *The Principle of Reason* (PR 46–48/86–89).

38. Ronell, "On the Misery of Theory without Poetry," 23.

39. This is the characterization given by Agamben in his "The End of the Poem" (109). The reading I am proposing is far closer to the understanding of poetic cadence in terms of a tension between meter and *phrasing*.

40. Anderson, ". . . Since the time," 120–21.

41. Indeed, Heidegger argues that the "B" version of the *Critique* disrupts this unity as Kant steps back from his own insight: "In the second edition of the *Critique of Pure Reason*, the transcendental power of imagination as it came to light in the impassioned course of its first projection was thrust aside and given a new interpretation—one favouring the understanding" (KPM 113/161); it "has forfeited its former independence" (KPM 116/165).

42. It is notable that the two Heidegger calls on to aid his attempt to think the uncanny in Sophocles's ode here, Parmenides and Hölderlin, both also wrote in verse, even if in a verse less removed (either as "thinker" or as one writing in German in the epoch of "metaphysics") from Heidegger's own mode of saying.

43. Simon Jarvis, "For a Poetics of Verse," *PMLA* 125, no. 4 (October 2010): 931.

44. Fynsk, *Language and Relation*, 17.

45. Fynsk specifies that he is using the term *allegory* in a nontechnical manner, which he then contrasts with Heidegger's own analysis, at the beginning of "The Origin of the Work of Art," of *allo agoreuei* (OBT 3/9, *Language and Relation*, 280). Bruns also suggests Heidegger's notion of *Erläuterung* as "more nearly resembles the allegorization of a text than the analysis of it" (*Heidegger's Estrangements*, 69). Bruns does, however, proceed to give a distinction of allegory other than that which Heidegger had in mind: "Allegory is the appropriation of dark texts; that is, it means taking a text differently from its literal sense because there is no taking the text literally—its literal sense is no sense at all: nothing can be made of it. . . . Allegory is a taking-off from the text rather than an exegesis that extracts something from the text in order to hold it up to the light" (69). This could, once

again, say more about the need to name the procedures of Heidegger's reading and writing than about the reading and writing itself.

46. Pound, *ABC of Reading*, 97. In the 1966 lecture "The End of Philosophy and the Task of Thinking," Heidegger opposes the *Lichtung* ('clearing') of the open to what he terms *Dickung* ('thickening', literally the dense undergrowth of a forest. TB 65/72). Although he does not make this explicit, it nevertheless offers the tantalizing possibility of following Heidegger's woodland analogy to portray *Dichtung* as itself a kind of *Dickung*: namely, a thickening of language which would serve to open up the clearing through its earthy density. Indeed, this poetic thickening accords powerfully with the account of the earth of the artwork and language discussed in Chapters 1 and 2. Allen notes that, while any claim of an etymological relation between *dichten* and *dicken* is *unsustainable* (*Ellipsis*, 93, 223), it is nevertheless crucial to Heidegger's own thinking: "That this thickness is also that of the composure of a poem is what justifies the subsequent statement that all art is essentially poetry (*Dichtung*). In this we hear nothing as much as a 'thickening' or 'condenzation' (*Verdichtung*) of appearance, as the appearance of appearance, which must now be thought in terms of the *Lichtung* as lightening, in both of its meanings" (80).

47. Wilhelm Waiblinger, *Phaëton* (Stuttgart: F. Franckh, 1823), 153–56; this history is recounted in greater detail in Krell, *Lunar Voices*, 65–66.

48. One of the most canonical instances of this thinking is to be found in Derrida's "The Double-Session," in *Dissemination,* trans. Barbara Johnson (Chicago: University of Chicago Press, 1981), 187–317. Here "rhythm" gives onto a repetition that would interrupt philosophy's desire for self-presence (279–82). See also the "outwork" (Preface) to *Dissemination,* esp. 43.

49. Allemann, *Heidegger und Hölderlin,* 182. Again, I am using the term *prosody* here where Krell and Allemann use the term *rhythm* in order to distinguish between the rhythms of verbal language (prosody) and the rhythmicity of beings' entry into appearance (rhythm).

50. Krell, *Lunar Voices,* 73. He in fact suggests that Heidegger's closest approximations to the language of poetry may . . . occur in his hardest, sparest prose' (74).

51. Fortuitously, the English translation of "sudden sight" for *jäher Blick* provides an extra alliteration.

52. Krell, discussing a passage from "Why Poets?" (*Unheil also Unheil spurt uns das Heile. Heiles er winkt rufend das Heilige. Heilges bindet das Göttliche. Göttliches nähert den Gott*), speaks of Heidegger's "strongly rhythmical line, which can be scanned as dactylic tetrameter and trimeter" (*Lunar Voices,* 72).

53. Ibid., 63.

Conclusion: A Poetics of Limit?

1. Werner Marx, *Is There a Measure on Earth? Foundations for a Non-Metaphysical Ethics,* trans. Thomas J. Nennon and Reginald Lily (Chicago: University of Chicago Press, 1987), 7, 10–11.

2. Jacques Rancière, *Politique de la littérature* (Paris: Galilée, 2007), 19.

3. Jacques Derrida, *Speech and Phenomena,* 78–79.

4. Ibid., 82.

5. Gilles Deleuze and Claire Parnet, *Dialogues,* trans. Hugh Tomlinson and Barbara Habberjam (New York: Columbia University Press, 1987), 17–18.

6. Ibid., 18.

7. Deleuze and Guattari, *Kafka: Toward a Minor Literature,* trans. Dana Polan (Minneapolis: University of Minnesota Press, 1986), 22. Deleuze and Guattari's "lignes de fuite" also alludes to the lines that gravitate toward the "vanishing point" (*point de fuite*) in linear perspective.

8. Paul Patton, *Deleuzian Concepts: Philosophy, Colonization, Politics* (Stanford, CA: Stanford University Press, 2010), 36. See also Jean-Jacques Lecercle, *Deleuze and Language* (London: Palgrave Macmillan, 2002), 27.

9. Deleuze and Guattari, *Kafka,* 22–23.

10. In this regard, two studies, both of which are based on sources from Heidegger's and Celan's libraries, stand out for their exhaustiveness and depth. James K. Lyon, *Paul Celan and Martin Heidegger: An Unresolved Conversation* (Baltimore, MD: Johns Hopkins University Press, 2006), and Hadrien France-Lanord, *Paul Celan et Martin Heidegger: le sens d'un dialogue* (Paris: Fayard, 2004).

11. This point is forcefully made by Ziarek, *Inflected Language: Towards a Hermeneutics of Nearness* (Albany: State University of New York Press, 1994), 174.

12. Ziarek, *Inflected Language,* 203–4.

13. Derek Attridge, *The Singularity of Literature* (London: Routledge, 2004), 128.

14. Ibid., 42.

15. Celan, "The Meridian," in *Paul Celan: Collected Prose* trans. and ed. Rosemarie Waldrop (New York: Routledge, 2003), 50.

16. Jonathan Culler, "Why Lyric?" *PMLA* 123, no. 1 (Jan 2008): 204.

17. "rechercher, devant une brisure des grands rythmes littéraires . . . et leur éparpillement en frissons articulés proches de l'instrumentation, un art d'achever la transposition, au Livre, de la symphonie ou uniment de reprendre notre bien." Stéphane Mallarmé, "Crise de vers," *Oeuvres complètes,* 367. My translation.

18. Ibid., 345.

19. Maurice Blanchot, "Le livre à venir," in *Le livre à venir* (Paris: Gallimard, 1959), 319.

20. Ezra Pound, *Personae: The Shorter Poems of Ezra Pound,* ed. Lea Baechler and A. Walton Litz (New York: New Directions, 1990), 111.

21. Ezra Pound, *The Cantos* (New York: New Directions, 1996), 538. That this line should mimic an *alexandrin* is a rather satisfying irony.

22. In his *ABC of Reading* (39) Pound gives a teleology from "inventors" ("Men who found a new process") to "masters" ("Men who combined a number of such processes, and who used them as well as or better than the inventors") and "diluters" ("Men who came after the first two kinds of writer, and couldn't do the job quite as well").

23. Theodor W. Adorno, "Commitment," trans. Frances McDonagh. *New Left Review* 87–88 (September/December 1974): 84. See also the assertion: "To write poetry after Auschwitz is barbaric," in "Cultural Criticism and Society," in *Prisms* trans. Samuel and Shierry Weber (Cambridge, MA: MIT Press, 1981), 33.

24. Wallace Stevens, *Collected Poems* (London: Faber, 1960), 110–11.

25. Phillip Stambovsky, *Philosophical Conceptualization and Literary Art* (Madison, NJ: Fairleigh Dickinson University Press, 2004), 177–78.

26. This analysis is developed powerfully by Bart Eeckhout, for whom it amounts to the two opposed conceptions of poetic language in Romanticism that M. H. Abrams depicted as the "mirror" (a representation of reality) and the "lamp" that brings the world to shine. *Wallace Stevens and the Limits of Reading and Writing* (Columbia and London: University of Missouri Press, 2002), 213–27.

27. See in this regard Alain Suberchicot, *Treize façons de regarder Wallace Stevens* (Paris: Harmattan, 1998), 93–95. For Suberchicot this is indicative of his thoroughgoing "poetic scepticism," which "one could conceive more broadly as a linguistic scepticism" and which is "too strong to allow a stability of tone" (95).

Bibliography

Adorno, T. W. "Commitment." Translated by Frances McDonagh. *New Left Review* 87–88 (September/December 1974): 75–89.

———. *Negative Dialectics.* Translated by E. B. Ashton. London: Routledge, 1990.

———. *Notes to Literature, vol. 2.* Translated by Shierry Weber Nicholsen. New York: Columbia University Press, 1992.

———. *Prisms.* Translated by Samuel and Shierry Weber. Cambridge, MA: MIT Press, 1981.

Agamben, Giorgio. *The End of the Poem: Studies in Poetics.* Translated by Daniel Heller-Roazen. Stanford, CA: Stanford University Press, 1999.

———. *Language and Death: The Place of Negativity.* Translated by Karen E. Pinkus with Michael Hardt. Minneapolis and London: University of Minnesota Press, 1991.

———. *The Open: Man and Animal.* Translated by Kevin Attell. Stanford, CA: Stanford University Press, 2004.

Aho, Kevin A. "The Missing Dialogue between Heidegger and Merleau-Ponty: On the Importance of the Zollikon Seminars." *Body & Society* 11, no. 2 (2005): 1–23.

———. *Heidegger's Neglect of the Body.* Albany: State University of New York Press, 2009.

Aler, Jan. "Heidegger's conception of language in *Being and Time.*" In *Martin Heidegger: Critical Assessments, vol. 4,* edited by Christopher Macann, 14–38. London: Routledge, 1992.

Allemann, Beda. *Hölderlin und Heidegger.* Zürich and Freiburg im Breisgau: Atlantis Verlag, 1954.

Allen, William S. *Ellipsis: Of Poetry and the Experience of Language after Heidegger, Hölderlin and Blanchot.* Albany: State University of New York Press, 2007.

Anderson, J. M. ". . . Since the time we are a dialogue and able to hear from one another." *Man and World* 10, no. 2 (1977): 115–36.

Aristotle. *Metaphysics.* Translated by Hugh Lawson-Tancred. Harmondsworth, UK: Penguin, 1998.

Attridge, Derek. *The Singularity of Literature.* London: Routledge, 2004.

Beistegui, Miguel de. *Heidegger and the Political: Dystopias.* London: Routledge, 1998.

———. *The New Heidegger.* London: Continuum, 2005.

———. *Thinking with Heidegger: Displacements.* Bloomington: Indiana University, 2003.

Benjamin, Walter. "The Task of the Translator." In *Illuminations,* edited by Hannah Arendt, 69–82. London: Cape, 1970.

Bernasconi, Robert. *The Question of Language in Heidegger's History of Being.* Atlantic Highlands, NJ: Humanities Press, 1985.

Bernstein, J. M. *The Fate of Art: Aesthetic Alienation from Kant to Adorno.* Oxford: Blackwell, 1992.

Blanchot, Maurice. "Le livre à venir." In *Le livre à venir,* 302–32. Paris: Gallimard, 1959.

Bolt, Barbara. *Art Beyond Representation.* London: I. B. Tauris, 2004.

Bourdieu, Pierre. *The Political Ontology of Martin Heidegger.* Translated by Peter Collier. Cambridge, UK: Polity, 1991.

Bowie, Andrew. *From Romanticism to Critical Theory: The Philosophy of German Literary Theory.* New York and London: Routledge, 1997.

Bruns, Gerald L. *Heidegger's Estrangements: Language, Truth and Poetry in the Later Writings.* New Haven, CT: Yale University Press, 1989.

Burton-Roberts, N., P. Carr, and G. Docherty, eds. *Phonological Knowledge: Conceptual and Empirical Issues.* Oxford: Oxford University Press, 2000.

Caputo, John. *Demythologizing Heidegger.* Bloomington: Indiana University Press, 1993.

Carman, Taylor. "Was Heidegger a Linguistic Idealist?" *Inquiry* 45, no. 2: 205–15.

Casenave, Gerald. "Heidegger and Metaphor." *Philosophy Today* 26, no. 2 (Summer 1982): 140–47.

Celan, Paul, *Breathturn.* Translated by Pierre Joris. New York: Sun and Moon Press, 1995.

———. *Collected Prose.* Translated and edited by Rosemarie Waldrop. New York: Routledge, 2003.

Crowell, Steven. "Making Logic Philosophical Again." In *Reading Heidegger from the Start,* edited by Theodor Kisiel and John van Buren, 55–72. Albany: State University of New York Press, 1994.

Culler, Jonathan. "Why Lyric?" *PMLA* 123, no. 1 (January 2008): 201–6.

Dahlstrom, Daniel. "Heidegger's Artworld." In *Heidegger: Politics, Art, and Technology,* edited by Karsten Harries and Christoph Jamme, 125–38. New York and London: Holmes and Meier, 1994.

Dastur, Françoise. *Heidegger: la question du logos.* Paris: J. Vrin, 2007.

de Man, Paul. *Aesthetic Ideology.* Minneapolis: University of Minnesota Press, 1996.

———. *Blindness and Insight: Essays in the Rhetoric of Contemporary Criticism,* edited by Wlad Godzich. 2nd ed. London: Methuen, 1983.

———. *The Resistance to Theory.* Manchester: Manchester University Press, 1986.

———. *Romanticism and Contemporary Criticism.* Edited by E. S. Burt, Kevin Newark, and Andrej Warminski. Baltimore, MD: Johns Hopkins University Press, 1992.

Deleuze, Gilles, and Claire Parnet. *Dialogues.* Translated by Hugh Tomlinson and Barbara Habberjam. New York: Columbia University Press, 1987.

Deleuze, Gilles, and Félix Guattari. *Kafka: Toward a Minor Literature.* Translated by Dana Polan. Minneapolis: University of Minnesota Press, 1986.

Derrida, Jacques. *Dissemination.* Translated by Barbara Johnson. Chicago: University of Chicago Press, 1981.

———. "*Geschlecht* I: Sexual Difference, Ontological Difference." In *Psyche: Inventions of the Other, vol. 2,* edited by Peggy Kamuf and Elizabeth Rottenberg, 7–26. Stanford, CA: Stanford University Press, 2008.

———. "Heidegger's Hand (*Geschlecht* II)." In *Psyche: Inventions of the Other, vol. 2,* edited by Peggy Kamuf and Elizabeth Rottenberg, 27–62. Stanford, CA: Stanford University Press, 2008.

———. *Of Spirit: Heidegger and the Question.* Translated by Geoffrey Bennington and Rachel Bowlby. Chicago: University of Chicago Press, 1989.

———. *Politics of Friendship.* Translated by George Collins. London: Verso, 2005.

———. "The Retrait of Metaphor." In *The Derrida Reader: Writing Performances,* edited by Julian Wolfreys, 102–30. Edinburgh: Edinburgh University Press, 1998.

———. *Specters of Marx: The State of the Debt, the Work of Mourning, and the New International.* Translated by Peggy Kamuf. London: Routledge, 2006.

———. *Speech and Phenomena, and Other Essays on Husserl's Theory of Signs.* Translated by David B. Allison. Evanston, IL: Northwestern University Press, 1973.

———. "White Mythology." In *Margins of Philosophy,* translated by Alan Bass, 207–73. Brighton, UK: Harvester Press, 1982.

Dreyfus, Hubert. *Being-in-the-World: A Commentary on Heidegger's Being and Time, Division I.* Cambridge, MA: MIT Press, 1990.

———. "Nihilism, Art, Technology, Politics." In *The Cambridge Companion to Heidegger,* edited by Charles Guignon, 345–72. Cambridge: Cambridge University Press, 2006.

Dreyfus, Hubert L., and Mark A. Wrathall, eds. *Heidegger Reexamined*. 4 vols. New York and London: Routledge, 2002.

Eeckhout, Bart. *Wallace Stevens and the Limits of Reading and Writing*. Columbia and London: University of Missouri Press, 2002.

Elden, Stuart. "Heidegger's Animals." *Continental Philosophy Review* 39, no. 3 (2006): 273–91.

Eliot, T. S. *Selected Essays*. London: Faber, 1951.

Farías, Victor. *Heidegger and Nazism*. Edited by Joseph Margolis and Tom Rockmore. Philadelphia: Temple University Press, 1989.

Feldman, Karen. "Heidegger and the Hypostasis of the Performative." *Angelaki* 9, no. 3 (2004): 157–67.

Fludernik, Monika. "Narratology in the Twenty-First Century: The Cognitive Approach to Narrative." *PMLA* 125, no. 4 (October 2010): 924–30.

Fóti, Véronique. *Heidegger and the Poets: poiēsis/sophia/technē*. Atlantic Highlands, NJ: Humanities Press International, 1992.

France-Lanord, Hadrien. *Paul Celan et Martin Heidegger: le sens d'un dialogue*. Paris: Fayard, 2004.

Fried, Michael. *Art and Objecthood: Essays and Reviews*. Chicago and London: Chicago University Press, 1998.

Fritsche, Johannes. *Historical Destiny and National Socialism in Being and Time*. Berkeley: University of California Press, 1999.

Froment-Meurice, Marc. *That is to Say . . . : Heidegger's Poetics*. Translated by Jan Plug. Stanford, CA: Stanford University Press, 1998.

Fynsk, Christopher. *Heidegger: Thought and Historicity*. Ithaca, NY: Cornell University Press, 1986.

———. *Language and Relation: . . . that there is language*. Stanford, CA: Stanford University Press, 1996.

———. "The Use of the Earth." http://abdn.ac.uk/modernthought/archive/publications/earth.php.

Gasché, Rodolphe. *Of Minimal Things: Studies on the Notion of Relation*. Stanford, CA: Stanford University Press, 1999.

Gethmann-Siefert, Annemarie. "Heidegger and Hölderlin: The over-usage of 'Poets in an impoverished time.'" in *Heidegger: Critical Assessments,* edited by Christopher Macann, 247–77. London: Routledge, 1992.

Gosetti-Ferencei, Jennifer. *Heidegger, Hölderlin, and the Subject of Poetic Language*. New York: Fordham University Press, 2004.

Greenberg, Clement. *Collected Essays and Criticism*. Vol. 4, *Modernism with a Vengeance, 1957–1969*. Chicago and London: Chicago University Press, 1993.

Greisch, Jean. *La Parole heureuse: Martin Heidegger entre les choses et les mots*. Paris: Beauchesne, 1987.

———. "Les mots et les roses: La métaphore chez Martin Heidegger." *Revue des Sciences Philosophiques et Théologiques* 57, no. 3 (1973): 433–55.

Guignon, Charles B. *Heidegger and the Problem of Knowledge*. Indianapolis, IN: Hackett, 1983.

————, ed. *The Cambridge Companion to Heidegger.* Cambridge: Cambridge University Press, 2006.

Gumbrecht, Hans Ulrich. "Martin Heidegger and his Japanese Interlocutors: About a Limit of Western Metaphysics." *Diacritics* 30, no. 4 (Winter 2000): 83–101.

Haar, Michel. *Heidegger and the Essence of Man.* Translated by William McNeill. Albany: State University of New York Press, 1993.

————. *Song of the Earth.* Translated by Reginald Lily. Bloomington: Indiana University Press, 1993. Originally published as *Chant de la terre: Heidegger et les assises de l'histoire de l'être* (Paris: L'Herne, 1987).

Halliburton, David. *Poetic Thinking: An Approach to Heidegger.* Chicago and London: University of Chicago Press, 1981.

Harries, Karsten. "Heidegger and Hölderlin: The Limits of Language." *The Personalist* 44 (1963): 5–23.

————. Introduction. In *Heidegger: Politics, Art, and Technology,* edited by Harries, Karsten and Christoph Jamme. New York and London: Holmes and Meier, 1994.

————. "Language and Silence." In *Martin Heidegger and the Question of Literature.* Edited by William V. Spanos, 155–72. Bloomington: Indiana University Press, 1979.

Harries, Karsten, and Christoph Jamme, eds. *Heidegger: Politics, Art, and Technology.* New York and London: Holmes and Meier, 1994.

Hegel, G. W. F. *Aesthetics: Lectures on Fine Art.* 2 vols. Translated by T. M. Knox. Oxford: Clarendon Press, 1975.

Heidegger, Martin. *Basic Problems of Phenomenology.* Translated by Albert Hofstadter. Bloomington: Indiana University Press, 1988. Originally published as *Die Grundprobleme der Phänomenologie* (Frankfurt am Main: Klostermann, 1975).

————. *Basic Writings.* Edited by David Farrell Krell. New York: Harper Collins, 1992.

————. *Being and Time.* Translated by John Macquarrie and Edward Robinson. Oxford: Blackwell, 1962. Translated by Stambaugh. Albany: State University of New York Press, 1996. Originally published as *Sein und Zeit* (Tübingen: M. Niemeyer, 1953).

————. *Elucidations of Hölderlin's Poetry.* Translated by Keith Hoeller. Amherst, NY: Humanity Books, 2000. Originally published as *Erläuterungen zu Hölderlins Dichtung* (Frankfurt am Main: V. Klostermann, 1951).

————. *The Essence of Truth: on Plato's cave allegory and Theaetetus.* Translated by Ted Sadler. London: Continuum, 2002. Originally published as *Vom Wesen der Wahrheit. Zu Platons Höhlengleichnis und Theätet* (Frankfurt am Main: Klostermann, 1988).

————. *Fundamental Concepts of Metaphysics.* Translated by William McNeill and Nicholas Walker. Bloomington: Indiana University Press, 1995. Originally published as *Die Grundbegriffe der Metaphysik: Welt, Endlichkeit, Einsamkeit* (Frankfurt am Main: Klostermann, 1992).

————. *Holzwege.* 2nd ed. Gesamtausgabe 5. Frankfurt am Main: Klostermann, 1977.

————. *Hölderlins Hymne, "Germanien" und "Der Rhein."* Gesamtausgabe 39. Frankfurt am Main: Klostermann, 1980.

————. *Hölderlins Hymne, "Andenken."* Gesamtausgabe 52. Frankfurt am Main: Klostermann, 1982.

————. *Introduction to Metaphysics.* Translated by Richard Polt and Gregory Fried. New Haven, CT: Yale Nota Bene, 2000. Originally published as *Einführung in die Metaphysik* (Tübingen: Niemeyer, 1966).

————. *Nietzsche I: The Will to Power as Art.* Translated by David Farrell Krell. New York: Harper and Row, 1979. Originally published as *Nietzsche: Der Wille zur Macht als Kunst* (Frankfurt am Main: Klostermann, 1985).

————. *Nietzsche II: The Eternal Recurrence of the Same.* Translated by David Farrell Krell. New York: Harper and Row, 1981. Originally published as *Nietzsches Metaphysische Grundstellung im abendländischen Denken: Die ewige Wiederkehr des Gleichen* (Frankfurt am Main: Klostermann, 1989).

————. *Off the Beaten Track.* Translated by Julian Young and Kenneth Haynes. Cambridge: Cambridge University Press, 2002. Originally published as *Holzwege* (Frankfurt am Main: Klostermann, 1950).

————. *On the Essence of Language: The Metaphysics of Language and the Essencing of the Word; Concerning Herder's Treatise On the Origin of Language.* Translated by Wanda Torres Gregory and Yvonne Unna. Albany: State University of New York Press, 2004. Originally published as *Zum Wesen der Sprache* (Frankfurt am Main: V. Klostermann, 1999).

————. *On the Way to Language.* Translated by Peter Hertz and Joan Stambaugh. New York: Harper and Row, 1971. Originally published as *Unterwegs zur Sprache* (Pfullingen: Neske, 1959).

————. "Only a God Can Save Us: The Spiegel Interview." In *The Heidegger Controversy,* edited by Richard Wolin, 91–116. New York: Columbia University Press, 1991.

————. *Parmenides.* Translated by André Schuwer and Richard Rojcewicz. Bloomington: Indiana University Press, 1992. Originally published as *Parmenides* (Frankfurt am Main: Klostermann, 1982).

————. *Pathmarks.* Edited by William McNeill. Cambridge: Cambridge University Press, 2001. Originally published as *Wegmarken* (Frankfurt am Main: Klostermann, 1967).

————. *Poetry Language Thought.* Translated by Albert Hofstadter. New York: Harper and Row, 1971. "Language" originally published as "Die Sprache" in *Unterwegs zur Sprache;* ". . . poetically man dwells . . ." originally published as ". . . dichterisch wohnet der Mensch . . ." in *Vorträge und Aufsätze* (Pfullingen: G. Neske, 1954).

————. *The Principle of Reason.* Translated by Reginald Lilly. Bloomington: Indiana University Press, 1991. Originally published as *Der Satz vom Grund* (Pfullingen: G. Neske, 1957).

———. *What is Called Thinking?* Translated by J. Glenn Gray and F. Wieck. New York: Harper and Row, 1972. Originally published as *Was heisst Denken?* (Tübingen: M. Niemeyer, 1954).

Herf, Jeffrey. *Reactionary Modernism: Technology, Culture, and Politics in Weimar and the Third Reich.* Cambridge: Cambridge University Press, 1984.

Hölderlin, Friedrich. *Essays and Letters on Theory.* Translated and edited by Thomas Pfau. Albany: State University of New York Press, 1988.

———. *Poems and Fragments.* Translated and edited by Michael Hamburger. 3rd ed. London: Anvil Press, 1994.

Hopkins, Gerard Manley. *The Journals and Papers of Gerard Manley Hopkins.* Edited by Humphry House. London: Oxford University Press, 1959.

Jarvis, Simon. "For a Poetics of Verse." *PMLA* 125, no. 4 (October 2010): 931–35.

———. "The Melodics of Long Poems." *Textual Practice* 24, no. 4 (2010): 607–21.

———. "Prosody as Cognition." *Critical Quarterly* 40, no. 4 (1998): 3–15.

Jünger, Carl. *Rhythmus und Sprache im deutschen Gedicht.* Stuttgart: Ernst Klett Verlag, 1952.

Kant, Immanuel. *Critique of Judgement.* Translated by Werner Pluhar. Indianapolis, IN: Hackett, 1986.

Kisiel, Theodor, and John van Buren, eds. *Reading Heidegger from the Start.* Albany: State University of New York Press, 1994.

Krell, David Farrell. *Daimon Life: Heidegger and Life-Philosophy.* Bloomington: Indiana University Press, 1992.

———. *Lunar Voices: of Tragedy, Poetry, Fiction, and Thought.* Chicago: University of Chicago Press, 1995.

Kockelmans, Joseph. "Heidegger on Metaphor and Metaphysics." In *Martin Heidegger: Critical Assessments,* edited by Christopher Macann, 293–320. London: Routledge 1992.

———, ed. *On Heidegger and Language.* Evanston IL: Northwestern University Press, 1972.

Kommerell, Max. *Briefe und Aufzeichnungen, 1919 –1944.* Edited by Inge Jen. Olten and Freiburg im Breisgau: Walter-Verlag, 1967.

Lacoue-Labarthe, Philippe. "The Caesura of the Speculative." In *Typography: Mimesis, Philosophy, Politics,* edited by Christopher Fynsk, 208–35. Stanford, CA: Stanford University Press, 1998. Originally published as "La césure du speculative," in *L'imitation des modernes,* 39–69 (Paris: Galilée, 1985).

———. *Heidegger, Art and Politics.* Translated by Chris Turner. Oxford: Basil Blackwell, 1990. Originally published as *La fiction du politique: Heidegger, art, politique* (Paris: C. Bourgeois, 1988).

Lafont, Cristina. *Heidegger, Language, and World-Disclosure.* Translated by Graham Harman. Cambridge: Cambridge University Press, 2000. Originally published as *Sprache und Welterschliessung: zur linguistischen Wende der Hermeneutik Heideggers* (Frankfurt am Main: Suhrkamp, 1994).

Lecercle, Jean-Jacques. *Deleuze and Language*. London: Palgrave Macmillan, 2002.

Löwith, Karl. "The Political Implications of Heidegger's Existentialism." In *The Heidegger Controversy*, edited by Richard Wolin, 168–85. New York: Columbia University Press, 1990.

Lyon, James K. *Paul Celan and Martin Heidegger: An Unresolved Conversation, 1951–70*. Baltimore, MD: Johns Hopkins University Press, 2006.

Macann, Christopher, ed. *Martin Heidegger: Critical Assessments*. London: Routledge 1992.

Mallarmé, Stéphane. *Oeuvres completes*. Edited by H. Mondor and G. Jean-Aubry. Paris: Gallimard, Bibliothèque de la Pléiade, 1992. First published 1945.

Mansbach, Abraham. *Beyond Subjectivism: Heidegger on Language and the Human Being*. Westport, CT, and London: Greenwood, 2002.

Marx, Werner. *Heidegger and the Tradition*. Translated by Theodore Kisiel and Murray Greene. Evanston, IL: Northwestern University Press, 1971.

———. *Is There a Measure on Earth? Foundations for a Non-Metaphysical Ethics*. Translated by Thomas J. Nennon and Reginald Lily. Chicago: University of Chicago Press, 1987.

Meschonnic, Henri. *Le Langage Heidegger*. Paris: Presses Universitaires de France, 1990.

———. "The Rhythm Party Manifesto." Translated by David Nowell Smith. *Thinking Verse* I (2011): 161–73.

Miller, J. Hillis. *Topographies*. Stanford, CA: Stanford University Press, 1996.

Moynihan, Robert. "Interview with Paul de Man." *Yale Review* 73, no. 4: 576–602.

Nancy, Jean-Luc. "On a Divine *Wink*." In *French Interpretations of Heidegger: An Exceptional Reception*, edited by François Raffoul and David Pettigrew, 167–86. Albany: State University of New York Press, 2008.

Nowell Smith, David. "The Poetry-Verse Distinction Revisited." *Thinking Verse* I (2011): 137–60.

———. "Mallarmé and the Ontologization of the Poem." In *Thinking Poetry: Philosophical Approaches to Nineteenth-Century French Poetry*, edited by Joseph Acquisto, 149–66 (New York: Palgrave Macmillan, 2013).

Ott, Hugo. *Martin Heidegger: A Political Life*. Translated by Allan Blunden. London: Fontana, 1988.

Patton, Paul. *Deleuzian Concepts: Philosophy, Colonization, Politics*. Stanford, CA: Stanford University Press, 2010.

Phillips, James. *Heidegger's Volk: Between National Socialism and Poetry*. Stanford, CA: Stanford University Press, 2005.

Polt, Richard. "Metaphysical Liberalism in Heidegger's *Beiträge zur Philosophie*." In *Heidegger Reexamined, vol. 3*, edited by Hubert L. Dreyfus and Mark A. Wrathall, 209–34. New York and London: Routledge, 2002.

Pope, Alexander. "Essay on Criticism." In *Alexander Pope: Pastoral Poetry and An Essay on Criticism,* edited by Émile Audra and Aubrey Williams, 233–326. London: Routledge, 1962.

Pound, Ezra. *ABC of Reading.* New York: New Directions, 2010.

———. *The Cantos.* New York: New Directions, 1996.

———. *Personae: The Shorter Poems of Ezra Pound.* Edited by Lea Baechler and A. Walton Litz. New York: New Directions, 1990.

Radloff, Bernhard. *Heidegger and the Question of National Socialism: Disclosure and Gestalt.* Toronto: University of Toronto Press, 2007.

Rancière, Jacques *Politique de la littérature.* Paris: Galilée, 2007.

Richardson, Fr. William. *Heidegger: Through Phenomenology to Thought.* The Hague: M. Nijhoff, 1963.

Ricoeur, Paul. *The Rule of Metaphor: Multi-disciplinary Studies of the Creation of Meaning in Language.* Translated by Robert Czerny with Kathleen McLauglin and John Costello. Toronto: University of Toronto Press, 1977.

Ronell, Avital. "On the Misery of Theory without Poetry: Heidegger's Reading of Hölderlin's 'Andenken.'" *PMLA* 120, no. 1 (2005): 16–32.

Rorty, Richard. *Essays on Heidegger and Others.* Vol. 2 of *Philosophical Papers.* Cambridge: Cambridge University Press, 1991.

Saussure, Ferdinand de. *Course in General Linguistics.* Translated by Wade Baskin. Edited by Charles Bally and Albert Sechehaye in collaboration with Albert Reidlinger. London: Fontana, 1974.

Schapiro, Meyer. *Theory and Philosophy of Art: Style, Artist, and Society.* New York: George Braziller, 1994.

Scott, Clive. "Translating Baudelaire." In *The Cambridge Companion to Baudelaire,* edited by Rosemary Lloyd, 193–205. Cambridge: Cambridge University Press, 2006.

Sheehan, Thomas. "Everyone has to tell the truth." *Continuum* I, no. 1 (Autumn 1990): 30–44.

———. "*Hermeneia* and *Apophansis:* The Early Heidegger's Reading of *De Interpretatione.*" In *Heidegger et l'idée de la phénoménologie.* Franco Volpi et al., 67–80. Dordrecht: Kluwer, 1988.

———. "On Movement and Destruction of Ontology." In *Heidegger Reexamined: Art, Poetry and Technology,* edited by Hubert L. Dreyfus and Mark A. Wrathall, 320–28. New York and London: Routledge, 2002.

———. "A Paradigm Shift in Heidegger Research." *Continental Philosophy Review* 22, no. 2 (2001): 1–20.

Shklovsky, Victor. *Theory of Prose.* Translated by Benjamin Sher. Elmwood Park, IL: Dalkey Archive Press, 1990.

Sinclair, Mark. *Heidegger, Aristotle, and the Work of Art.* Basingstoke, UK: Palgrave Macmillan, 2006.

Staiger, Emil. *Basic Concepts of Poetics.* Translated by Janette C. Hudson and Luanne T. Frank. University Park: Pennsylvania University Press, 1991.

Stambovsky, Phillip. *Philosophical Conceptualization and Literary Art.* Madison, WI: Farleigh Dickinson University Press, 2004.

Steiner, George. *Heidegger.* London: Fontana, 1978.

Stellardi, Giuseppe. *Heidegger and Derrida on Philosophy and Metaphor: Imperfect Thought.* Amherst, NY: Humanity Books, 2000.

Stevens, Wallace. *Collected Poems.* London: Faber, 1960.

Suberchicot, Alain. *Treize façons de regarder Wallace Stevens.* Paris: Harmattan, 1998.

Taminiaux, Jacques. "The Husserlian Heritage in Heidegger's Notion of the Self." In *Reading Heidegger from the Start,* edited by Theodor Kisiel and John van Buren, 269–92 Albany State University of New York Press, 1994..

Tiffany, Daniel. *Toy Medium: Materialism and Modern Lyric.* Chicago: University of Chicago Press, 2000.

Trask, R. L., and Peter Stockwell. *Language and Linguistics: The Key Concepts.* London: Routledge, 2007.

Tynianov, Yuri. *The Problem of Verse Language.* Translated by Michael Sosa and Brent Harvey. Ann Arbor, MI: Ardis, 1981.

Valéry, Paul. *Rhumbs.* Paris: Société des Médecins Bibliophiles, 1929.

Volpi, Franco, et al. *Heidegger et l'idée de la phénoménologie.* Dordrecht: Kluwer, 1988.

Waiblinger, Wilhelm. *Phaëton.* Stuttgart: F. Franckh, 1823.

Warminski, Andrzej. "Monstrous History: Heidegger reading Hölderlin." *Yale French Studies* 77 (1990): 193–209.

———. *Readings in Interpretation: Hölderlin, Hegel, Heidegger.* Minneapolis: Minnesota University Press, 1987.

Wennerstrom, Ann. *The Music of Everyday Speech: Prosody and Discourse Analysis.* Oxford: Oxford University Press, 2001.

White, David. *Heidegger and the Language of Poetry.* Lincoln: University of Nebraska Press, 1978.

Wolin, Richard, ed. *The Heidegger Controversy: A Critical Reader.* 2nd ed. Cambridge, MA, and London: MIT Press, 1993.

Wolin, Richard. *The Politics of Being: The Political Thought of Martin Heidegger.* New York: Columbia University Press, 1990.

Wright, Kathleen. "Heidegger and the Authorisation of Hölderlin's Poetry." In *Heidegger: Politics, Art and Technology,* edited by Karsten Harries and Christoph Jamme, 164–74. New York and London: Holmes and Meier, 1994.

Young, Julian. *Heidegger, Philosophy, Nazism.* Cambridge: Cambridge University Press, 1997.

———. *Heidegger's Philosophy of Art.* Cambridge: Cambridge University Press, 2001.

Ziarek, Krzysztof. *The Historicity of Experience: Modernity, the Avant-Garde, and the Event.* Evanston IL: Northwestern University Press, 2001.

———. *Inflected Language: Towards a Hermeneutics of Nearness.* Albany: State University of New York Press, 1994.

Zimmerman, Michael. *Heidegger's Confrontation with Modernity: Technology, Politics, and Art.* Bloomington: Indiana University Press, 1990.

Index

created work, 27–28, 32, 34, 45, 140–46, 187
Crowell, Steven, 81
Culler, Jonathan, 188

Dahlstrom, Daniel, 215n1
Dasein, 28–33, 68, 80–83, 117–18, 127, 145–46
Dastur, Françoise, 68, 80, 210n42
deconstruction, 6, 92, 184
Deleuze, Gilles, 184–85
de Man, Paul, 22, 70–71, 105, 128, 142, 154, 156, 217n30
Derrida, Jacques, 73, 78, 92, 94, 103–4, 109, 114, 118, 128, 153, 183–84, 219n48
Dichten, 138–39, 169, 179; and *Denken*, 147–48, 152, 162–64
Dichtung, 2–5, 8–9, 20–21, 59, 162–63, 197n1, 219n46
discourse (*Rede*), 15–16, 63–69, 79–84, 97, 206n5, 209n41
Dreyfus, Hubert, 200n32, 206n5
Dürer, Albrecht, 42, 193

earth, 13–15, 61, 91–92, 125–28, 130–31, 145, 165–72; and world, 31–42, 45, 55, 85–88,
ecstasis, 13, 117, 145–47, 164, 187, 211n49
Eeckhout, Bart, 221n26
eidos, 41
Elden, Stuart, 118
Eliot, T. S., 150–51
enjambment, 7–8, 160, 169–72
equipmentality, 26–30, 147
Ereignis, 5, 96–99, 148, 193
Erläuterung, 1, 17, 137–38, 156, 218n45
excess, 8–9, 41, 78–79, 83, 90, 131–33, 183
exegesis, 138–39, 154–56, 181, 187
existential, 64–65, 69, 80

Farìas, Victor, 10
Feldman, Karen, 107, 108, 129, 213n23
finite transcendence, 23, 31–33, 83, 145, 200n5
Flaubert, Gustave, 182
form: artistic form, 2–7, 14–15, 19–25, 54–55, 59, 85–86, 99, 154, 182; and

matter, 24–29, 36–40. *See also morphe;* technique
Fóti, Véronique, 153–55, 167, 205n44
fourfold, the, 55, 91, 165–67
Fried, Gregory, 57, 199n26
Fried, Michael, 26
Fritsche, Johannes, 199n30
Froment–Meurice, Marc, 36, 70–71, 85, 92, 204n37, 208n29
Fuge, jointure, 9, 42, 46–53, 58–9, 95, 167–73 passim, 177, 204n41
Fynsk, Christopher, 22, 32, 42, 90, 92, 98, 148, 153, 165, 201n15, 218n45

Gasché, Rodolphe, 146–47
gathering, 41–47, 51–53, 58–59, 65–67, 73–74, 87, 92, 122
George, Stefan, 7, 57–58, 137, 173–78, 191, 194
Gestalt, 15, 35–36, 41, 44–48, 50, 57–59, 122, 130–33, 140–41, 189
gesture, 75–79, 119–20, 129, 188
Gethmann-Sifert, Annemarie, 198n24, 217n32
Greenberg, Clement, 26, 201n11
Greisch, Jean, 103–4, 107, 128–29, 208n28
Guignon, Charles, 67–68, 207n13
Gumbrecht, Hans Ulrich, 77, 209n35, 216n9

Haar, Michel, 37, 42, 85
Halliburton, David, 205n44, 207n22, 209n36, 215n6
harmony: diatonic, 38, 182; *einstimmen*, 91, 99, 126, 130
Harries, Karsten, 152, 208n32, 216n6, 217n20, 218n32
hearing, 81–82, 102, 114–20, 124, 129, 131, 133, 146, 157, 174
Hegel, G. W. F., 34, 115, 208n31
Heidegger, Martin, works of: "Anaxi-mander's Saying," 50–51, 106–7, 110–11, 149; *Basic Problems of Phenomenology*, 210n47; *Being and Time*, 28, 30–31, 51, 65–68, 80–84, 115, 145, 203n33; "The Concept and Essence of *Phusis* in Aris-

Ronell, Avital, 156, 158
Rorty, Richard, 201n12, 213n15

Saussure, Ferdinand de, 68–69, 206n4, 207n22
saying, 15–16, 56, 66, 70–75, 90–99, 126, 130, 134, 175–78, 187, 207n22, 209n36
Scott, Clive, 150
seeing, 79, 102, 114–17, 121–22, 128–29, 182
sensuous/nonsensuous, 4, 16, 25, 63, 69, 86, 102, 114–17, 121–32, 172, 183
Sheehan, Thomas, 5, 49, 197n3, 202n28, 204n37, 208n24
Shklovsky, Viktor, 33, 201n19
showing, 31, 69–72, 75, 86, 95–97, 129–30, 183, 208n29
sign, signification, 25, 36, 44, 62–88 passim, 102, 112, 119, 123–24, 130, 132–33, 171, 183–85, 206n4, 207n20, 208n26, 209n38
silence, 8, 16, 43, 46, 58, 64, 84–98, 125, 175, 178, 180, 183, 189, 194
Sinclair, Mark, 36
Sophocles, 56–57, 141, 144, 149–53 passim, 160–63
sound, 16, 69, 84–91, 115, 124–25, 133; and sense, 8–10, 54, 61–62, 99, 157–58, 184; sounding, 3, 16, 19–24, 29–30, 38, 40, 43–44, 54–59, 63–64, 75, 84–98, 112, 120–35, 163, 189, 193–95
Staiger, Emil, 52, 205n43
Stambaugh, Joan, 73, 207n10, 210n44
Stambovsky, Phillip, 191–92
Steiner, George, 137
Stellardi, Giuseppe, 104, 105, 109–11, 213n31
Stevens, Wallace, 191–95
Stimmung, 31–32, 81–84, 126–27, 158
strife, 35–37, 40–42, 45, 87–88
Suberchicot, Alain, 221n27
symbolic images, 12, 25, 101–2, 104, 115–16

technique, 2, 7, 27, 38, 42–43, 59, 133, 150–51, 171, 189

Tezuka, Tomio, 76–77
temporality, 6, 37, 48–52, 56, 80, 168, 176–77, 209n41
Theophrastus, 110–11
Trakl, Georg, 52, 53, 104, 112, 153–55, 191, 216n6; "Ein Winterabend," 2, 53, 55, 73–74, 89, 93, 165–68, 175
trope, 5, 25, 58, 109, 112, 128, 131–33, 157–58, 179–80, 194–95, 212n11
truth, 12, 20–48 passim, 59, 70, 104, 106–7, 111, 112–13, 140–45, 166–67, 195, 200n7, 204n37. *See also aletheia*
Tynianov, Yuri, 205n48

uncanniness, 12, 30–34, 56–57, 83–84, 112–13, 145–46, 149–51, 159–60, 184, 218n42

Valéry, Paul, 157–58
Van Gogh, Vincent, 28, 200n8, 202n29, 215n5
verbal language, 15–16, 62–99 passim, 120–134 passim, 171, 177–79, 183, 189
voice, 4, 15–16, 63, 81–99 passim, 120–34 passim, 169, 183–85, 189, 193, 195
Volk, 13–14, 182–83

Warminski, Andrej, 152, 156, 199n25, 217n19
withdrawal, 13–14, 28–33, 36, 38, 40–41, 61, 72–73, 85–88, 90, 92, 125–26, 146–47, 154–55, 175
work-character, 45, 138, 140–41, 158
work-material, 13, 14, 20, 25–26, 31, 35–37, 40, 45, 59, 98
world, 5, 9, 22–23, 28–31, 63–69, 81–83, 85, 91, 115, 118–19, 126–27, 165–68, 182, 191–93
Wright, Kathleen, 157–58, 199n25, 217n32

Young, Julian, 10, 41 52, 198n22, 202n29, 204n37, 215n5, 216n11

Ziarek, Krzysztof, 187, 202n20, 220n11
Zimmerman, Michael, 10

Perspectives in Continental Philosophy
John D. Caputo, series editor

John D. Caputo, ed., *Deconstruction in a Nutshell: A Conversation with Jacques Derrida*.

Michael Strawser, *Both/And: Reading Kierkegaard—From Irony to Edification*.

Michael D. Barber, *Ethical Hermeneutics: Rationality in Enrique Dussel's Philosophy of Liberation*.

James H. Olthuis, ed., *Knowing* Other-*wise: Philosophy at the Threshold of Spirituality*.

James Swindal, *Reflection Revisited: Jürgen Habermas's Discursive Theory of Truth*.

Richard Kearney, *Poetics of Imagining: Modern and Postmodern*. Second edition.

Thomas W. Busch, *Circulating Being: From Embodiment to Incorporation—Essays on Late Existentialism*.

Edith Wyschogrod, *Emmanuel Levinas: The Problem of Ethical Metaphysics*. Second edition.

Francis J. Ambrosio, ed., *The Question of Christian Philosophy Today*.

Jeffrey Bloechl, ed., *The Face of the Other and the Trace of God: Essays on the Philosophy of Emmanuel Levinas*.

Ilse N. Bulhof and Laurens ten Kate, eds., *Flight of the Gods: Philosophical Perspectives on Negative Theology*.

Trish Glazebrook, *Heidegger's Philosophy of Science*.

Kevin Hart, *The Trespass of the Sign: Deconstruction, Theology, and Philosophy*.

Mark C. Taylor, *Journeys to Selfhood: Hegel and Kierkegaard*. Second edition.

Dominique Janicaud, Jean-François Courtine, Jean-Louis Chrétien, Michel Henry, Jean-Luc Marion, and Paul Ricoeur, *Phenomenology and the "Theological Turn": The French Debate*.

Karl Jaspers, *The Question of German Guilt*. Introduction by Joseph W. Koterski, S.J.

Jean-Luc Marion, *The Idol and Distance: Five Studies*. Translated with an introduction by Thomas A. Carlson.

Jeffrey Dudiak, *The Intrigue of Ethics: A Reading of the Idea of Discourse in the Thought of Emmanuel Levinas.*

Robyn Horner, *Rethinking God as Gift: Marion, Derrida, and the Limits of Phenomenology.*

Mark Dooley, *The Politics of Exodus: Søren Kierkegaard's Ethics of Responsibility.*

Merold Westphal, *Overcoming Onto-Theology: Toward a Postmodern Christian Faith.*

Edith Wyschogrod, Jean-Joseph Goux, and Eric Boynton, eds., *The Enigma of Gift and Sacrifice.*

Stanislas Breton, *The Word and the Cross.* Translated with an introduction by Jacquelyn Porter.

Jean-Luc Marion, *Prolegomena to Charity.* Translated by Stephen E. Lewis.

Peter H. Spader, *Scheler's Ethical Personalism: Its Logic, Development, and Promise.*

Jean-Louis Chrétien, *The Unforgettable and the Unhoped For.* Translated by Jeffrey Bloechl.

Don Cupitt, *Is Nothing Sacred? The Non-Realist Philosophy of Religion: Selected Essays.*

Jean-Luc Marion, *In Excess: Studies of Saturated Phenomena.* Translated by Robyn Horner and Vincent Berraud.

Phillip Goodchild, *Rethinking Philosophy of Religion: Approaches from Continental Philosophy.*

William J. Richardson, S.J., *Heidegger: Through Phenomenology to Thought.*

Jeffrey Andrew Barash, *Martin Heidegger and the Problem of Historical Meaning.*

Jean-Louis Chrétien, *Hand to Hand: Listening to the Work of Art.* Translated by Stephen E. Lewis.

Jean-Louis Chrétien, *The Call and the Response.* Translated with an introduction by Anne Davenport.

D. C. Schindler, *Han Urs von Balthasar and the Dramatic Structure of Truth: A Philosophical Investigation.*

Julian Wolfreys, ed., *Thinking Difference: Critics in Conversation.*

Allen Scult, *Being Jewish/Reading Heidegger: An Ontological Encounter.*

Richard Kearney, *Debates in Continental Philosophy: Conversations with Contemporary Thinkers.*

Jennifer Anna Gosetti-Ferencei, *Heidegger, Hölderlin, and the Subject of Poetic Language: Toward a New Poetics of Dasein.*

Jolita Pons, *Stealing a Gift: Kierkegaard's Pseudonyms and the Bible.*

Jean-Yves Lacoste, *Experience and the Absolute: Disputed Questions on the Humanity of Man.* Translated by Mark Raftery-Skehan.

Charles P. Bigger, *Between Chora and the Good: Metaphor's Metaphysical Neighborhood.*

Dominique Janicaud, *Phenomenology "Wide Open": After the French Debate.* Translated by Charles N. Cabral.

Ian Leask and Eoin Cassidy, eds., *Givenness and God: Questions of Jean-Luc Marion.*

Jacques Derrida, *Sovereignties in Question: The Poetics of Paul Celan.* Edited by Thomas Dutoit and Outi Pasanen.

William Desmond, *Is There a Sabbath for Thought? Between Religion and Philosophy.*

Bruce Ellis Benson and Norman Wirzba, eds., *The Phenomenology of Prayer.*

S. Clark Buckner and Matthew Statler, eds., *Styles of Piety: Practicing Philosophy after the Death of God.*

Kevin Hart and Barbara Wall, eds., *The Experience of God: A Postmodern Response.*

John Panteleimon Manoussakis, *After God: Richard Kearney and the Religious Turn in Continental Philosophy.*

John Martis, *Philippe Lacoue-Labarthe: Representation and the Loss of the Subject.*

Jean-Luc Nancy, *The Ground of the Image.*

Edith Wyschogrod, *Crossover Queries: Dwelling with Negatives, Embodying Philosophy's Others.*

Gerald Bruns, *On the Anarchy of Poetry and Philosophy: A Guide for the Unruly.*

Brian Treanor, *Aspects of Alterity: Levinas, Marcel, and the Contemporary Debate.*

Simon Morgan Wortham, *Counter-Institutions: Jacques Derrida and the Question of the University.*

Leonard Lawlor, *The Implications of Immanence: Toward a New Concept of Life.*

Clayton Crockett, *Interstices of the Sublime: Theology and Psychoanalytic Theory.*

Bettina Bergo, Joseph Cohen, and Raphael Zagury-Orly, eds., *Judeities: Questions for Jacques Derrida.* Translated by Bettina Bergo and Michael B. Smith.

Jean-Luc Marion, *On the Ego and on God: Further Cartesian Questions.* Translated by Christina M. Gschwandtner.

Jean-Luc Nancy, *Philosophical Chronicles.* Translated by Franson Manjali.

Jean-Luc Nancy, *Dis-Enclosure: The Deconstruction of Christianity.* Translated by Bettina Bergo, Gabriel Malenfant, and Michael B. Smith.

Andrea Hurst, *Derrida Vis-à-vis Lacan: Interweaving Deconstruction and Psychoanalysis.*

Jean-Luc Nancy, *Noli me tangere: On the Raising of the Body.* Translated by Sarah Clift, Pascale-Anne Brault, and Michael Naas.

Jacques Derrida, *The Animal That Therefore I Am.* Edited by Marie-Louise Mallet, translated by David Wills.

Jean-Luc Marion, *The Visible and the Revealed.* Translated by Christina M. Gschwandtner and others.

Michel Henry, *Material Phenomenology.* Translated by Scott Davidson.

Jean-Luc Nancy, *Corpus.* Translated by Richard A. Rand.

Joshua Kates, *Fielding Derrida.*

Michael Naas, *Derrida From Now On.*

Shannon Sullivan and Dennis J. Schmidt, eds., *Difficulties of Ethical Life.*

Catherine Malabou, *What Should We Do with Our Brain?* Translated by Sebastian Rand, Introduction by Marc Jeannerod.

Claude Romano, *Event and World.* Translated by Shane Mackinlay.

Vanessa Lemm, *Nietzsche's Animal Philosophy: Culture, Politics, and the Animality of the Human Being.*

B. Keith Putt, ed., *Gazing Through a Prism Darkly: Reflections on Merold Westphal's Hermeneutical Epistemology.*

Eric Boynton and Martin Kavka, eds., *Saintly Influence: Edith Wyschogrod and the Possibilities of Philosophy of Religion.*

Shane Mackinlay, *Interpreting Excess: Jean-Luc Marion, Saturated Phenomena, and Hermeneutics.*

Kevin Hart and Michael A. Signer, eds., *The Exorbitant: Emmanuel Levinas Between Jews and Christians.*

Bruce Ellis Benson and Norman Wirzba, eds., *Words of Life: New Theological Turns in French Phenomenology.*

William Robert, *Trials: Of Antigone and Jesus.*

Brian Treanor and Henry Isaac Venema, eds., *A Passion for the Possible: Thinking with Paul Ricoeur.*

Kas Saghafi, *Apparitions—Of Derrida's Other.*

Nick Mansfield, *The God Who Deconstructs Himself: Sovereignty and Subjectivity Between Freud, Bataille, and Derrida.*

Don Ihde, *Heidegger's Technologies: Postphenomenological Perspectives.*

Françoise Dastur, *Questioning Phenomenology.* Translated by Robert Vallier.

Suzi Adams, *Castoriadis's Ontology: Being and Creation.*

Richard Kearney and Kascha Semonovitch, eds., *Phenomenologies of the Stranger: Between Hostility and Hospitality.*

Michael Naas, *Miracle and Machine: Jacques Derrida and the Two Sources of Religion, Science, and the Media.*

Alena Alexandrova, Ignaas Devisch, Laurens ten Kate, and Aukje van Rooden, *Re-treating Religion: Deconstructing Christianity with Jean-Luc Nancy.* Preamble by Jean-Luc Nancy.

Emmanuel Falque, *The Metamorphosis of Finitude: An Essay on Birth and Resurrection.* Translated by George Hughes.

Scott M. Campbell, *The Early Heidegger's Philosophy of Life: Facticity, Being, and Language.*

Françoise Dastur, *How Are We to Confront Death? An Introduction to Philosophy.* Translated by Robert Vallier. Foreword by David Farrell Krell.

Christina M. Gschwandtner, *Postmodern Apologetics? Arguments for God in Contemporary Philosophy.*

Ben Morgan, *On Becoming God: Late Medieval Mysticism and the Modern Western Self.*

Neal DeRoo, *Futurity in Phenomenology: Promise and Method in Husserl, Levinas, and Derrida.*

Sarah LaChance Adams and Caroline R. Lundquist eds., *Coming to Life: Philosophies of Pregnancy, Childbirth, and Mothering.*

Thomas Claviez, ed., *The Conditions of Hospitality: Ethics, Politics, and Aesthetics on the Threshold of the Possible.*

Roland Faber and Jeremy Fackenthal, eds., *Theopoetic Folds: Philosophizing Multifariousness.*

Jean-Luc Marion, *The Essential Writings.* Edited by Kevin Hart.

Adam S. Miller, *Speculative Grace: Bruno Latour and Object-Oriented Theology.*

Jean-Luc Nancy, *Corpus II: Writings on Sexuality.*

David Nowell Smith, *Sounding/Silence: Martin Heidegger at the Limits of Poetics.*